Teaching Music in the Urban Classroom, Volume I

A Guide to Survival, Success, and Reform

Edited by
Carol Frierson-Campbell

Published in partnership with
National Association for Music Education
Frances S. Ponick, Executive Editor

Rowman & Littlefield Education
Lanham, Maryland • Toronto • Oxford
2006

Published in partnership with
National Association for Music Education

Published in the United States of America
by Rowman & Littlefield Education
A Division of Rowman & Littlefield Publishers, Inc.
A wholly owned subsidiary of The Rowman & Littlefield Publishing Group, Inc.
4501 Forbes Boulevard, Suite 200, Lanham, Maryland 20706
www.rowmaneducation.com

PO Box 317
Oxford
OX2 9RU, UK

British Library Cataloguing in Publication Information Available

Library of Congress Cataloging-in-Publication Data

Teaching music in the urban classroom : a guide to survival, success, and reform / [edited by] Carol Frierson-Campbell.
p. cm.
"Published in partnership with National Association for Music Education."
Includes bibliographical references.
ISBN-13: 978-1-57886-460-7 (hardcover : alk. paper)
ISBN-10: 1-57886-460-7 (hardcover : alk. paper)
ISBN-13: 978-1-57886-461-4 (pbk. : alk. paper)
ISBN-10: 1-57886-461-5 (pbk. : alk. paper)
1. Music—Instruction and study. 2. Education, Urban—Social aspects. 3. City children—Education. I. Frierson-Campbell, Carol, 1961–
MT1.T387 2006
780.71—dc22 2005037240

™ The paper used in this publication meets the minimum requirements of American National Standard for Information Sciences—Permanence of Paper for Printed Library Materials, ANSI/NISO Z39.48-1992. Manufactured in the United States of America.

Contents

Foreword

I had the privilege and pleasure of teaching and supervising music in a very large inner-city school district, the Denver Public Schools, for 20 years. Teaching instrumental music in this diverse urban environment was quite challenging, but it was one of the best experiences of my career.

Why did I become a music teacher who so thoroughly enjoyed teaching Native American, Hispanic, Asian, African American, Caucasian, or any other kid? Because music teachers nurtured and mentored me when I was just another little African American kid in their classrooms. Those long-term thinkers believed in my future and became involved in my life as role models. At nearly every stage in my career since, music educators stepped forth to help me out. I am grateful enough to them to want more kids—a *lot* more—to get what I got.

Even when they're slogging through the day, dedicated music educators keep their eyes on their students' futures. It is extraordinarily gratifying to meet students who come back to visit (and even to thank us) after they have grown up.

Yet how many of these former students chose music education as a career? Where are the future leaders in music education today? Many of them live in urban neighborhoods. Many of them are marginalized. They're shy. They're afraid. Sometimes they're the ones who mouth off the most. Some of them may even become gang leaders, which is definitely not the best way to apply one's talents. What about the future for these kids?

The theme of reform permeates this book, but reform is what changes the future. For me, "reform" means more music educators, and more music educators from diverse and urban backgrounds. I don't mean fewer Caucasian teachers and more African American teachers; I mean more of *everybody*. The profession needs people like you, who have picked up this book and started reading it.

You can change not only your students, but also the profession. Students taught by inspired music teachers become inspired themselves. Some of them become leaders. If these leaders become music educators, they will truly influence music education on local, state, and national levels.

Too often, reform is fueled by emotion—a lot of hot air and good intentions that sputter out when the "feel-good" fades away. *Teaching Music in the Urban Classroom* adds an essential ingredient to reform: its how-tos, narratives, and reflections are based on solid research and real experiences. Every contributor has harnessed emotion to reason.

Keep reading past this foreword. You'll discover a thoughtful, caring narrative that covers myriad aspects of teaching music in difficult—and diverse—environments.

—Willie L. Hill Jr.
past president, MENC: The National Association for Music Education
past president, IAJE: The International Association for Jazz Education
director, Fine Arts Center, University of Massachusetts-Amherst

Acknowledgments

This volume is the result of many hours of work on the part of the chapter authors, and of a shared vision on the part of many others. It began for me when Diane Falk-Romaine, the music department chair at William Paterson University, invited me to get involved with the New Jersey Teacher Quality Enhancement Consortium, a grant-supported outreach project between the university and three urban school districts in the region. Leslie Agard-Jones, dean of the College of Education, supported the involvement of music teachers from these districts, and Dean Ofelia Garcia of the College of the Arts and Communication supported the interdisciplinary collaboration between the two colleges. Grant administrators Michael Chirichello, Bob Ross, and Stephanie Koprowski-McGowan provided financial and logistical support for the music education project.

Three things became obvious very quickly: (1) the challenges faced by music educators in these urban schools were difficult by any standards; (2) even amidst the challenges, many good musical things were happening in urban schools that deserved attention; and (3) too few people were paying attention. A conversation with Nick Santoro, then president of the New Jersey Music Educators Association, led to the creation of an "Urban Issues" position on the board of that organization, and current president Frank Phillips appointed me to that position. Nick also introduced me to the Urban Music Leadership Conference, and eventually to Ardene Shafer, former assistant executive director of Member Services and Publications at the National Association for Music Educators (MENC). Ardene shared my vision for a book that would restart the conversation about urban music education at the national level.

This book was first inspired by the music teachers of Paterson, Passaic, and Garfield, New Jersey, who willingly shared their stories and their dedication to teaching music in urban settings. The vision would not have become a reality without the support of MENC. In addition to Ardene, David Circle—current president—provided support for the book and the "Urban Issues" initiative throughout his presidency. Fran Ponick, director of Academic and Book Publications, provided incredibly patient advice throughout the editing process. My sincerest thanks go to all of the contributing authors for their ideas, assistance, and patient revision. A special debt of gratitude is owed to Frank Abrahams for his help and advice during the reviewing process. Other friends and colleagues who have provided advice and direction include Mickey Flagg and Susan Conkling. Thanks are also due to graduate students David Hull and Abigail Riccards for help with copyediting. Finally, a special thanks to my husband, Bob Campbell, who still "makes my heart sing!"

Introduction: Perspectives on Music in Urban Schools

Carol Frierson-Campbell

Addressing issues specific to urban schools is not new to the music education profession. In 1967, attendees at the Music Educators National Conference (MENC) landmark Tanglewood Symposium "sought to reappraise and evaluate basic assumptions about music in the 'educative' forces and institutions of our communities" (Choate, 1968, p. iii). That conversation included luminaries from across the educational, musical, and political spectrum, whose purpose was to set a future direction for music education in "a nation that had only recently reached a fair degree of consensus on civil rights" (Mark, 2000, p. 9). The resulting document is a testimony to complexity of this vision.

Clearly the issues we call "urban" in today's world were part of the discussion. In a blistering speech, David McAllester accused the profession of a kind of blindness in which "the controlling middle class in the United States does not *see* the lower classes and the poor among them" (Choate, 1968, p. 138). McAllester noted that those in "the Establishment" were "profoundly unwilling to face the invisible culture" or to admit that "the invisible culture has a rugged vitality of its own" (p. 138). The declaration reflects this concern: "The music education profession must contribute its skills, proficiencies, and insights toward assisting in the solution of urgent social problems as in the 'inner city' or other areas with culturally deprived individuals" (p. 139).

In 1970, MENC dedicated a full issue of the *Music Educators Journal* to "Facing the Music in Urban Education." Charles Fowler, then editor of the journal, suggested that the profession's cultural shortsightedness was reaching epidemic status. His description, while dated, resonates with many present-day concerns:

> In the ghetto, music teachers find that every ideal they were taught to adhere to seems to be open to attack or, at the least, seriously questioned. Worst of all, the so-called "tried and true" approaches fail to work. Music teachers in the ghetto soon discover an enormous gap. Not a generation gap, but a much more confusing and devastating one—a gap between their middle class values and the particular values held by their students. There is often a vast difference between the teacher's and the student's cultures. The disadvantaged student isn't particularly interested in learning the names of the instruments of the orchestra. He isn't "turned on" by cowboy songs. He won't easily enthuse over studying stringed instruments. He doesn't want our Lincoln Centers. He isn't interested in classical music; in fact he'll tell you with complete certainty how dull it sounds compared to James Brown or Aretha Franklin. The old image, the old ways, and the old music education curriculum are developing cracks. They don't work in the ghetto. Not only that, there is evidence that what happens on the front lines is becoming an epidemic that is certain to spread to the suburbs and beyond. (pp. 9–10)

Perhaps because of the renewal of the nation's highly politicized school reform efforts, urban music education was not a frequent topic for discussion during the 1980s. At the start of the following decade, Warrick Carter (1993) sought to move the profession forward with a commentary entitled "Minority Participation in Music Programs," in which he exhorted music educators to "work to change the climate of school music to be more welcoming for minority students" (p. 227). Carter's eloquent plea continues to inspire the profession:

> Please, no more hyperbole or philosophical papers; rather, we need Herculean deeds and actions to change the situation. If not, school music programs will continue to miss out on the participation of some of the country's best young musical minds. Young minority musicians will continue to make music, but they will not make music in the schools. (p. 227)

In 1995, June Hinckley, then president of MENC, reiterated the importance of music education for urban students who had lost musical opportunities that had been available to their older brothers and sisters. Hinckley described a population of urban youth who "saw the elimination of music programs as one more expression of a lack of caring on the part of the school leaders and the community at large" (p. 33). As the 21st century approached, Hinckley and others hosted the Housewright Symposium to "look at what . . . we as music professionals might do to insure that future generations would continue to experience the deep joy that we know as practicing musicians"

(Hinckley, 2000, p. 1). Intending to refocus the conversation that began at Tanglewood, the symposium and resulting document sought to answer questions critical to the future of music education:

- Why do humans value music?
- Why study music?
- How can the skills and knowledge called for in the national standards best be taught?
- How can all people continue to be involved in meaningful music participation?
- How will societal and technological changes affect the teaching of music?
- What should be the relationship between schools and other sources of music learning? (Madsen, 2000).

Paul Lehman's address related to the skills and knowledge question presents a compelling vision of the future of music education. He predicts that the nature of the 21st-century music program "will reflect the wide range of diversity that exists in the United States" (2000, p. 95). Further,

> Regardless of his or her field of specialization, every music teacher will be able to teach courses open to students lacking the time, background, or interest to participate in the school's select performing groups. Because oral traditions and aural learning are key to most of the musical styles of the world, awareness of these traditions and facility in teaching them will be essential for music educators. (p. 98)

The Housewright Declaration that summarized the event continues to stress the importance of making school music available to all students with this statement: "All persons, regardless of age, cultural heritage, ability, venue, or financial circumstance deserve to participate fully in the best music experiences possible" (Madsen, 2000, p. 219).

As a music educator, I came to the issue of urban music education relatively recently. After 12-plus years of teaching music in the small towns of northern New York State, I took a university teaching position in suburban New Jersey. My experience in urban schools began with my first field observation. On that day I visited two university students—one placed in a high school in Paterson, a city near the university, and a second in a new elementary school in the town where the university is located. My visit to the Paterson school fell on the day after a former student had been murdered in a fight. Guards and police were everywhere in the school, for fear that there would be retribution for the crime. Students' grief hung heavy in the air. A poster had been hung in one hallway for students to place their condolences to the victim's family.

My visit to the music classrooms was an eye-opener. The choir director proudly showed me photographs and news clips from 30 years prior, when the school had been nationally recognized for its state-of-the-art design. Yet on this day it was in lockdown mode. The spacious auditorium, once a performance center for the arts, had become a television studio. In the band room, the director taught a group of approximately 25 students (five students each day) from a school of over 1,200. The choir director struggled to reach the group of students who did not see the connection between the classical music she taught and the reality of their daily lives.

I went from the Paterson school to the suburban elementary school, where the beginning band was rehearsing in the science lab because the new band room had not yet been completed. The only security evident was a buzzer on the front door and a requirement to sign in at the office. The day's most pressing issue was deciding what kind of fish should go in the pond of the newly constructed science room. I returned to the university determined to explore ways that music educators could respond effectively to students in urban environments. It has since become clear to me that contexts traditionally considered "urban"—multiculturalism, interdisciplinarity, assessment, and educational activism—color every aspect of the music education profession.

Toward the end of my public school tenure, I was fortunate to attend a lecture by Dr. James Garbarino, an expert on youth violence. One of his many good points was the idea that "social epidemics" begin in areas of high need and social stress, and eventually move from those borders into the society at large. He noted that people who are not from high-needs areas are often blind to social epidemics because they are "not our problem," but that eventually these issues become universal. My visits to the urban schools in the region where I now live and work brought this idea of "social epidemic" to a new light.

Malcolm Gladwell further illuminates the concept of social epidemics in his book *The Tipping Point*. Gladwell (2000) believes that social epidemics—good ones like urban renewal and bad ones like random violence—"spread just like viruses do" (p. 7). They are "tipped" from inconsequential to epidemic status by incremental changes in the status quo. His thesis is that it is possible to learn to "tip" such changes by understanding how change works. This is why the present conversation is so important. The change needed in urban music education is not only that music should be at the center of the curriculum in urban schools; it is also that culturally relevant music should be a creative force at the center of reform in urban education.

At its most basic level, this change begins in the classroom. Music teachers are at the forefront of change, of improving the status of music and education in urban schools. But others beyond the classroom—administrators, teacher educators, researchers, and policy makers—control much of what happens in urban music classrooms and schools. Still others—school reformers, advocates for the poor, activists from diverse cultures, and members of the communities served by urban educators—have important insights about the change process that must be acknowledged. While "urban issues" have been at the forefront of the music education conversation for almost 40 years, they have not yet reached the "tipping point" needed to make MENC's mission "to advance music education by encouraging the study and making of music by all" a reality in all urban schools. It is diverse voices, distinct and yet united, that will tip the equation in the direction of change.

The purpose of this book is to bring new voices to this conversation. Authors include graduate students, practicing music teachers from cities large and small, teacher educators and researchers, administrators, and even businesspeople involved in arts-based school reform. We represent a diversity of opinions, but are united in our concern about the role of music in urban education. We met during MENC's 2005 Eastern Division Convention to define what the book would be about. Some felt that we should define *urban* from the get-go, acknowledging the political, cultural, and economic pieces of the puzzle. Others felt we should dispense with philosophizing and politicizing and just talk about getting the job done—reaching kids in urban schools. Ultimately, we decided that our goal would be to stimulate further discourse with the hope of tipping the profession to renewed action. We expect that our readers will like what some authors have to say and disagree with others. We hope you raise your voice to agree, to dissent, or to make points that we have neglected to make. This too is part of the conversation.

CULTURAL RESPONSIVITY

> Music educators' concern for diversity will include, for example, attention to differences in learning style, cultural or ethnic background, age, gender, emotional needs, physical needs, and family structure. (Lehman, 2000, p. 98)

Whether because of rigid training or professional nearsightedness, the cultural disconnect between music teachers and urban students is a theme that permeates the discussion of music in urban schools. It is sometimes an uncomfortable issue, and one that inspires many different opinions. MENC's (2002) revised Strategic Plan recognizes the importance of "diversifying music instruction" for students, and includes "Music for all" as one of four Strategic Directions for the future of music education (p. 8). Because this issue arises throughout the history of school music education with such frequency and passion, it will be the first one explored in this book. We begin with Cathy Benedict, who uses the concept of "other" to challenge music teachers to consider whether the cultural assumptions they bring into the classroom somehow limit their engagements with their students. She suggests that taking on a transformative pedagogy to advocate for social change will enable music educators to develop students' musical capacities and thereby transform the profession.

Donna T. Emmanuel reminds us that "culture is a complex and multilayered concept." Donna describes how a biracial student (Hispanic and Anglo) in a music education immersion internship came to recognize that her own cultural assumptions were a barrier between her and the Latino students in the urban school where she was teaching. The words of this young teacher provide food for thought, especially for those who prepare music teachers to work in urban schools. While language was not a barrier for this young teacher, it is a barrier between students and music teachers in many urban schools. Particularly in secondary music classes, teachers depend heavily on verbal communication to convey musical knowledge. As a result, English-language learners may not understand much of what happens in those classes. Regina Carlow shares a process known as *dialogue journals* to help music teachers reach out to limited English proficiency (LEP) students.

Teachers who work to develop a high degree of cultural understanding with their students are known as *culturally relevant* pedagogues. In the final chapter in this section, Kathy M. Robinson offers the practices of four such music teachers as models to the profession. Each of them has learned to go beyond their middle-class backgrounds to use the cultural knowledge, prior experiences, and performance styles of diverse cultures to make learning more appropriate and effective for urban students.

MUSIC TEACHER STORIES

> One does not have to stretch the imagination too far or be too perceptive to realize that music educators in America have a tremendous responsibility to develop a wider pool of culturally diverse students . . . who will be both talented in music performance and exhibit music literacy, understanding, skills, and knowledge that qualify them to enter college and university programs as music majors for the purpose of joining the music profession as teachers and administrators. (Spearman, 2000, p. 163)

The music teachers who deal with the realities of urban schooling on a daily basis are in many ways the experts. Janice Smith and Carlos R. Abril share the stories of some of those teachers. Janice teaches in an urban university, and several of her graduate students teach in urban settings. Upon hearing that this book was forthcoming, they asked Janice to write a chapter that presented the reality of novice music teachers learning to negotiate urban schools. Their stories provide insight to those who plan professional development and teacher education for urban music teachers. Carlos Abril describes the professional lives of three teachers at a different place in their careers. These experienced music teachers have developed successful methods for providing high-quality and meaningful music programs for students.

TEACHING STRATEGIES

> Music teachers who are successful in the urban setting must share successful teaching strategies so that new teachers can benefit from their experience in spanning what is often a cultural void between teacher and learner. (Hinckley, 1995, p. 20)

Music teachers from urban schools seldom have an opportunity to share their strategies with others in their districts, much less with the profession at large. The "Teaching Strategies" section in this book recognizes the importance of bringing practicing music teachers into the conversation about music in urban schools. Acknowledging the challenges of teaching in "a school culture bent on test preparation," Elizabeth Ann McAnally begins this section by sharing the strategies she uses in her music classroom to motivate students. Elizabeth suggests that creating classrooms where students feel safe, teaching content that is relevant to students, and making cross-curricular connections will motivate urban music students to learn.

Daniel Abrahams uses *differentiated instruction* to reach the students in his urban choral ensemble. He finds that this approach raises the "level of involvement for every student by encouraging reflective learning, advanced critical thinking skills, problem solving and creativity . . . in urban settings and beyond." Kevin Mixon provides strategies that have helped him to build a successful music program in a city in upstate New York: an initial survey, culturally relevant recruiting, support from parents and school colleagues, and administrative support. Jeanne Porcino Dolamore presents the *String Chorale Concept* as an alternative teaching strategy for string programs in urban schools. Jeanne suggests that a choral approach to string teaching can help string teachers meet high musical standards, embrace diversity of culture and economic level, and involve the community in string education. Karen Iken discusses an action research study in which she examined the impacts of instrumental music education on urban students. She finds, interestingly enough, that her research not only helped her understand her students, but changed her perceptions as their teacher.

ALTERNATIVE TEACHING MODELS

> To find the true values of a culture and the ways in which music is reflective of those values, we must look beneath the surface. (Palmer, 2002, p. 33)

Alternative teaching models based on philosophical ideals can provide direction for those seeking to make stronger connections across cultural boundaries. Frank Abrahams and Patrick K. Schmidt challenge music educators to seek alternative pedagogies that deal directly with urban issues. They suggest that the tenets of *Critical Pedagogy for Music Education* help music teachers connect directly to the worlds and realities of urban students. As Terry Gates (2000) noted during the Housewright Symposium, "Unity and diversity are both important parts of this landscape in compulsory schooling, and music makes both unity and diversity audible in ways that language does not" (p. 69). Edward Green and Alan Shapiro present *Aesthetic Realism* as a way to approach that reality in the music class. Based on the core principle that "all beauty is a making one of opposites, and the making one of opposites is what we are going after in ourselves," these authors have found that this bias-free concept can serve as a bridge between faculty and students who have very different musical backgrounds.

The common denominator between all of these issues—cultural responsivity, student learning, and music teacher growth—is professional development. Without opportunities to work with each other, their non-music peers, and those beyond their schools and universities, music teachers are left out of the professional discussions that define the role of music in urban education. The final chapter in this volume describes a situation where participation in school reform efforts was not expected by, required of, or available to urban music teachers. Contrasting this with Thiessen and Barrett's (2002) vision of "reform-minded music teachers," I suggest that music will remain outside the larger school reform vision unless music educators seek and are given opportunities to join the conversation.

A familiar parable describes a scene in which a person has lost their keys in a dark alley and is searching painstakingly under a lamppost. As James Garbarino (1999) tells it, an old friend happens by and offers to help in the search for the lost keys. This proves to be a difficult task, so the friend calls in reinforcements. This includes a "campaign" ("Find the keys! Find the keys!"), a "more systematic approach," a "behavioral approach," a "psychoanalytical approach," and finally a "literary-historical approach." The futility of the search becomes clear when the key-seeker confesses that the keys were lost "about a hundred yards up the road," but the light was better under the lamppost (p. 179–180).

My first encounter with music education in the urban setting left me wondering how I and others in the profession had been left "in the dark" about the realities of urban education and the difficulties involved in addressing the musical needs of urban students. Upon reflection, it seems instead that a long-standing epidemic of social blindness has allowed us *to stay in the light*—that the privilege of our ethnicity, or our economic or educational status has let us believe that the answers to these difficult problems lie in places where they are easy to see. They do not. If they did, the collective wisdom of the many musician-educators that serve American schools in so many capacities would have solved them long ago.

If music is good for children, then it belongs at the center of education, urban and otherwise. For this to occur, music educators must join forces with others in the corridors and communities in which they work. Administrators, teacher educators, researchers, policy makers, school reformers, advocates for the poor, activists from diverse cultures, and members of urban communities must join their distinct voices together in an effort to bring the transformational power of music to the core of urban education. The tipping point will occur when each of us moves forward individually and collectively to make this difference.

REFERENCES

Carter, Warrick L. (1993). Minority participation in music programs. In M. Mark (Ed.) (2002), *Music education: Source readings from ancient Greece to today*, 2nd ed. (pp. 227–228). New York: Routledge.

Choate, R. A. (Ed.). (1968). *Documentary report of the Tanglewood Symposium.* Washington, DC: Music Educators National Conference.

Fowler, C. (Ed.). (1970). Facing the music in urban education [special issue]. *Music Educators Journal.* Washington, DC: Music Educators National Conference.

Garbarino, J. (1999). *Lost boys.* New York: Free Press.

Gates, J. T. (2000). Why study music? In C. Madsen (Ed.), *Vision 2020: The Housewright Symposium on the future of music education* (pp. 57–82). Reston, VA: MENC.

Gladwell, Malcolm. (2000). *The tipping point: How little things can make a big difference.* Boston: Little, Brown and Company.

Hinckley, J. (1995). Urban music education: Providing for students. *Music Educators Journal*, 82(1), 32–36. Retrieved July 1, 2005, from the Academic Search Premier database.

———. (2000). Introduction. In C. Madsen (Ed.), *Vision 2020: The Housewright Symposium on the future of music education* (pp. 1–3). Reston, VA: MENC.

Lehman, P. (2000). How can the skills and knowledge called for in the national standards best be taught? In C. Madsen (Ed.), *Vision 2020: The Housewright Symposium on the future of music education* (pp. 89–107). Reston, VA: MENC.

McAllester, D. (1968). Curriculum must assume a place at the center of music: A minority report. In R. A. Choate (Ed.), *Documentary report of the Tanglewood Symposium* (p. 138). Washington, DC: Music Educators National Conference.

Madsen, C. K. (Ed.). (2000). *Vision 2020: The Housewright Symposium on the future of music education*. Reston, VA: MENC.

Mark, M. M. (2000). MENC from Tanglewood to the present. In C. K. Madsen (Ed.), *Vision 2020: The Housewright Symposium on the future of music education* (pp. 5–22). Reston, VA: MENC.

MENC: The National Association for Music Education. (2002). Strategic plan. Retrieved August 30, 2005, from www.menc.org/information/admin/strategic-plan.html

Palmer, A. J. Multicultural music education: Pathways and byways, purpose and serendipity. In B. Riemer (Ed.), *World musics and music education: Facing the issues* (pp. 31–53). Reston, VA: MENC.

Spearman, C. E. (2000). How will societal and technological changes affect the teaching of music? In C. K. Madsen (Ed.), *Vision 2020: The Housewright Symposium on the future of music education* (pp. 155–184). Reston, VA: MENC.

Thiessen, D., & Barrett, J. R. (2002). Reform-minded music teachers: A more comprehensive image of teaching for music teacher education. In R. Colwell and C. Richardson (Eds.), *The new handbook of research on music teaching and learning* (pp. 759–785). New York: Oxford.

I

CULTURAL RESPONSIVITY

1

Defining Ourselves as Other: Envisioning Transformative Possibilities

Cathy Benedict

> Outsider is commonly the term used to describe people new to a place or people who do not know the ways of a place. The use of the term outsider indicates that a person does not properly understand the behavior expected of people in a town, region, or nation. Outsiders are often despised and suspected of being troublemakers. They are people "out of place." (Cresswell, 1996, pp. 25–26)

For teachers, urban settings are often looked upon as placements of desperation. How has this become so? Who can we blame? They see only the difficulties; they see urban schools as places where "quality" music programs don't stand a chance. There are the usual suspects of course: the apparent larger-than-life behavioral problems, parental noninvolvement issues, and cultural tensions, as well as the perceived lack of skills and understandings children bring to the classroom. The list feels endless and efforts seem futile.

We would benefit from considering the reasons such negative images have become embedded in our consciousness. While these issues may seem very real, it is necessary in any educative situation to address assumptions. Chief among those that we must consider when examining urban education is the notion of *who we are* as teachers and whether our beliefs and assumptions somehow perpetuate these perceived "problems" in urban music education. I am suggesting that we challenge ourselves to see these issues not as "givens," but as situations that had and have human agency.

In taking on this challenge, we might ask ourselves whether we have played a role in creating and perpetuating these situations. Of course, none of us seeks to do this directly, but we must continually remind ourselves that "larger social and economic factors . . . impinge on individuals' lives and their life chances" (Ladson-Billings, 2001, p. 106). The title of this chapter suggests that seeing ourselves as the "other," or the outsider, rather than the *savior*, or the bearer of "correct" culture and cultural understanding, will better enable us to engage in transformative possibilities.

So—What does it mean to see ourselves as "other," and what does this have to do with transformation? All of us "know" that music education needs to "fight" for its rightful place of legitimacy within a curriculum. Who has time for transformation when our efforts need to be channeled toward advocacy? Who has time for transformation when we are teaching "children who have never known the joy of having music in their lives, [giving] them a gift that they will never forget" (Reninger, 2004)?

The purpose of this chapter is to examine the ways in which the particular geographical situatedness of the urban school contributes to the ways music educators, administrators, researchers, and policy makers envision their positions and engage with students. Of particular interest are those engagements that view students as bereft of culture, musical experiences, and lacking in "appropriate skills." I seek to suggest that an educative process that focuses on a very particular model of cultural transmission and method actually serves to punish our students—rather than celebrate diversity—to negate the very cultures they bring to our classrooms and lives. Ultimately this process serves to punish us as well, preventing opportunities for all of us to experience community, to engage in reciprocal experiences that will allow the eradication of "otherness."

THE TAKEN-FOR-GRANTEDNESS OF THE URBAN SETTING AND "OTHER"

How did urban education become the last refuge of desperation? Why have urban settings become almost synonymous with troubled students and difficult teaching situations? Certainly *someone* is responsible. The easiest person to blame is the student, particularly the "type" of student who may attend urban schools. Many of these schools had past "glory days" in which most students graduated and went off to college: some to become statesmen, scholars, even Nobel laureates. This was expected and even considered "normal" behavior and yet now, urban schools often struggle just to retain students.

Cresswell writes, "The geographical setting of actions plays a central role in defining our judgment of whether actions are good or bad" (1996, p. 9).

The ramifications of this statement are vast and circular. The geographical setting of the urban school contributes to the ways we see our students. This setting consequently affects how we see ourselves, including the ways in which we engage in pedagogy, curriculum development, assessment practices, research, and eventually policy. While our actions are mostly well intended, unless we question how "society" defines terms such as *at risk*, *disadvantaged*, and *culture*, the ramifications of these assumptions—often set in play by the geographical setting—cloud our actions. If we allow them to go unexamined, we end up ascribing very particular meanings to what we think of as music, culture, and our practice. We need to step back and check whether our assumptions about students—differences in their perceptions of discipline and of structure, differences between their sense of order and our own—stem from our particular dominant status quo experiences. Do we assume students "should" behave in certain ways because those are the expectations from our own culture?

Cresswell continues: "But value and meaning are not inherent in any space or place—indeed, they must be created, reproduced, and defended from heresy" (1996, p. 9). Heresy, false doctrine—We work very hard to defend and advocate our particular culture from these things. Seeing our students as "others" allows us to define ourselves as "out of place" in the urban setting, *their* setting. Doing so enables us not only to abdicate responsibility for actions that perpetuate a system of dominance and social injustice, but also to perpetuate a version of "in place," *our* setting, confident of our well-meaning, yet unexamined mission. Is it this power, this ability to "make the rules" and define what appropriate behavior is and is not in a classroom and society, that we are convinced we must defend?

Were each of us—music educators, researchers, administrators, and policy makers—to take on this task of seeing ourselves as "other" (or, more importantly, realizing that there is no "other"), we might begin to see the ways in which we take for granted our ability to move in and out of the urban setting with ease. This might make us more willing to take on the responsibility for challenging a system of assumptions, oppression, and injustice. In this case heresy would become the act of *not* challenging assumptions. Clearly, contemplating the transformative possibilities of urban settings is a complicated journey as we examine this sense of "otherness" from many perspectives.

The National Collaborative on Diversity in the Teaching Force (2004) sifted through the statistics collected by the National Center for Education Statistics (2003) and came up with some rather powerful facts, one of which is that 90% of American public school teachers are White, while 40% of students are of color. While the term *White* is problematic in itself, this statistic suggests that *White* teachers work regularly in settings in which they are the minority—the other. Does this matter? Well, it does and it does not. And while it may seem easy and obvious to go with the "it does not" answer, this assumption, gone unchecked, can become the foundation for a pedagogy of neglect.

> Typically, white middle-class perspective teachers have little or no understanding of their own culture. Notions of whiteness are taken for granted. They are rarely interrogated. But being white is not merely about biology. It is about choosing a system of privilege and power. (Ladson-Billings, 2001, p. 96)

The commonness of Whiteness in our society spawns a culture in which the experiences of the White teacher become the normative yardstick by which to measure all experience. A recent study by Mazzei (2004) considered the ways White teachers regarded their "racial identity." Mazzei found that even when they were the minority population in schools, White teachers continued to see their experiences as "normative" and those of their students as "other" (p. 26). This inability to see Whiteness as a particular positioning and privilege in society "coupled with a cultural taboo learned early by many Whites that it is impolite not to notice color or differences, produces silences that are meaning-full" (p. 30).

THE DEFICIT MODEL

Some educators choose to view the problems of urban education as a collection of perceived deficits that students bring to the classroom. This includes an assumption that students are lacking in the skills and knowledge that are "necessary" to succeed in schools. Unfortunately, framing the problems of urban schooling, choosing to examine students and their environments (including parent and communities) from a deficit model serves to negate the possibility of realizing the potential of each student.

We must consider whether the deficit model allows (or perhaps even encourages) blame to be placed on the students for the difficulties that arise in urban settings. We must likewise be cautious about using words such as *underprivileged*, *disadvantaged*, *deprived*, *neglected*, and even *poor*. What does it mean when music teacher educators frame issues of urban education through the deficit model, when novice teachers learn to see urban settings as places of "warfare," and see their pedagogical training as preparation for "survival in the trenches"? These poor choices of language, coupled with a profound lack of knowledge of cultural practices and parental issues, sets up a "safe" and seemingly immutable barrier between "us" and "them." While these particular practices may seem innocuous, left unexamined they are at best unhelpful and at worst deceitful and even insidious.

Allowing our thought processes to be framed with a deficit-based analysis lets us forget, as Ladson-Billings reminds us, the "larger social and economic factors that impinge on individuals' lives and their life chances" (2001, p. 106). Using descriptors such as *underserved*, rather than *underprivileged*, helps to place the responsibility back on those who have privilege in this world and forces us to consider that we are complicit in the larger and social and economic factors that are impinging on our students' lives. A student of Ladson-Billings once pointed out that our assumptions are often sifted through the expectations of a "Western philosophy toward education" (p. 199). In a similar fashion, music educators often "expect" students to behave in certain ways, to come from certain kinds of home environments, and to lack the specific experiences that will prepare them for "our" music education agenda. The deficit model may also obfuscate the cultural differences between the ways that families from different cultures address the educative system.

> Some teachers assume that the "right" way for students and their parents to respond to school is the way they (and their parents) responded to school. When parents fail to come to school and participate in school activities, teachers may assume that the parents don't care about education. Teachers (like all of us) may attribute meanings to parents' and students' behaviors that are incorrect. (Ladson-Billings, 2001, p. 83)

Malia'iaupuni, a spokesperson for the native peoples of the Hawaiian Islands, addresses the deficit model in this way: "deficits-based approaches often miss the expertise that exists in our communities and families, viewing instead outside experts as the only ones capable of 'fixing' our problems" (2004, p. 29). Rather than thinking of us as experts, Malia'iaupuni calls on us as teachers to draw on the strengths of each individual. She challenges us to create a "positive space for greater voice and empowerment of a marginalized collective" (p. 29). So for music educators, it isn't just a matter of including a "broad range of genres, styles, and periods, including music from outside the art music traditions, music from the various cultures from the various musical cultures of the world" (MENC, 1994, pp. 3–4). The challenge is in examining our assumptions and situations and creating a "space for greater voice and empowerment" so that, as Malia'iaupuni reminds us, we may be better able to "challenge sociocultural and political processes of domination" (2004, p. 30).

COLOR-BLIND TEACHING AND THE PEDAGOGY OF NEGLECT AND IRRELEVANCY

Cultural aversion is the reluctance of teachers and administrators to discuss race and race-related issues like ethnicity, culture, prejudice, equality, and social justice. This color-blind philosophy is linked to edu-

> cators' uncomfortableness in discussing race, their lack of knowledge of the cultural heritage of their students and the students' peers, and their fears and anxieties that open consideration of differences might incite racial discord or perhaps upset a fragile, often unpredictable, racial harmony. (Jordan Irvine, 1991, p. 26)

I would imagine that each of us came to the teaching force wanting to teach "all kinds" of students. The alternative suggests a person none of us wants to be, or even to associate with. No teacher comes to the profession with the intention to create situations that would be disrespectful and "incite racial discord." However, those meaning-full silences that Mazzei discovered around the racial identity of people of privilege can render us incapable of considering the ways in which color-blind pedagogy plays out in music education—ways that might seem incomprehensible, a pedagogy that in fact

> denies the legitimacy of students' heritage and race and often contributes to a cycle of misunderstanding that leads to unstated and unvented hostility between teachers and students, which often results in more misunderstanding and confrontations. (Jordan Irvine, 1991, p. 27)

Each of us has been "schooled" on the importance of addressing diversity and multiculturalism in our classrooms. MENC (1994) has been at the forefront of articulating this mission:

> The music studied should reflect the multimusical diversity of America's pluralistic culture. It should include a broad range of genres, styles, and periods, including music from outside the art music traditions, music from the various cultures form the various musical cultures of the world. (pp. 3–4)

To suggest that music education does not reflect multiculturalism, or to deny the presence of music educators at the forefront of the multiculturalism movement—as defined by varied repertoire and cultural contexts—would be nonsense. And yet, in our music classrooms, how do we address the physical characteristics of race? In what ways has our "color-blind" philosophy prevented us from truly engaging in a process of multiculturalism? As Jordan Irvine points out, color-blind teaching has devastating effects when allowed to go by unexamined. It is worth quoting her at length:

> By ignoring students' most obvious physical characteristic, race, these teachers are also disregarding students' unique cultural behaviors, beliefs, and perceptions—important factors that teachers should incorporate, not eliminate, in their instructional strategies and individualized approaches to learning. When teachers ignore students' race and claim that they treat all children the same, they usually mean that their model of the ideal student is white and middle-

> class and that all students are treated as if they are or should be both white and middle-class. Such treatment contributes to perceptions of inferiority about black culture and life and to denial and self-hatred by black children. (1991, p. 54)

The implications of these words are powerful. And while as music teachers, it almost seems that we are above these accusations, the question of how we treat our students in our classes remains. How do we "incorporate . . . instructional strategies and individualized approaches to learning" to recognize and challenge structures of oppression, to acknowledge "students' unique cultural behaviors"?

Some of us rely on a method of teaching music: Orff, Kodály, Gordon, Suzuki. We may believe that when we "teach to" the standards as discrete units, so as to check them off a list, we are relying on a particular method of teaching. We find comfort in the fact that these methods enable us to teach each of our students fairly and equally, to treat everyone identically. Could it be that this reliance on method renders us blind to the differences in our students? Is our understanding of Western music "as a universal language" actually an attempt to assimilate our students into "our" musical culture—albeit with the inclusion of diverse musics and cultural contexts? Valenzuela, addressing the Mexican American population in the United States notes that

> Students' cultural world and their structural position must also be fully apprehended, with school-based adults deliberately bringing issues of race, difference, and power into central focus. This approach necessitates abandoning the notion of a color-blind curriculum and a neutral assimilation process. (1999, p. 109)

How can music educators use this pedagogical stance of questioning, challenging issues of power and inferiority, as suggested by Valenzuela, Ladson-Billings, and others? How does this differ from believing that our purpose as educators is to "give our students a leg up on life"? How does thinking of our students as "less fortunate" people who have never known the joy of music in their lives serve to fulfill the MENC goal that the primary purpose of music education is "to improve the quality of life for all students by developing their capacities to participate fully in their musical culture" (1994, p. 2)? How does a repertoire of diverse music and the examination of the cultural context really address each of our students and their structural positioning in the world? And finally, is any of this multiculturalism? Ladson-Billings (2001) reminds us:

> "Helping the less fortunate" can become a lens through which teachers see their role. Gone is the need to really help students become educated enough to develop intellectual, political, cultural, and economic independence. Such an

> approach to teaching diverse groups of students renders their culture irrelevant. (p. 82)

Thus, it is not enough to simply "reflect the multimusical diversity of America's pluralistic culture" (MENC, 1994, pp. 3–4). Music educators, administrators, researchers, and policy makers must accept the challenge to look beyond the idea of "improving the quality of life" and address the political and structural positioning of our students so that transformative experiences are not only musically, but socially oriented.

Seeing ourselves as rescuers, and the urban setting—the students and their cultures—as deficits, impedes our interpretation of liberation, which comes only when all persons engage in actions that move them toward a fuller humanity and social justice. This is a transformative process, just as multiculturalism is a process, rather than a noun or an adjective (Sleeter, 2002). Banks and Banks (2004) define multiculturalism as

> A reform movement designed to change the total educational environment so that students from diverse racial and ethnic groups, both gender groups, exceptional students, and students from each social-class will experience equal educational opportunities in schools, colleges, and universities. A major assumption of multicultural education is that some students, because of their particular racial, ethnic, gender, and cultural characteristics, have a better chance of succeeding in educational institutions as they are currently structured than do students who belong to other groups or who have different cultural and gender characteristics. (p. 451)

Including diverse musics is an important first step, as is contextualizing those musics. But just teaching about differences is not enough. . . . there is another critical step. We must also allow and encourage stories to be told. Pedagogy that leads toward societal transformation requires opportunities for these stories and narratives to take place in all classes including performing ensembles, general music, and even music theory. Such stories might include discussions of those whose voices and musics are missing, as well as reasons why certain composers and musics have been privileged. The stories must be enmeshed with the constant narrative of what it means to understand diverse musics and cultures, and consideration of whether we can ever fully understand cultures that differ from our own.

This means taking on habits of mind that will allow us to ask difficult questions such as these: Which students are not being served in our programs and how are we complicit in that arrangement? How do our word choices prevent social transformation? And most importantly, How can I continually question my own assumptions so that I may help my students question theirs?

These kinds of questions lead toward what Ladson-Billings refers to as "culturally relevant pedagogy": a pedagogy that is based on "student achievement, cultural competence and a sense of sociopolitical consciousness" (2001, p. 144). We must consider whether a "color-blind" approach to teaching music negates the goal of cultural relevance and even serves to perpetuate models of oppression. We must examine the temptation to think that we can address deeper and systemic issues of oppression simply by including a diverse repertoire of music. Will relying on the belief that music is a "universal language" magically wipe away all differences and create the coveted level playing field? Students can certainly identify with music of their cultures, and even differences in music. Yet how much more profound if they can affiliate their life experiences with issues and situations that are addressed in the curriculum, thus becoming tied more closely to the goals of a socially and ideologically aware music curriculum.

LINGERING QUESTIONS

The lingering question that hovers over all that we do is the purpose of music education. There are at least two parts to this question: the musical purpose and the larger, societal purpose that addresses the ways we engage with others to broaden the ideal of "quality of life." An examination of this larger purpose begins with each of us individually. We must consider our methods; there are serious limitations inherent in following a method that does not allow us to know and see each child for who they are. Rather than accepting the idea that our lives are predestined by cultural differences, we need to find ways to acknowledge and make sense of how our students live in the world. As such we need to be mindful of believing that our worldview is the only worldview and be wary of this particular positioning of power.

> Indeed, in the educational institutions of this country, the possibilities for poor people and for people of color to define themselves, to determine the self each should be, involve a power that lies outside of the self. It is others who determine how they should act, how they are to be judged. When one "we" gets to determine standards for all "wes," then some "wes" are in trouble! (Delpit, 1995, p. xv)

On multiple levels, music teacher "wes" ought to take this missive to heart. Too often others outside the discipline have been allowed to define who we are and what we can be. As a result, an inordinate amount of our time and effort is spent on advocacy. How can we take control of our own reality and advocate policy that allows us to do what we do best; that is, to enable all persons to define and express who they are? Can we construe advocacy as something bigger than standards and trappings of arts education? We are positioned to address the broader educative goal of democratic inquiry and critique. Transformation, however, begins with who we are and the assumptions we bring to any educative setting.

In January of 1970, *Music Educators Journal* devoted an entire issue to a special report called "Facing the Music in Urban Education." In bold letters, music educators were told that an "educational revolution is underway," in which the "front lines are the ghetto schools." The bold declaration continued with wartime metaphors, suggesting "command headquarters" and "combat troops," language that has evolved only slightly in the 35 years since its publication. It is a difficult volume to read through. On the one hand, we can be comforted by the progress we have made. But comparing the 1970s "lingo" of that issue with that of the current era tells us how much farther we need to go.

The title of this chapter suggests that we should learn to see ourselves as "other." The real need, however, is not to see our students or ourselves as outsiders, but rather to "come to see that everybody is cultural and multicultural" (Erickson, 2004, p. 55). If our primary purpose as music educators is to improve the quality of life for all students, then taking on transformative pedagogy to advocate for social change, rather than relying on methodologies that suggest that the universal language of music transcends all, would enable us not only to develop our students' capacities to participate fully in their musical cultures, but our own capacities to transform culture as well.

REFERENCES

Banks, C., & Banks, J. (Eds.). (2004). *Multicultural education: Issues and perspectives*. Hoboken, NJ: Wiley.

Cresswell, T. (1996). *In place/out of place: Geography, ideology, and transgression*. Minneapolis: University of Minnesota Press.

Delpit, L. (1995). *Other people's children: Cultural conflict in the classroom*. New York: The New Press.

Erickson, F. (2004). Culture in Society and in Educational Practices. In C. Banks & J. Banks (Eds.), *Multicultural education: Issues and perspectives*. Hoboken, NJ: Wiley.

Fowler, C. (Ed.). (1970). Special Report. *Music Educators Journal*, 56(5), 90.

Jordan Irvine, J. (1991). *Black students and school failure: Policies, practices, and prescriptions*. Westport, CT: Praeger.

Ladson-Billings, G. (2001). *Crossing over to Canaan: The journey of new teachers in diverse classrooms*. San Francisco: Jossey-Bass.

Malia'iaupuni, S. (2004). Ka'akalai Ku Kanaka: A call for strengths-based approaches from a Native Hawaiian perspective. *American Educational Research Association*, 33(9), 29–36.

Mazzei, L. (2004). Silent Listenings: Deconstructive practices in discourse-based research. *American Educational Research Association*, 33(2), 21–30.

Music Educators National Conference (MENC). (1994). *National standards for arts education: What every young American should know and be able to do in the arts.* Reston, VA: MENC.

Reninger, R. (2004). Setting your sights on the inner city—The joys and challenges of urban music education, *MENC Collegiate NewsLink, December2004*. Retrieved from www.menc.org/networks/collegiate/newslink/archives/04dec/December2000Newslink. html on July 7, 2005.

Sleeter, C. (2002). Rethinking our schools. Retrieved from www.rethinkingschools.org/archive/15_02/Int152.shtml on September 1, 2005.

Valenzuela, A. (1999). *Subtractive schooling: U.S.-Mexican youth and the politics of caring*. Albany: State University Press of New York.

2

Cultural Clashes: The Complexity of Identifying Urban Culture

Donna T. Emmanuel

CHANGING OUR PERSPECTIVES

Many of the terms commonly used in conversations about urban schooling—*cultural diversity*, *inner-city*, *at-risk*, *urban*, *multicultural*, and *others*—carry with them sets of assumptions based on the misconception that culture itself can be "fixed" or constant. In fact, the "belief systems and cultural practices associated with cultural groups are always under negotiation with new generations and new material as well as with social conditions" (Lee, 2003, p. 3). Changes within cultural groups occur because of many types of societal influences. One of those influences is the way groups typically identified as minority (such as those in urban settings) are viewed by members of the dominant culture.

Research has shown that educators in general tend to fit a typical profile, that of White, female, and middle class. This group fits within the category of "dominant culture" in the United States. It is common for educators who fit this profile to have preconceived beliefs about schools and students in urban areas. These might include that the environment is dangerous, that students do not want to learn, that students are loud and unruly, that there is little parental involvement because parents do not value education, and that these are inherent characteristics. These stereotypes are examples of how members of the dominant culture tend to value and devalue certain cultural differences (Southwest Education Development Lab, 1999). These perspectives have an impact on those who are typically identified as cultural "others." Rather than reflecting the true nature of a cultural group, these perspectives are often inaccurately and socially constructed.

A "typical" teacher new to the urban setting might assume, based on these perceptions, that his or her role is to impose his or her own brand of knowledge, to "save" underprivileged youth, or to do a good deed for humanity. This is what Paolo Freire (1982) calls *cultural invasion*, when teachers draw from their own values, ideologies, and social worlds to determine what is best for those who are different from them. These simplistic perceptions and preconceived attitudes about urban students and schools can cause educators to perpetuate cultural conflict and as a result be less effective in the classroom. In order to find common ground with their culturally diverse students, teachers must understand that culture is a complex and ever-changing phenomenon.

It is vital for music educators in urban areas to realize that individual identities are constantly evolving rather than to make simplistic generalizations about members of urban cultural groups. We must remember that categorizing students as members of a certain cultural group does not assure that every individual within that cultural group shares the same belief systems or characteristics (Lee, 2003, p. 4). Instead we must come to understand individuals in urban classrooms as participants in their own cultural practices while also being aware of the larger contexts of social, political, and economic influences that exist in urban settings.

This chapter describes an experience that brought the complexity and multilayeredness of the concept of culture to light for a specific participant in a music education immersion internship. Her journey toward coming to terms with her identity as an individual and as a future music educator is instructive to those of us who would understand the cultural dilemmas often presented in urban school settings, whether we are in-service teachers, preservice teachers, teacher educators, or administrators.

THE IMMERSION INTERNSHIP

It was during an undergraduate-level immersion internship that this particular participant confronted her own quest for identity. The project was offered as a university course for credit and had two components: one week of orientation on a Big Ten university campus in the United States where participants examined their own beliefs and attitudes concerning teaching in a culturally diverse setting and two weeks of immersion internship in urban Detroit, Michigan, which included team-teaching at a primary site and observation in a variety of schools. The immersion internship was part of a study on developing intercultural competence among preservice music educators (Emmanuel, 2002). The concept of intercultural competence is vitally important in the field of urban music teacher education because preservice teachers' experiences within their own cultures, as well as their personal histories that form those experiences, influence the formation of knowledge, attitudes, beliefs, and values. In turn, teachers' knowledge, attitudes, beliefs, and values influence their perceptions of students' behaviors and actions, and their interpretations of both verbal and nonverbal communications. Teachers must recognize and understand their own worldviews in order to understand the worldviews of the students, and thus be effective in working with students from diverse cultural backgrounds.

This experience was defined as an *immersion internship* because during the immersion weeks of this course, the instructor and participants lived together in one apartment located in downtown Detroit. The elementary school where the participants spent most of their time observing and teaching was located in a predominantly Hispanic neighborhood downtown. This course was made available for undergraduates and graduates in the music education program with a limit on the size of the class, offered as a fifth-year elective for all music education majors. Five students registered for the class.

During the orientation week, the participants read selected texts, participated in carefully chosen activities and discussions, and viewed two films. Each of these sources was chosen to help participants examine the beliefs and attitudes they might have about teaching in a culturally diverse urban area, and how those beliefs and attitudes originated. Texts included *Savage Inequalities* by Jonathan Kozol (1991), *The Bluest Eye* by Toni Morrison (1970), and *The Art of Crossing Cultures* by Craig Stortie (1990). Other activities included creating a set of ground rules by which all participants would abide, writing and sharing detailed autobiographies to discover the similarities and differences among the participants, interviewing close relatives about their cultural histories, exploring the word *multicultural*, identifying cultural aspects of ourselves, and taking a multicultural awareness quiz. The films included *Blue Eyed* by Strigel, Verhaag, and Elliott (1996) and *The Color of Fear* by Lee Mun Wah (1994). All participants began keeping journals this week and continued throughout the immersion weeks.

During the immersion weeks the students observed in the primary site, taught short lessons in teams, observed music educators in a variety of urban settings (including middle and high school band and choral programs), and gradually taught longer segments individually. All the classes they observed were located in downtown Detroit and were in both traditional public schools and magnet schools. By the end of the two-week session, most of the participants were teaching entire class periods at multiple grade levels.

All participants in the study were concerned with being "inquisitive ethnographers," which arose from a primary purpose of the study. Often internships focus on the nuts and bolts of teaching rather than gathering rich, thick data in the form of reflection on the teaching experience. The participants in this study were required to journal and take field notes daily in order to be able to revisit and reflect upon their experiences. This component of the course proved to be extremely powerful, as evidenced by new awarenesses gained by the participants months after the internship was completed. Only by examining the ethnographic data they collected were they able to come to these new realizations.

From a practical point of view, it is challenging to design, develop, and implement immersion experiences such as this one. Finding a location for all participants to live together for a period of time is often the most difficult task. Another task is establishing a relationship with urban school administrators to choose a primary site and other observation sites. There may be a short window of time for such an internship to take place—before public schools are out but after the university spring semester has ended. Because the topics discussed are often personal and controversial, it is important to establish an environment of safety and trust among all the participants. There must be an experienced instructor who can act as guide and interpreter for behaviors and incidents that might be witnessed. Adding to the difficulty is that there are few true immersion internships that are documented and so few models exist. In spite of these challenges, the results of these experiences can be life-changing, making them valuable in urban teacher preparation.

Camille

The participant discussed in this chapter, Camille (a pseudonym), is biracial, Latina, and Anglo. At the time of the internship, this young woman had already spent a good portion of her life trying to discover her identity. Her father was of Caribbean, Spanish, and Mayan descent, and was from a part of Belize located close to Mexico. Camille had visited her grandmother and other relatives in Belize on several occasions. While she strongly identified with her Latina background, she felt her peers categorized her as Anglo based on her fair skin. Upon learning that the immersion experience would take place in a predominantly Hispanic section of downtown Detroit, Camille made many assumptions based on her Latina identity. These assumptions and the conflicts they created first appeared in journal entries she made during the immersion internship. A powerful writer and thinker, she continued this exploration after the internship had ended. Four months after the immersion experience, she wrote a paper titled "Dancing Betwixt and Between the Metaphysical Self." Her words are powerful, and are included here.

A Search for Identity

Camille's first identity conflict revolved around concerns about how she would fit or would not fit in this urban setting, and what role she would play as a participant in a study. She also encountered conflict concerning the several roles she was taking on during the internship. Concerned whether what she had learned in college would be effective in an urban setting with students of diverse cultural backgrounds, she was gingerly experimenting with classroom management techniques. She was discovering what it meant to be a teacher. She was also becoming a novice researcher, gathering data and recording it in her daily journal. These same conflicts might be experienced by any beginning music teacher who finds himself or herself in an urban field placement for the first time. Camille discussed how she began to navigate these multiple roles.

> I began to search inside and ask questions such as "What role would I play in this experience? How will these students view me?" Unfortunately, [it] is after participating in the study that I realize this unique cultural immersion forced me to balance between separate identities. As a novice teacher, I planned on using this experience to improve instruction skills and polish my teaching technique. On the other hand, as [a] subject of the greater ethnographic dissertation study, I was also challenged to engage in this experience on a personal level. . . . I was forced to dance betwixt and between contrary roles of a teacher and research subject.

Camille examined each of these roles in the context of being a novice teacher and identifying herself as Latina. She chose labels to identify these developing identities: Persona Number One: A Novice Teacher in Uncharted Territory and Persona Number Two: A Naïve Mestiza American. She began examining the assumptions that she carried with her, first looking at those concerning her role as a preservice teacher, then at her assumptions concerning urban settings. These led to a shift in the way she viewed her own identity and initial steps toward reconstructing that identity.

> I primarily decided to embark on the journey with the intention of gaining practical and professional experience within a diverse setting under structured and direct supervision. I saw this experience as an opportunity to challenge academic theories learned in methods classes. I wanted to see if the knowledge acquired in my years of academic training applied to "real" world situations. It was upon entering into the project as a naïve and relatively inexperienced educator that I tried to prepare in my mind the type of environment I would encounter in Detroit. However, the assumptions I formulated before entering into the research field could not have prepared me for what I would encounter in urban Detroit. Clearly, from this preliminary exposure to my research environment, my notes suggest that this was my first experience with urban poverty.
>
> I had to search for a new identity as a music educator within this unfamiliar environment. Before agreeing to participate in the dissertation I was a sheltered college student with no real "world experience." After traveling to Detroit, I realized that my previously formulated and romanticized goals, such as show-

> ing my prospective students that life does not have to be what one is given, reaching out to the marginalized children lost in the education system, giving each child encouragement and individualized direction and showing my prospective students that musical expression is a basic human need, seemed incredibly simplistic. I had to determine if my romanticized goals would accommodate these forgotten members of society. If not, I had to figure out a way to reach them by separating myself from previous stereotypes and perceptions regarding urban education. It was this initial trip into Detroit that separated me from my sheltered outlook on society and forced me to cross the threshold towards reality. I was stuck somewhere between.

Camille went into this experience thinking that somehow the status of these urban students was deficient and that she would be able to instill in them a sense of purpose in rising above their current status. This way of thinking, that these students need to be rescued, is common in novice teachers who choose to go into an urban setting. This is again based on simplistic generalizations about students in urban areas, and until this stereotypical thinking is challenged, these teachers will be unsuccessful. It took the immersion internship experience and continued reflection for Camille to realize that these stereotypical beliefs would create barriers rather than allow her to connect with her students.

Cultural Clashes

The conflict that Camille encountered centered largely on her perception of herself as Latina and her assumption that the Hispanic students we would be working with would affirm this perception. She anticipated that the students would behave in a certain way because they shared her Latin background. Since she had experienced identity conflict throughout her own life, she was looking for validation of herself as Latina and assumed that these students would provide that validation. A pivotal event, a Cinco de Mayo celebration in the elementary school, served as the catalyst for Camille's cultural conflict.

> I vividly remember standing outside the elementary general music classroom feeling very "white." I was uncomfortable with the possibility that those around me looked at the color of my skin and judged me as a rich, snobby, white girl. Parents stood along the lockers and brick walls lining the main hallway. It was then that it happened. To my surprise the eye of a woman in her late thirties immediately caught my attention and I smiled at her with the innocent hope of establishing a connection within the communal audience. Alas, she glared at me sending a begrudging smirk in my direction as if to clearly insinuate that I, an outsider to this community, was intruding. It was at this moment I realized I was not welcome. I was an outsider.

> I naively assumed I would be able to bond with some of the students to a certain extent because I believed we shared a common Hispanic heritage. As a child of mixed races, Hispanic and Caucasian, I looked at this opportunity as a chance to reach out to the Hispanic community. I wanted to be accepted as a person of Hispanic heritage. I wanted to be labeled Hispanic, Mestiza, or Latina because I thought it meant I had a chance to connect with my surroundings on a cultural level. I wanted to be one of them. . . . I romanticized about the possibility of connecting with the Latino students in our fieldwork by using my cultural roots and Spanish surname to establish a path toward commonality. I held these students close to my heart and took it upon myself to attempt to personally connect with them on a cultural level.

Upon reflection Camille realized that much of the conflict occurred because of the assumptions she made about this particular cultural group. These assumptions were based on her own personal history and the experiences she had connecting with the Central American part of her family as well as her desire to identify herself as Latina. She realized that these were stereotypical assumptions and that this particular cultural group had evolved based on different societal influences they encountered in their urban environment.

> I found myself wrestling with my previous expectations and assumptions of traditional Mexican heritage and was faced with the vivid snippets of urban reality. I expected to see a traditional celebration of Mexican heritage at the student assembly. Instead, I witnessed an urbanized American Mexican culture that did not have any connection to the nostalgic memories told to me by my Yucatan Grandmother. I opened myself up to disillusionment by raising personal expectations and attempting to connect to my surroundings based on treasured cultural memories. I believe I experienced culture shock when I was shocked to see behaviors that didn't coincide with what I imagined I would observe. I didn't see my Grandmother's Mexico. I was confused, trapped between previous perceptions of my surroundings and that of romanticized memories.
>
> My journal, for example, expounds upon this juxtaposition between cultural perceptions in the following statement. "Culturally there were some shocking behaviors. I am familiar with the Latin culture and found movements [of the dancers] suggestive and inappropriate. Kids were dancing sexy and singing songs about infidelity. Totally inappropriate for school behavior." This statement was made after witnessing a group of young Mexican children dancing to non-traditional mass media club music. I found this offensive and not representative of the Mexican culture I expected to encounter. My journal also stated, "The only thing I can think of is that with this culture, physicality . . . [is] a large part of the Latin lifestyle. Latinos are very passionate and sensual people who take pride in their humanness." In retrospective analysis, it appears as if I made this statement due to my struggle to understand why these events happened within the public school setting. And in result, I ended up generalizing about a culture I thought I had connections to. . . . the reality of the situation lead me to realize that I held stereotypical ideas of the Mexican/Latin American

> culture. I would never understand the cultural significance of the Cinco de Mayo celebration since I am not a member of their struggle, their community, or their urban lifestyle.

Camille realized that in order to interpret behaviors she witnessed that created conflict for her, she had only her past experiences to rely upon. This is an example of how personal histories and experiences form belief systems and how those impact perceptions. Unless an educator examines those beliefs, as Camille was beginning to do, he or she will continue to misinterpret both verbal and nonverbal behaviors and perpetuate cultural conflict.

A New Definition

The realizations that Camille had forced her to reconsider the conflicts she had with her own identity. She realized that before she could begin to come to some kind of common ground with students that are somehow different from her, she would have to continue to explore her own identity, beliefs, and attitudes. She was confronted with the difficulties of identifying cultural characteristics, attitudes, and behaviors. As a preservice teacher, Camille came to the powerful realization that assumptions and preconceptions have a tremendous impact on the way teachers engage in the teaching process, the way they interact with students, and the expectations they hold for those students. She ultimately came to a new understanding of how culture might be defined and what implications this had for her as a future teacher.

> Looking back, I realize that I will probably never discern my place in the world as a Hispanic American within society. I will have to come to terms with my ethnicity and identity as a person of mixed races. The desire to branch out to cultural roots will always be there, but the extent that I place personal expectations on identity categorization will ultimately change. I will have to learn to be content with my place in society as a child of mixed races. I will have to overcome feelings of inadequacy in order to view the Hispanic culture without personal baggage.
>
> As an educator, my experience in Detroit helped me to see that cultural awareness and self-discovery are one and the same. This experience taught me that educators have a responsibility to look past prior assumptions and enter into unknown territory with a passionate intent to learn more about their surroundings, their skills, and their craft. I will possibly never fully understand other cultures, but it is [in] the process of learning about myself that I can attempt to learn about my students.
>
> I feel that experiences such as the Detroit project are a necessary step in crossing the threshold between idealism and reality. In conclusion, I am not quite sure where my career will take me in the future. I now better understand that culture is subjective and dependent upon environmental elements and is largely dependent upon personal history. And the most important lesson

learned from this ethnographic experience is that I have a long way to go before I will fully discern my mission as a music educator, as a citizen looking for social justice, and as an inquisitive ethnographer. In reality, I am on my way towards enlightenment. I simply just have to let myself dance.

CONCLUSION

The knowledge base that is most important for teaching is that which is created in context. With this as a core belief, faculty and teachers should empower future music educators through learning opportunities that are contextual and relevant to a career in teaching in urban settings. Although immersion internships like this one require extensive planning and implementation time, they can be vital components in conjunction with other culturally relevant coursework.

Ongoing research with successful music teachers in urban schools could contribute to the ongoing dialogue among all these participants. Camille's powerful reflections and realizations that emerged four months after the immersion internship are strong indicators that research should be longitudinal. These kinds of experiences can often be overwhelming, and participants need time to sort through their experiences. Longitudinal research could indicate if changes in assumptions and attitudes might be long-lasting. Music education research should also continue to look at ways of developing intercultural competence rather than focusing solely on "multicultural" awareness.

In this experience, Camille encountered many cultural clashes based on her assumptions about the rapport she would have with Hispanic students. It is important to consider that Camille, the students she encountered, and the setting in which these experiences occurred all have complex cultural underpinnings. Describing the primary school site as predominantly "Hispanic" did not completely represent the cultural picture of this setting. The students were Mexican, Mexican American, Puerto Rican, and Cuban. Their Latino cultures merged with the culture of the inner city, as well as with American popular culture, to create a complex blend of sociocultural influences. Camille discovered that the urban Hispanic culture had few commonalities with her memories of her grandmother in Belize, and the fact that she spoke Spanish meant little to the students in this urban school.

Historically, music education at the college and university level has done little to prepare future music educators to deal with the complexity of culture. By focusing on a specific "multicultural" repertoire, we may have inadvertently encouraged the stereotypical view that particular cultural groups can be associated with specific behaviors and characteristics. The results of this young woman's foray into urban culture indicate that outside perceptions of particular cultural groups, including those typically identified as "urban," often hold inaccuracies that lead to misinterpretations of behaviors and attitudes. In other words, the concept of cultural identity as we often define it is much too simplistic to be of real value when dealing with diverse cultures in the urban classroom.

The most powerful lesson for all of us, no matter what role we play in the educational process, is that successful teaching in culturally challenging settings requires that we begin by examining our own sets of assumptions, beliefs, and attitudes about people who are somehow different from us. We must reflect upon how our own personal histories and experiences have created the lenses through which we view the world, and come to understand that the world may look very different to someone else. Before we can begin to try to make connections with culturally diverse students, particularly those in urban schools, we must understand that the sets of beliefs and behaviors we carry with us impact the way we interact with our students, the way we interpret their actions, and the way we view the teaching and learning process.

REFERENCES

Emmanuel, D. (2002). A music education immersion internship: Pre-service teachers' beliefs concerning teaching music in a culturally diverse setting (Ph.D. dissertation, Michigan State University). *Digital Dissertations*, AA7 3064224.

Freire, P. (1982). *Pedagogy of the oppressed*. New York: Continuum.

Kozol, J. (1991). *Savage inequalities*. New York: Crown.

Lee, C. (2003). Why we need to re-think race and ethnicity in educational research. *Educational Researcher*, 32(5), 3–5.

Morrison, T. (1970). *The bluest eye*. New York: Plume.

Sodowsky, G., Kwan, K-L., & Pannu, R. (1995). Ethnic identity of Asians in the United States. In J. Ponterotto, J. Casas, L. Suzuki, & C. Alexander (Eds.), *Handbook of multicultural counseling* (pp. 123–154). Thousand Oaks, CA: Sage.

Southwest Educational Development Lab. (1999). Disability, diversity, and dissemination: A review of the literature on topics related to increasing the utilization of rehabilitation research outcomes among diverse consumer groups. Austin, TX: National Center for the Dissemination of Disability Research (ERIC Document Reproduction Service No. ED 436 907).

Stortie, C. (1990). *The art of crossing cultures*. Yarmouth, ME: Intercultural Press.

Strigel, C., Verhaag, B., & Elliott, J. (1996). *Blue eyed* [video recording]. San Francisco: California Newsreel.

Wah, L. (1994). *The color of fear* [video recording]. Berkeley, CA: Stir-Fry Productions.

3

Building *Confianza*: Using Dialogue Journals with English-Language Learners in Urban Schools

Regina Carlow

The young Anglo teacher walked 20 freshman and sophomore girls into a practice room for an alto sectional. She scanned the mostly non-White faces and wondered how many of the students could be classified as beginning English-language learners (ELLs). Because the school's demographics were quite diverse, she knew that the group in front of her probably included recent immigrants. She also knew that many of her students were first- and second-generation students, as well as African American students—but at first glance, she had no way of knowing any individual student's country of origin, much less anyone's linguistic abilities. She explained that she would play through the entire piece on the piano once, and then would challenge students to find where she stopped in the music. The girls were respectfully silent as she played through the piece, but she sensed that many of them neither understood her verbal instructions nor could follow the musical score that she was playing.

BACKGROUND

The classroom depicted in the above scenario is representative of the widespread phenomenon of English language learner (ELL) students in mainstream settings in urban classrooms. Additionally, because of the content-specific language involved in individual subject areas, the infusion of ELL students in U.S. schools has produced wide knowledge gaps about how to build both language and subject matter learning simultaneously (Ruiz-de-Velasco, 2000). These demographic changes have created unique challenges for the education of all racial minority and immigrant children, but most especially for teachers of ELL students in secondary urban schools.

One subpopulation of ELL students that is at great risk for failure is immigrant teens that arrive in U.S. urban school systems with significant gaps in their previous schooling. Many of these children are not fully literate in their native languages, much less in English. The meeting of students from diverse cultural groups and recent immigrants with interrupted schooling can create disharmony and distrust in the school, and it can lead to an increase in bullying and other unsafe behavior, as well as student disenfranchisement. Because of this, greater attention must be paid to the educational needs of older (middle and high school) beginning ELL students and the challenges facing the high-poverty secondary schools in which they are enrolled.

By the time younger immigrant children reach adolescence, their first languages are usually established well enough to support the learning of a second language without intense first-language support. However, because it frequently takes five to seven years to acquire a second language at a level of proficiency adequate to begin to engage proficiently in ordinary high school classroom activities, students who immigrate to the United States as adolescents are at a distinct disadvantage (Corson, 2001). ELL students' success in school is often determined by their abilities to use central concepts, discourse practices, and canons that are associated with the various academic cultures that they experience in school. In addition, there are larger social and cultural issues that shape the education of ELL students in urban secondary schools, such as prejudice, social alienation, and gang activities (Walqui, 2000).

Through interaction with parents, peers, and teachers, learners may be led beyond their comfort zone. Nevertheless, opportunities to use oral or written language interactively are often missing in many secondary music classrooms. As in all mainstreamed classes, ELL students must be able to interpret and understand directions, instructions, and grading information in both written and spoken form delivered by the teacher to the students in music classes. In secondary musical performance ensembles, verbal discourse is often centered on teacher instructions and oral critiques of students' performance. Students are not usually required to respond orally, but they are held responsible for knowing the information given either orally or in writing by their teacher. Additionally, while music students are often required to demonstrate musical competence through a series of tasks that do not necessarily require English proficiency, ELL students are frequently unable to discern the meaning behind much of the verbal discourse in the classroom and sometimes perform at a minimal level or not at all.

FORMING POSITIVE RELATIONSHIPS WITH ELL STUDENTS

During the early years of the multicultural music education movement, it was assumed that by integrating multicultural materials into the music curriculum, all students would come to better understand the myriad of diverse cultures within our society. Through this exposure, students would develop empathy for members of these cultures and appreciate the contributions of these cultures to the music of all humanity (Burton, 1997). Positive relationships and negotiation between students and teachers involve mutual respect, shared responsibility, and mutual commitment to learning goals, as well as effective communication and feedback. However, the difficulty in forming relationships with linguistically and culturally dissimilar students often presents a challenge for the monolingual educators who continue to follow traditional curricular norms that were put in place at the start of the twentieth century.

Monzó and Rueda (2001) suggest that teachers who emphasized a concern for students' emotional and social welfare played a significant role in helping ELL students to navigate learning in a new language. These authors called this process "building *confianza*." This concept is based on the belief that a significant part of teaching ELL students is mediating the social and emotional needs of these students in a way that lets the students know that they are valued and important members of the classroom community.

Examining personal accounts of students' past and present musical experiences allows music educators to have a unique opportunity to know their students. Bishop and Glynn (2003) suggested that knowledge of students' life experiences promotes the construction of *power-sharing* relationships in the classroom. Teachers may allow students to be "experts on their own lives" as they tell their stories and affirm their own heritage, culture, and beliefs (Delpit, 1995).

My personal interest in the musical experiences of English-language learners (ELL students) in music classrooms stems from more than 20 years as a general and choral music teacher. I spent many of those years in urban settings in which I encountered recent immigrants who were struggling to learn English. I had many questions about the difficulties that my high school ELL students faced. I noted their minimal participation during class, their limited involvement in extracurricular activities, an absence of traditional parental support, and what I interpreted as no buy-in to the goals of my choral program. I found that few ELL students enrolled for choir beyond one year and discovered that other choral teachers in my school district faced the same dilemmas with ELL students.

Because of this, I framed a yearlong research project to explore ELL students' experiences of singing in a high school chorus in the United States. I based my research on a quotation that I had found in *Releasing the Imagination* (1995), by Maxine Greene, an educational philosopher and teacher: "To help the diverse students we know [to] articulate their stories is not only to help them pursue the meanings of their lives, [but also] to find out *how* things are happening and to keep posing questions about the why" (p. 165). I was moved by the notion of hearing students' voices, specifically the stories of students in secondary music classes who might otherwise be invisible.

One of the ways in which I was able to hear the stories and voices of these students was through dialogue journals. A dialogue journal is a conversational narrative, written rather than spoken, through which individual students of any age can carry on private discussions with their teacher (Peyton, 1993). This chapter describes how journal writing can facilitate ELL students' successful participation and can help them to build a sense of *confianza* (confidence) in music classrooms.

FINDING SPACE FOR CONVERSATION

I became convinced that to teach students from a culture different from my own, I would have to adapt my instruction and assessment procedures and take into account my ELL students' educational and musical backgrounds. After interviewing a number of ESOL (English for speakers of other languages) teachers and asking them about strategies for helping their students to succeed in content-area classes, I found that they viewed interactive journal writing as an important part of their classes. This spurred me to try a similar tactic.

A district-wide writing initiative in all content area classes required that daily writing activities be incorporated into all classes. To add the writing component to my teaching, I had to reevaluate my rehearsal practices and put an extra activity in my always-overcrowded rehearsal plan. I soon discovered the difficulty of creating space and time for what Greene (1995) called "continuous and authentic personal encounters," particularly with the ELL students in my classroom.

At first, I focused my writing assignments on students' impressions of listening lessons and on their reactions to specific pieces of music (Larsen & Merrion, 1987). Later, I began to extend my questions to areas of music that interested them and asked about connections that they might make between the music we performed in class and the music to which they listened at home and with friends. Gradually, I allowed students to select their own topics. Many of their entries and responses astounded me and provided me with information about circumstances and events in their lives that would have remained unknown to me with my continued reliance upon the traditional rehearsal format that I had used for years.

The ELL students often struggled with these writing tasks more than did the students who were fluent in English, yet because the ELL students were accustomed to regular journal writing assignments in their ESOL classes, they were able to keep up. Some were able to respond only in brief fragments or pictures. In spite of these limitations, these journals soon provided me with a window into my students' lives.

Maria, a young woman from Panama, wrote of how a piece of music that we sang reminded her of her brother, who had been murdered the year before she had come to the United States. She confessed that she knew that she had been difficult in class lately, but as the anniversary of her brother's death was approaching, she wrote, "I am so sad days that I can't get on bus. When I hear 'How Do I Say Goodbye,' I get crying. It make me miss him and remember him at the same time. Please excuse my tears" (personal communication, September 1999).

Jorge, a young immigrant student from El Salvador, who was in an entry-level ELL class, chose to draw his journal entries. One entry depicted a chorus of men standing in front of a flag from El Salvador singing with their arms linked. I responded by saying: "Jorge, I would love to learn more about singing in your country." In his next journal entry, he listed the names of his favorite singers and their songs and offered to talk to me after class. His entry provided an opportunity for a meeting that would not have happened otherwise.

To learn more about how ELL students perceived their experiences in music class, I initiated a yearlong study situated in a colleague's secondary choral classroom. This study involved the use of dialogue journals with recent immigrant students who were in varying stages of learning English. While this study was done in a suburban school with a high number of recent immigrant students, I found many of the same themes that had surfaced in my own teaching in urban schools. Immediately, I discovered that linguistic incompatibilities greatly affected the teacher/student relationship in the classroom. The teacher was unaware of ELL students' linguistic abilities and musical backgrounds. Students participated minimally in the class. Some cited confusion, some boredom, while others said that they were afraid that they would sing at the wrong time during rehearsal. I found my own monolingual status to be a major obstacle in communicating with these ELL students. Consequently, my relationship with them started as one that relied heavily on a computer-based translation system and gradually changed to communicating in English.

Although there are drawbacks to computer-based translation programs, the format suited these students' need for immediate communication in their own language. My regular presence in the choral classroom, coupled with scheduled time for dialogue journal activities, provided the ELL students with a means for opening and maintaining a channel of communication with a sympathetic adult at school. In the paragraphs that follow, I will offer a detailed explanation of dialogue journals and their use with ELL students in music classrooms.

SETTING THE STAGE

When introducing the concept of an ongoing dialogue with students, it is essential to discuss the unique ways in which musicians and conductors communicate with and understand each other. This immediately highlights the difficulties that ELL students face on a daily basis in class. Invite the class to brainstorm possible ways to keep their non-English-speaking classmates in the discussion. Bilingual students might act as peer translators for these initial discussions.

The next step involves listing possible topics that promote connections between musicians. This list might include evaluating rehearsals, describing music listening preferences, or expressing feelings about current or future repertoire. As this activity involves writing, it is a good idea to provide a scribe for beginning ELL students so that they may see their own language displayed next to the English version. A bilingual student, teacher, or community volunteer can be used to translate on the spot for this activity. This sends a message that all students in the classroom are valued.

If translators are not available or if the school has adopted an English-only policy for ELL students, Reiss (2005) suggested the following ways to keep non-English speaking students involved in the discussion.

1. Slow down. Speak at a slightly slower pace. Pause at natural breaks in a phrase or sentence for an extra second or two.
2. Enunciate, and use gestures. The easiest way to do this is to highlight intonation and important words by raising or lowering voice level and pitch.
3. Simplify speech by avoiding contractions and the overuse of pronouns. Try to repeat names and other nouns more frequently than one might normally.
4. Explain idioms and limit their use. Ensemble conductors tend to color instructions with imagery that might cause confusion among ELL students.
5. Use a word wall that highlights key concept-area terms. Write these terms on small cards or strips of paper, and post them in a designated

place in the classroom. When using a word, point to the word or ask students to define the term.

DIALOGUE JOURNAL SPECIFICS

Initially, it is important to stress that writing in the journal is required for all students, regardless of their linguistic ability. Additionally, it is helpful to specify a predetermined minimum length for the writing, as well as to emphasize that correct grammar, punctuation, and spelling are not required. A key component of using dialogue journals is that students will receive regular written responses to their entries from their teacher and that the journal is a private conversation between student and teacher. Teacher response rate depends on a number of factors, including class size and the composition of the class. When working with an entire class, it is essential to set aside time for students to read the teacher's response, as well as time for students to write back to the teacher. This can be done in the early parts of the class: before the bell has rung or while roll is being taken. Students need a designated place to leave and pick up their journals, such as a crate, shelf, or box that ensures confidentiality.

Translation software programs are available for purchase and on the Internet, affording each ELL student an immediate means to communicate in his or her native language. Electronic and traditional dictionaries that translate words, phrases, or short paragraphs can also be used to facilitate journal writing. These are generally inexpensive and can serve as an excellent springboard for conversations with ELL students. As with all written translation programs, there are disadvantages, including word limits and the production of word-for-word translations, which can be stilted. Often, these programs do not take into account the use of idioms and content-specific terms. This can cause confusion in a music class, where many key words have dual meanings.

Despite the drawbacks of translation software, dictionaries, and Internet sites, they can be used to bridge initial communication gaps between monolingual teachers and beginning ELL students because they afford an immediate form of communication. Ayres (2001) noted that bridge building requires someone to "lay the first plank" and that schools are often structured around the notion that students should "lay the first, the second, and virtually every plank after that" (p. 75). He argued that teachers must act as the architect for the bridge and that to do that, they must know their students to know where to put the first plank. By using a computer program, Internet program, or handheld translator, no matter how limited, teachers can take that first step to invite ELL students into a continual written dialogue between student and teacher. While there are many forms of journal writing that are suitable for classroom use, learning logs and analytic notebooks are two formats that work well in the music classroom.

Learning Logs

Learning logs contain short pieces of reflective writing (which are neither edited nor graded) used as a venue to promote genuine consideration of classroom activities. For example, during the last few minutes of the class session, the teacher might ask students to describe the rehearsal in as much detail as possible. When working with ELL students, teachers should provide a numbered written outline in a worksheet format. For example:

1. Today we sang/played __________, __________, and __________.
2. The first thing we did was ______________________________.
3. The second thing we did was ____________________________.
4. The last thing we did was _______________________________.
5. Today I learned _____________________________________.

Beginning ELL students might also demonstrate their learning by drawing sequenced pictures or charts using numbers depicting several stages or stages of the rehearsal.

A vocal-range assessment page is especially useful with ELL boys who are working through various stages of the voice change. Students are instructed to document the range of the entire piece, as well as their own voice part. Then during sectionals, each boy documents his own vocal range, noting changes on a weekly basis. Learning logs make students aware of daily class activities. This awareness reinforces abstract concepts, such as breathing or tone placement. Using this type of journal is especially valuable if scheduled prior to a break or at the end of class.

Analytic Notebooks

Analytic notebooks involve writing an analysis of reactions to works of art. In the music classroom, such notebooks are most commonly used for written analyses of listening lessons. A homework assignment using this format might look like this: "Listen to two pieces of music, one that you like and one that you do not like. List all the reasons why you think that one is good and all the reasons why the other is not." Alternatively, the teacher might design a lesson around a particular piece of repertoire that the group is performing, highlighting a different arrangement of the selection, and could instruct the students to note similarities and differences. To assist ELL students with the language required in this activity, word walls and vocabulary lists should be reviewed so that the students can succeed with such a task.

Students may also use analytic notebooks to comment on their own performance. Again, this type of writing works best with ELL students when they have been prepared in advance for the task through a review of vocabulary and definitions, as well as a suggested or prescribed written format. When writing in an analytic notebook, ELL students may be more comfortable writing in cooperative learning groups, which require each person in the group to contribute something in writing to the notebook.

SUMMARY: BUILDING *CONFIANZA*

Positive relationships between ELL students and monolingual teachers involve mutual respect, shared responsibility, and mutual commitment to learning goals, as well as effective communication and feedback. These kinds of relationships are much easier to achieve between teachers and students who are linguistically and culturally similar to one another. When teachers have little understanding of their students' educational and linguistic backgrounds, forming effective relationships is challenging, and ELL students and those from culturally divergent backgrounds often sense that they are a burden or that they are not welcome in the classroom.

In effect, dialogue journals provide an opportunity for ELL students to express themselves freely about issues that interest or concern them. Dialogue journals also serve to provide teachers with crucial background information about their students. As students begin to feel surer and more confident of their ability to speak and write in English, they gain *confianza*. Teacher/student interactions and the relationships that are fostered through ongoing dialogue play a significant role in student learning and achievement. Providing ELL students a venue to share their thoughts, concerns, and opinions enables them to begin to view their own contributions and previous experiences as valuable. Consequently, teachers and students become jointly responsible for creating a climate of high-level musical and intellectual interaction in urban music classrooms.

REFERENCES

Ayers, W. (2001). *To teach: The journey of a teacher*. New York: Teachers College Press.

Bishop, R., & Glynn, T. (2003). *Culture counts: Changing power relations in education*. London: Zed Books.

Burton, B. (1997). The role of multicultural music education in a multicultural society. In R. Rideout (Ed.), *On the sociology of music education* (pp. 81–84). Norman: University of Oklahoma.

Corson, D. (2001). *Language diversity and education*. Mahwah, NJ: Lawrence Erlbaum.

Delpit, L. (1995). *Other people's children: Cultural conflict in the classroom*. New York: New Press.

Greene, M. (1995). *Releasing the imagination: Essays on education, the arts, and social change*. San Francisco: Jossey-Bass.

Larsen, C., & Merrion, M. (1987). Documenting the aesthetic experience. In T. Fulwiler (Ed.), *The journal book* (pp. 254–260). Portsmouth, NH: Boynton/Cook.

Monzó, L. D., & Rueda, R. (2001). *Sociocultural factors in social relationships: Examining Latino teachers' and paraeducators' interactions with Latino students*. Santa Cruz, CA: Center for Research on Education, Diversity and Excellence.

Peyton, J. K. (1993). Teacher questions in written interaction: Promoting student participation in dialogue. In J. K. Peyton & J. Staton (Eds.), *Dialogue journals in the multilingual classroom: Building language fluency and writing skills through written interaction* (pp. 155–174). Norwood, NJ: Ablex.

Reiss, J. (2005). *ESOL strategies for teaching content: Facilitating instruction for English language learners*. Saddle River, NJ: Pearson.

Ruiz-de-Velasco, J. (2000, December 1). *Overlooked & underserved: Immigrant students in U.S. secondary schools*. Retrieved September 20, 2004, from www.urban.org/JorgeRuizdeVelasco.

Walqui, A. (2000, June). Strategies for success: Engaging immigrant students in secondary schools [electronic version]. Center for Applied Linguistics. Retrieved September 17, 2004, from www.cal.org/resources/digest/0003strategies.html.

4

White Teacher, Students of Color: Culturally Responsive Pedagogy for Elementary General Music in Communities of Color

Kathy M. Robinson

In Leanne's urban elementary general music classroom, students are finishing a lesson on the cello by listening to Yo-Yo Ma play an unaccompanied Bach Cello Suite. When it is time to leave, the class files out to the strains of Bach with the exception of one little girl, a seven-year-old Laotian girl, who remains to talk with Leanne. The conversation begins:

Student (S): I have to play this for my mommy—Can I take this home?
Leanne (L): Of course. Why do you want your mom to hear this?
S: Because it will make her happy.
L: You want to make her happy? Why do you need to make your mother happy?
S: 'Cause last night in bed it was hot and she had her clothes off and I saw all the scars on her back and I asked her what they were from and she told me that she was whipped when she was a slave. . . .

(Leanne tries to retain her composure, not act shocked so the girl will "let it all out," but every cell in her being is trying not to cry.)

S: I think my mom—she has a hard time going to sleep. She has nightmares. I think that if she heard this music that she could . . . and when she sees that he has slanty eyes—who's playing the music—then she will really love it!

What would you have said or done next if you were this teacher? What would you feel comfortable doing? Would you ever be involved in a conversation like this? How responsive could you be to this child's world both humanistically and musically?

This conversation may be more common in our U.S. classrooms than we might believe; many of our students live lives beyond our comprehension. Major demographic shifts are changing the colors and the cultures of our U.S. society. Today's schools serve a more ethnically, linguistically, and culturally diverse population than ever before in our history. "The demographic breakdown in the 100 largest school districts in the United States includes Latinos at 31.7% and African Americans at 29.4%; furthermore, in the 500 largest school districts in the country, Latinos and African Americans account for 52% of the student's population" (Young, 2002). "By the year 2050, the average U.S. resident will trace his or her descent to Africa, Asia, the Hispanic world, the Pacific Islands, the Middle East almost anywhere but white Europe" (Taylor, 1990, p. 1), and the United States will mirror the rest of the present world populace as a majority non-White nation (Davis, 1996).

In urban schools children of color are the majority. These children are and will continue to be, well into the future, served by teachers and other school authority figures of whom 88–90% are of a middle-class White European background. The gulf between music educators, 94% of whom are White, and urban students is even wider (U.S. Bureau of the Census, 1999). It is clear that U.S. teachers and many of their students lie in geographically, ethnically, linguistically, and socioeconomically different worlds. This poses one of urban education's greatest challenges.

Culture is a powerful variable that influences the teaching and learning processes (Irvine, 2001); "it is at the heart of all that we do in the name of education, whether that is curriculum, instruction, administration, or performance assessment" (Gay, 2000, p. 8). An individual's culture influences not only their "values, beliefs and social interactions but also how they view the world, what they consider important, what they attend to, and how they learn and interpret information" (Chisholm, 1994, p. 45). In *Other People's Children*, Delpit (1995) reminds us that people are experts on their own lives and "to deny their own expert knowledge is to disempower them" (p. 33). "Young children in particular know how to behave in their community and at home, but they experience frustration in settings that do not share the same norm" (Hobgood, 2001, p. 1). Many children of color experience this frustration, this discontinuity when they attend school and find that their home culture does not "fit" with the school culture. These children may become alienated and disengaged, and are clearly at a disadvantage in the learning process (Sheets, 1999; Irvine, 2001; Delpit, 1995; Ladson-Billings, 1998).

This gulf between teacher/educational system and students of color can be narrowed if teachers whose background does not match that of their student make an effort to learn about the norms, beliefs, values, customs, and learning styles of their students and apply that knowledge in their classroom content, perspectives, and instructional techniques.

When teachers are responsive to the varied learning and communication styles of their students of color, their pedagogy is said to be *culturally responsive*. Culturally responsive teaching (CRT) uses "the cultural characteristics, experiences, and perspectives of ethnically diverse students as conduits for teaching them more effectively" (Gay, 2002, p. 106). It teaches "to and through the strengths of these students" (Gay, 2000, p. 29).

Culturally responsive teaching is an outgrowth of the multicultural education movement, which began in the 1970s to address racial and ethnic inequalities in our educational system. Specifically, the theory of CRT developed from studies of teachers working with African American students (Foster, 1997; Delpit, 1995; Ladson-Billings, 1994; Irvine, 1990) and serious concerns regarding the academic achievement of poor students and students of color. Research shows that CRT "is based on the assumption that when academic knowledge and skills are situated within the lived experiences and frames of reference of students, they are more personally meaningful, have higher interest appeal and are learned more easily and thoroughly" (Gay, 2002, p. 106). CRT acknowledges that teaching is a form of social interaction and promotes development of personal relationships as well as planning for and carrying out instruction (Irvine, 2001). CR teachers devote time, both in and out of school, to students and view them as members of their extended family (Ladson-Billings, 1994).

U.S. educational pedagogy has always been culturally responsive to its majority culture—middle-class Western European Americans. Educators used to believe that this pedagogy was universally acceptable for all students. Students of color who did not adapt failed because their behavior, language, and customs were different; they were labeled as "disadvantaged," "deprived," or "deficient." For many educators this early thinking about diversity changed to one of "color-blindness," in which matters of race were repressed or silenced, giving way to the attitude that racism is over, the "playing field" is leveled, and differences are nonexistent or "whited out." A contrasting perspective held by others is that of a "cultural mismatch," which acknowledges that cultures are different, assumes one is not superior to the other, and believes that diverse students fail because their cultural values and traits do not match those of the dominant White culture (Manning & Baruth, 2000). Conversely, CR teachers view difference as a quality not to be melted away, but as an asset that enriches schools and society. CR teachers act on their beliefs; they begin with knowing students and what they bring with them from their families, communities, and experiences and continue by using that knowledge to help students be more successful learners and better human beings.

While the relationship between teaching, learning, and culture is well known, misunderstandings and misperceptions regarding CRT are prevalent. CRT is *not* aligned with political correctness (PC), which is a surface-level way of being and doing that avoids topics or ideas that might offend anyone with respect to gender, race, or ethnic background in order to conform to a "social standard" rather than show respect and value for people who have been historically marginalized. CR teachers respect, value, and know about diverse cultures and experiences; they also understand the roles of power, privilege, and oppression in our society and are willing to directly address inequity and injustice to develop sociopolitical consciousness in their students (Gay, 2004; Ladson-Billings, 1998).

In schools with diverse students, teachers of any ethnicity, not just teachers of color, are capable of being effective CR educators. Effectiveness depends more on knowledge, sensitivity, personal comfort, and mind-set of teachers than ethnicity. CRT is more of an attitude than method in working with students of color. This attitude is a catalyst for changing the roles of teacher and student and it can act as a vehicle for social change. Understanding the difficulties students of color may have faced both inside and outside of school doesn't mean that CR teachers have lower standards for their students. They have high expectations for their students of color and clearly and consistently communicate those expectations to them (Ladson-Billings, 1994).

CULTURALLY RESPONSIVE TEACHING

Geneva Gay (2000), in her award-winning book *Culturally Responsive Teaching: Theory, Research, and Practice* and subsequent article, Preparing for Culturally Responsive Teaching (2002), identifies five essential elements of CRT.

1. Developing a knowledge base about cultural diversity
2. Including ethnic and culturally diverse content in the curriculum
3. Demonstrating caring and building a learning community
4. Cross-cultural communications
5. Cultural congruity in classroom instruction

These five elements of CRT will be explored in this chapter through the pedagogy of three urban elementary general music educators with more than 80 collective years of experience working with elementary school children of color. I have come to know these teachers, their pedagogy, and their students over a period of six years and have formally interviewed each of them about CRT at the end of the 2004–2005 school year. All of the teachers work in a Northeastern urban school district that serves 220,000 residents and is among the top 15 school districts in the nation in child poverty. Collectively, the teachers are of European heritage, have master's degrees and at least two years of Orff Schulwerk levels training, and have members of their immediate family whose ethnicity is different from their own. They are known throughout their district as exemplary teachers. While these teachers have much in common they and their culturally responsive classrooms are very different from one another. All personal names used in this article are pseudonyms.

Gina Craig is an ethnically proud Italian American woman who graduated from the same urban school district where she has taught elementary general music for more than 29 years. Her school is located in an inner-city neighborhood that used to be *the* place to live for well-to-do African Americans. It has since become a much poorer community with many challenges. Ms. Craig's students are very active, inquisitive learners who are 99% African American. Gina has shared her culturally responsive classroom with my undergraduate and graduate students for several years.

Leanne Nevis is an effervescent, dramatic woman who loves to dance and has taught elementary general music for more than 15 years. Her K-6 school is located just south of the city center, and 80% of its children are recent immigrants to the United States, from primarily Africa and the Middle East, and most know little English when they arrive. All students are bussed to the school from other areas of the city. The school motto is "the world in our school."

Kathryn Montgomery personifies the professional music educator and lifelong learner and has been a role model for all music teachers in this school district. Her K-6 school serves a population of African American, Latino, and European American students, and is the center for Deaf Education in the district. All students are bussed to the school from other areas of the city. Kathryn, who also developed and led the Character Education program at her school, retired at the end of the last school year after serving this district for more than 30 years.

FIVE ESSENTIAL ELEMENTS OF CULTURALLY RESPONSIVE TEACHING

Developing a Knowledge Base about Cultural Diversity

Understanding the cultural characteristics and contributions of different ethnic groups is a first step in development of the knowledge base needed for culturally responsive teaching. A culture's preference for self-sufficiency versus cooperative problem solving, or authoritarian versus lenient styles of child-rearing, and their communications styles and gender roles are understandings that can help a teacher respond better to a diverse community of students. CRT requires not only general knowledge about various groups of people, but also suggests that teachers gain detailed knowledge of the specific contributions of the ethnic groups represented in their own schools.

Over the years Gina has developed her knowledge base of African American culture in a variety of informal and formal ways. She has taken two courses—*African American Literature and Music* and *Gospel Piano Style*—and attended "as many performances of African Americans making music as possible." Listening to jazz, reading books, attending movies, and "paying close attention to the kids" has also given her much insight into the African American "mind-set and worldview." Gina credits the *African American Literature and Music* class for getting her to understand oral versus "literate" (written) traditions and to think deeply about and grow to respect oral tradition.

> What I got out of that class was [that] note reading is a wonderful thing and people have been able to save music with it. But there is this whole other way that is probably the most basic—more important than reading. You've got to keep that in mind. . . . We want to educate, but at the same time we don't want to slight those. . . . You've got to be really careful about that. Some of the greatest musicians did not note read.

Leanne has learned about her children's cultures primarily through her students and their families. Leanne makes quite a few visits to the homes of students to learn cultural information, including songs and dances from family members. She often audio or videotapes this music making to share with her students when parents and other family members are too shy to come to the school and share. Leanne has even created a sample videotape of the parents of former students to convince new parents that it "would mean so much to their child even if they acted like it wouldn't." Leanne wants her students to become culturally competent—"to grow in understanding and respect for their cultures of origin" (Ladson-Billings, 2002, p. 111) and to "know and praise their own and each other's cultural heritages" (Gay, 2000, p. 29).

One of Leanne's former students from Sudan remembers her parents' sharing as "the worst and the best day of my life."

> Both my mother and my father came in to teach a dance at briefing [weekly assembly]. At first I thought I was going to die and never be able to show my face again in this school and now—[as a senior in high school]—it's the only thing I remember about elementary school. I remember that I was a little embarrassed and a little proud and I didn't know which one was the most. . . .

> If my parents die, it would be what I would say at their funeral. They came to my elementary school and taught a dance that they did at their wedding in front of everyone.

Leanne continues:

> And because they got a standing ovation from everyone clapping so hard and affirming them and saying how beautiful—how wonderful. It made it so authentic. So I have decided that the only way I can make something authentic is to get someone who actually did it--knows it—loves it.

All immigrant children in Leanne's school had to complete paperwork before enrolling, so she has found the translators from the district's placement center to be another valuable resource for cultural information when she has students from countries unfamiliar to her.

> Songs and dances break down the walls better than any other thing that I have seen. My dream is to finally get such a repertoire that no matter what country somebody comes from, we have something that would go—You're from this country and on their first day in class you take out the video of the choir that sang it three years ago and you play it for them and they are like—"Oh, there's a piece of home that I get right here and maybe this place isn't so horrible," because we deal with the culture shock thing so drastically. We had some little babies this year that never stopped crying. They are just in such emotional pain.

Kathryn too has learned much from her students, especially before and after school when she has often held dance classes or drumming ensembles.

> This year I did samba . . . in the morning before the school day starts and my room is right next to the bus loop and they come up and hear the samba music and every Hispanic kid in the building is in my room. I know the basic steps of samba so they are surprised that I know that . . . but I don't know the cultural stuff that goes with that dance, but I learn it from the kids because I'm not on teacher time, I'm on my own time . . . so we are more free to experience each other and I dance with the kids and I say "OK show me what you know how to do" and they learn from me and I learn from them, and to me that's the only way to get that.

Being an avid dancer in styles from ballroom to African, Kathryn uses people from the dance classes she attends as cultural resources. She also gleans information by attending world music concerts and taking summer courses in world musics and culture in the classroom, and from print resources such as *Roots and Branches* (Campbell, McCullough Brabson, & Tucker, 1994). When she was unable to find children's songs from Puerto Rico (the home country of most of her Latino students), her Puerto Rican master's intern from my university helped her learn songs and other cultural information that she used in her classroom.

Including Ethnic and Culturally Diverse Content in the Curriculum

Simply learning a culture's traits and practices is not enough. Culturally responsive teachers also must learn how to convert this content "into culturally responsive curriculum designs and instructional strategies" (Gay, 2002, p. 108). Gay divides content into formal, symbolic, and societal curricula, each of which offers opportunities to engage students with cultural diversity.

Formal music education curricula are sanctioned by school districts and other educational bodies and are supported by approved textbooks and other print, audio, and video materials. While in the past 10 years the ethnic and cultural content of these materials has improved greatly, CR teachers must recognize the strengths and weaknesses of this material and adapt it to improve its quality (as Kathryn did for her Latino students). Gay (2002) identifies several unfortunate trends in formal curricula of which CR teachers should be cautious:

> avoiding controversial issues such as racism, historical atrocities, powerlessness and hegemony; focusing on a few high profile individuals repeatedly and ignoring the actions of groups; giving more attention to African Americans than other groups of color; decontextualizing women, their issues and their actions from their race and ethnicity; ignoring poverty; and, emphasizing factual information while minimizing other kinds of knowledge (such as values, attitudes, feelings, experiences, and ethics). (p. 108)

To counter these trends, culturally relevant teachers address controversy head-on, include content and perspectives from a variety of ethnic groups and cultures, and most importantly contextualize curricular material by addressing issues of race, class, ethnicity, and gender.

To discuss such issues, Gina features lessons on African American musicians Louis Armstrong, Ray Charles, and Marian Anderson and song lyrics from "The Dream of Martin Luther King," "Paddy Works on the Railroad," and "Drill ye Tarriers." She finds it "amazing" that the students enjoy those discussions; they especially like the ones that address "someone not being treated fairly and someone standing up for the underdog." Gina has found that it is not only African American materials that resonate with her students. Her children love the story of *Amahl and the Night Visitors*:

> There's something about his character the children really relate to. [Amahl's] not a child that has had everything handed to him. He hasn't had life so easy. He gets in a little bit of trouble with his mother. He lies. She's going to spank

> him. They really get into that scene. She talks to him—"If you don't learn to tell the truth I'm going to have to spank you."

Beethoven has also captivated her fourth graders:

> The fact that people thought he was crazy and he again didn't have life so easy. They see that. . . . In fourth grade I end the year with Beethoven. They'll hear *Fur Elise* and I heard at least five kids say "That's my song. *Fur Elise*! That's my song."

While highlighting her students' culture is very important, Gina tries to remind herself that she must have balance in the curriculum.

> It's wonderful that they know who Louis Armstrong is, but if they don't know who Beethoven is I've done them a disservice. You can't make them Black smart and world stupid. You have to really look at the big picture—the *big* picture. Who's important period—and how do I get them to a place where the kids—that they'll learn.

Kathryn believes that it is important to include content and perspectives on Native American, Latino, Asian, and African American cultures in her classroom. As a member of the district curriculum writing team, she made sure that the new curriculum addressed those cultures. Leanne believes context to be "all important" in her classroom and believes that music must touch the "heart and soul" of her children. She has found herself increasingly addressing music's power to heal in the classroom as a result of the conversation with her Laotian student found at the beginning of this chapter. Both Leanne and Gina credit the child-centered, experiential Orff Schulwerk approach to teaching music with helping them, in Gina's words, "hit [her] students' hearts as well as their minds."

The *symbolic* curriculum, which includes bulletin boards, images, icons, awards, decorations, mottoes, artifacts, and the like, can be a powerful force in culturally relevant teaching. CR teachers know that students can learn important lessons from these "symbols" and use them as catalysts to increase knowledge, skills, and values. CR teachers also make sure that a variety of ethnicities, cultures, genders, and time periods are represented and that the material portrayed is accurate and unbiased. They know that students "value what is present and devalue that which is absent" (Gay, 2002, p. 108).

The classrooms of Kathryn, Leanne, and Gina are filled with pictures, instruments, and other artifacts from a variety of cultures and traditions that they often refer to as they are teaching. When Gina began teaching she was frustrated with not being able to find pictures of famous Black musicians about whom she wanted to teach. Finding a few books with tiny pictures was inadequate, so she resorted to making silhouettes of these musicians and placing them on her bulletin boards. She remarked: "You can imagine my joy when I started to see these catalogs coming out with . . . posters of African American musicians." Gina credits Black History Month with forcing educators in her school "to get things [of African American culture] up on bulletin boards." Some of her colleagues are

> bothered by that [Black History Month] because they think it's like [this] segregation kind of thing again. But now what I'm seeing as a result of Black History Month is that people at school are paying more attention to women's history, there's Hispanic/Latino. . . .

Kathryn keeps a display of ethnic instruments in her room, which she strategically puts out to pique her children's interest. This practice always elicits questions and serves as "an opening to talk about this culture." Kathryn also creates bulletin boards outside of her classroom on the "heritage of the month," and she strategically arranges for children to stop by when walking them to and from their classrooms. She is pleased that some of her "most quiet kids that have never said anything" are sparked by the display. One of her young autistic students who was quite withdrawn became very excited when she recognized instruments and artifacts that were also in her home and "unbelievably" started talking with Kathryn about her heritage. The next day she "showed up with her mother with all of her cultural heritage stuff from her adoption and asked 'Could I please talk about it and present it to the class?'" She did, and her mother told Kathryn what an incredibly meaningful event this was in her daughter's life.

The *societal* curriculum, the third type, is concerned about the "knowledge, ideas and impressions about ethnic groups that are portrayed" on television and in newspapers, movies, and magazines (Gay, 2002, p. 109). Unfortunately, "what is seen on television is more influential and memorable that what is learned from books in classrooms" (Gay, 2002, p. 109). This information is often incorrect and often stereotypes people of color. CR teachers understand the influence these images have on students and work to counteract them in their classrooms.

Kathryn uses her cultural heritage bulletin boards to address the hurtful nature of stereotypes. Teaching the children appropriate ways to ask about another's cultural heritage is especially important to her because of the Korean heritage of her children.

Demonstrating Cultural Caring and Building a Learning Community

People of diverse cultures communicate, learn, and even define the importance of learning in different ways. Each culture also has its own expectations for learning. Thus, a third essential element of CRT is "creating classroom climates that are conducive to learning for ethnically diverse students" (Gay, 2002, p. 109). CR teachers know how to use their students' cultures and experiences to improve their academic achievement and widen their horizons (Gay, 2002). They care deeply about their students, have the highest expectations for them, and work hard to help students achieve these goals.

To forge a closer bond with her students, Gina wanted to be able to match the style in which they were singing outside of school. She recalls moving out of her comfort zone on two occasions:

> I was not trained as a by-ear musician by any means but I knew functional piano and made myself come up with an accompaniment that would fit the style of what she [one of her students] was singing. And it was a big event in the school that she was able to sing in her Black style and I was able to play as close as possible to a Black style that a White person probably could.

Gina remembers a similar situation with the spiritual "Children Go Where I Send Thee" and deems that as a "huge moment" in her teaching career.

> That showed me what I had to do for each and every student to see where they're coming from and try to adjust to it instead of them always adjusting to me. If I was going to be credible as a teacher I had to also show this other side.

Bonding more closely with her students in no way changes the high expectations she has for them in the classroom and concert venue. Gina does not give her students permission to fail. I have seen her demonstrate for the students what an A, B, or C graded effort looks like in their classroom activity; I've also witnessed her stop during a choir selection in her spring concert to remind the students *who they were* and *where they were* and in the next moment helping them create beautiful music together.

Accompanying individual students at events in the African American community has helped Gina forge a closer relationship with her school community. She remembers vividly:

> I walked into the room and I realized I . . . was the only White person there and I'm playing "Lift Every Voice and Sing"—the Black national anthem. The acceptance of me was astounding. I mean they gathered around me, they sat me down, they brought me food, they couldn't have thanked me enough for taking this little small part of my day to come and play for this boy.

After attending several such events with this student she

> came to understand the celebrating that the African Americans do in this city—and the customs—and not to be worried if people are late for example. It was good for me to experience the real ethnicity of it.

Gina marks this as a key experience in her career and she relishes the relationship that has developed: "They'll call me Sister Craig. I love it."

Leanne wants her students to believe that they are the most beautiful and talented children in the world. Quite a few of her students are afraid to speak, fearing that their English is not good enough and they will be criticized or ostracized. While on bus duty one day Leanne observed a young Chinese girl who had never spoken in school since she arrived, talking excitedly in Mandarin to her brother on the school bus. Witnessing this exchange prompted a home visit, and eventually to the child reading a poem she created to an amazed audience in a school assembly. It was the first time anyone at school had heard her speak.

Hoping to connect more deeply with her female African students, Leanne wrote a grant to bring a West African dance residency to her school. She was ecstatic to see how much the girls learned about themselves and how good they felt when their dancing abilities were affirmed. The culminating event in this residency was an evening dance session with parents, friends, teachers, and students. Leanne remembers:

> It was the most powerful, most unbelievable thing you've ever seen. . . . where you would see a 30-pound girl from Thailand dancing with a 300-pound African American guy on the same dance floor—both laughing so hard they were crying. Only in this school. I love this school. It was worth going through the hassle of writing the grant.

Building community *among* diverse learners is another essential element of CRT. Many students of color come from ethnicities where group needs take priority over those of the individual; people help each other perform and they work together toward a common goal. CR teachers emphasize the development of the whole child and teach social, political, cultural, personal, and academic knowledge simultaneously with skills.

The work that it takes to create community in the school and the classroom should not be underestimated. In her earliest days of teaching, Kathryn found it extremely difficult to bring together children whose community was separated from the context of their school. In the 1970s one of her schools was 90% European American and 10% African American. The White students who were bussed to the school were enrolled in a magnet Major Achievement Program (MAP) and rarely encountered the students from the African American neighborhood. These Black children were treated as second-class citizens in their school, and as a result treated others poorly. As the fourth music teacher in two years, Kathryn was charged with creating performance groups that reflected the neighborhood. It took time to develop the trust of the African American students, but she never gave up. She remembers: "I refused to quit. I refused to go home and say 'I can't do this,' so I stayed." When the students and Kathryn did come together in their spring concert:

> the magnetism that went from the stage to me was overpowering. . . . They understood what I was trying to get out of them and I wasn't there to be mean to them but I wasn't going to take this nonsense behavior that they were giving me and that was such an overwhelming experience to have come from the bottom where we were, to what we reached at that point. And it was basically just trying to understand their culture and allow[ing] them to show their culture and be who they were.

Cross-Cultural Communication

"What we talk about; how we talk about it; what we see, attend to, or ignore; how we think and what we think about" (Porter and Samovar, 1991, p. 21) is highly influenced by culture and ethnicity and is at the core of the fourth essential element of CRT. The kinds of verbal communication that are sanctioned in our schools are primarily of a European "passive receptive" style (Irvine, 2001). In this style, one person talks while the others listen passively. Students share in discussion only when it is solicited by the teacher, and teachers usually ask questions that converge on one correct answer. Conversely, most people of color communicate in an active participatory style where the speaker solicits verbal response from the listeners. The roles of speaker and listener are "fluid and are interchangeable" (Gay, 2002, p. 111). CR teachers know how to interpret the communication styles of their students of color, and they modify classroom communications to accommodate them and strengthen their voices and achievement.

Among verbal communication styles, differences in pronunciation and vocabulary may also be found. There are varying standards, too, for acceptable loudness, tempo, rhythm, pitch, attentiveness, and response time across cultures. Many Native American societies place high value on reflection and tend therefore not to make immediate responses during conversation. The opposite is true for many African Americans (Taylor, 1990). Other considerations in discussions and conversations across cultures include: What is spoken and left unspoken? When is it appropriate to interrupt or defer to others? Who asks direct and who asks indirect questions (Irvine, 2001)?

While the spoken word is important, nonverbal communication actually comprises 65% of all communication. Interpersonal space, frequency of touching, styles of walking, eye glances, dress, and personal presentation vary greatly among cultures and ethnicities (Irvine, 2001). In some cultures people in conversations stand close enough to touch, and in others a distance is kept to show respect (Taylor, 1990). For some Latinos showing respect means not looking authority figures in the eyes, while European Americans consider such an act to be disrespectful (Davis, 1996). Lack of understanding regarding different communication styles can foster miscommunications and conflicts, which can alienate students and make them feel unwelcome in school.

Gina agrees with her principal that her African American students need to know how to speak proper English when they "go for a job interview," but she has some difficulty with correcting them in the classroom.

> I don't want to stop the child from saying what they're really thinking so I can't say that in every single circumstance I correct them. I'm more apt to do it when we're doing informal things—after school washing the boards and they'll say something and I'll say something teasingly with them. Sometimes I'll say to the kids "now you know you're presenting yourself to the public when we're giving a concert. It's kind of like a wedding. You don't just run down the aisle with your fancy dress on—You have this little show—That's what we're doing here." You approach it from that—the kids take it better.

Gina, like Delpit (1995), believes that the "children have a right to their own language and should be allowed to express themselves in their own language" without penalty (p. 37). She also admits that after nearly 30 years in her school, she doesn't always hear the Black English. Sometimes she finds little phrases of her students' coming out of her mouth:

> To me it's the love thing which has taken over. You love each other. You're with each other all day long. You're talking to each other and something comes out that is not just standard English, but everybody knows what you mean. Sometimes you do it on purpose with a sense of humor. The kids just laugh. They know. They understand. They accept it. They know where you're coming from. They know that you're not making fun. You're just trying to make your point.

Cultural Congruity in Classroom Instruction

Responding to ethnic diversity in the delivery of instruction is the final and perhaps most important element of CRT because it requires educators to implement what they have learned in their pedagogy and match their instructional techniques to the learning styles of their students of color. Native Americans, Latinos, and African American students whose cultures are communal can benefit from using a variety of cooperative learning arrangements in the classroom. These learners also respond positively to storytelling and case studies. African American child-rearing practices tend to include more time spent with a maternal figure and more physical and verbal contact with family and community members than European Americans (Chimezie, 1988). Classroom activities congruous with African American learning styles incorporate motion, movement, music, frequent changes in activities, and drama (Shade, Kelly, & Oberg, 1997; Ladson-Billings, 1994; Irvine, 2001; Davis, 1996).

Research indicates that many teachers' perceptions of students' race, class, and/or gender negatively influence their expectations for behavior and academic performance (Gollnick and Chinn, 1998; Delpit, 1995). This cultural mismatch between teachers and students "has denied to ethnically different students the right to grapple with learning challenges from the point of strength and relevance found in their own cultural frames of reference" (Gay, 2002, p. 114). In other words, U.S. education has placed these students in "double jeopardy" by requiring them to "master tasks under unnatural situations" (Gay, 2002, p. 114).

Culture also impacts cognitive learning styles: the preferred way that people receive, process, store, and retrieve information (Irvine, 2001). Research suggests that most students of color tend to be field-dependent learners rather than field-independent learners (Shade, et al., 1997; Manning and Baruth, 2000; Hale Benson, 1986). African American and Latino learners are identified as field dependent and, according to Irvine's (2001) synthesis of the research, tend to:

- Respond to things in terms of the whole instead of the isolated parts;
- Prefer group learning situations;
- Prefer inferential reasoning;
- Approximate space and numbers rather that adhere to exactness or accuracy;
- Focus on people rather than things;
- Prefer learning by doing;
- Be more proficient in nonverbal than verbal communications;
- Prefer learning characterized by variation in activities;
- Prefer kinesthetic, active, hands-on instructional activities (p. 490).

It is important to note that these learning preferences are not mutually exclusive and that learners could, at different times, exhibit qualities of both (Irvine & York, 1995).

A core belief of learning-styles research is that children of color learn better when teaching matches their preferred way of learning (Irvine & York, 1995). While learning-styles research can be helpful in getting to know and understand children of color, educators should be cautious in its interpretation and should use it only as starting point. Research captures the most frequent (modal) communication and learning styles of a large percentage of a particular group of people, which does not imply that all members of that group share the same traits or styles (Weinstein, Tomlinson-Clarke, & Curran, 2004). The cultural influence on learning styles can be mediated by variables such as socioeconomic status, age, gender, education, and degree of cultural affiliation.

Culturally responsive educators know that learning styles do not correspond to intellectual abilities and thus plan experiences that are stimulating and challenging for their students. They also devote considerable instructional time to building bridges connecting children's prior knowledge to new knowledge. Gina, Kathryn, and Leanne have each developed a considerable repertoire of well-thought-out, intentional strategies to use in teaching their students of color, many of which have been previously mentioned: Orff approach, movement and dance, use of self and traditional culture bearers in the classroom, storytelling, and drama.

Students' academic achievement is higher in classrooms that use culturally relevant examples and congruent instructional practices or strategies (Gay, 2000, 2002; Irvine 2001). Within their many years of teaching, each of these teachers changed their instructional practices and curricular content over the years in response to the changing demographics of their schools. These changes did not always come easily. In trying to match her students' musical style and to create decidedly African American traditions at her school, Gina had "to be a little courageous to try. How do I know I'm going to be able to do that? . . . I wasn't born into it." She encourages teachers to be open-minded and not set up roadblocks for themselves.

Gina has found that she "loves being in the heart of the culture" and experiencing firsthand "the vibes." She's witnessed Black folks "talking out in the middle of the sermon," affirming the minister and his message, and she understands when that happens in her classroom. Her *school* rules include the ubiquitous "Raise your hand and wait to be called on," but for her children she finds that rule stifling and very restrictive. About this interaction style, she tells her student teachers:

> You're going to know when it's OK. And you're going to know when it's not OK. Because when it's OK, it's real learning happening. When it's not OK, it's chaos, so you've got to judge it.

Creating traditions based on African American music and dance to end her school concerts became important to Gina.

> Alvin Ailey [dance troupe] was pivotal in the kind of teacher I became. They do this thing called *Revelation* at the end of almost every performance. That lit me up like nothing else I had ever seen. . . . And I just said that children's performances could be like that—a little rinky-dink school. That's how I got the idea of finding something that the audience loves and then just doing it. That becomes part of the tradition of the school. That "Rhythm of Life"—That's how it came to be.

Kathryn gave up presenting large-scale musicals at her school of almost 30 years because the school changed from a neighborhood school to a bussed school population with weaker language skills:

I had to change my whole way of what I used to do with kids. . . . What can I do that will work with *these* kids? I didn't go on and say well you can't do this—you must be stupid. The kids need something entirely different than I used to do. And you just kind of find what works, so my program has changed tremendously from what I used to do because the kids changed so much.

CONCLUSION

Culturally Responsive Teaching in elementary general music education purposefully incorporates the cultural knowledge, experience, and frames of reference of ethnically diverse students to make learning more relevant for students whose cultural, ethnic, linguistic, racial, and social class backgrounds differ from that of the majority, most especially their teachers. Kathryn, Gina, and Leanne are passionate, caring, and dedicated European American teachers working in communities of color where they will do whatever it takes to ensure that every child is achieving and continually moving toward realizing his or her potential. Through their words, we are drawn into their classrooms, their hearts, and their minds regarding working effectively with their diverse learners. We can gain a sense of the depth involved and the commitment required to engage in culturally responsive practices. From samba to West African dance, from cooperative learning to Orff pedagogy, from Beethoven to jazz, and from storytelling to drama, their classrooms, each unique, are vibrant models for culturally responsive pedagogy.

Kathryn, Gina, and Leanne didn't begin teaching with all the skills and understandings they now possess. Each, in their own way, has embarked on a lifelong journey of learning, understanding, and growing both personally and professionally. They were, and still are, willing to move out of their comfort zones, and they are willing to fail, but always hoping to succeed. It is my hope that you can see yourself in their struggles and their triumphs and are encouraged and willing to reflect upon your own cultural responsiveness and to take action in the interest of teaching our students of color more effectively. Given the changing demographics of our U.S. students, a commitment to continuous development of our culturally responsive pedagogy is an imperative.

To ponder the rewards of teaching and learning in urban communities of color, Gina turns to her own musical experience. In her childhood, she was a member of the prestigious Inner Junior Choir that brought children from all over the city together for a high-level choral experience.

For me it was a wonderful opportunity to be responsive to other cultures. I'll never forget . . . a Jewish person was there and a black person was there. . . . Neither one of them went to my school. . . . So I remember learning about Hanukah for the first time from that Jewish girl. . . . I remember when Martin

> Luther King was shot—talking to the Black girl next to me. What a great experience! That's why urban schools could be so "all that." 'Cause where else are you going to get all that? That was one of the reasons I wanted to teach in urban schools.

Teaching elementary general music in urban communities of color can clearly be "all that."

REFERENCES

Au, K., & Blake, K. (2003). Cultural identity and learning to teach in a diverse community: Findings from a collective case study. *Journal of Teacher Education*, 54 (3), 192–205.

Campbell, P. S., McCullough Brabson, E., & Tucker, J. C. (1994). *Roots and branches.* Danbury, CT: World Music Press.

Chimezie, A. (1988). Black children's characteristics and the schools: A selective adaptation approach. *The Western Journal of Black Studies*, 12 (2), 77–85.

Chisholm, I. M. (1994). Preparing teachers for multicultural classrooms. *The Journal of Educational Issues of Language Minority Students* (14), 43–68.

Davis, L. (1996). Equality in education: An agenda for urban schools. *Equity and Excellence in Education*, 29(1), 61–67.

Delpit, L. (1995). *Other people's children: Culture and conflict in the classroom.* New York: The New Press.

Delpit, L., & Dowdy, J. K. (Eds.). (2002). *The skin that we speak. Thoughts on language and culture in the classroom.* New York: The New Press.

Foster, M. (1995). African American teachers and culturally relevant pedagogy. In J. A. Banks & C. A. M. Banks (Eds.), *Handbook of research on multicultural education* (pp. 570–581). New York: Macmillan.

———. (1997). *Black teachers on teaching.* New York: New Press.

Gay, G. (2000). *Culturally responsive teaching: Theory, research and practice.* New York: Teachers College Press.

———. (2002). Preparing for culturally responsive teaching. *Journal of Teacher Education*, 53(2), 106–116.

———. (2004). The importance of multicultural education. *Educational Leadership*, 61(4), 30–35.

Gollnick, D. M., & Chinn, P. C. (1998). *Multicultural education in a pluralistic society.* Columbus, OH: Merrill.

Hale Benson, J. (1986). *Black children: Their roots, culture, and learning styles.* Baltimore: Johns Hopkins University Press.

Hobgood, B. (2001, November). When teachers don't understand. Learn North Carolina (52). Retrieved May 22, 2005, from www.learnnc.org/articles/understand 0404.

Irvine, J. J. (1990). *Black students and school failure: Policies, practices, and prescriptions.* Westport, CT: Greenwood.

———. (2001). The critical elements of culturally responsive pedagogy: A synthesis of the research. In J. Irvine & B. Armento (Eds.), *Culturally responsive teaching: Lesson planning for elementary and middle grades* (pp. 3–17). New York: McGraw-Hill.

Irvine, J. J., & York, D. E. (1995). Learning styles and culturally diverse students: A literature review. In *Handbook of research on multicultural education* (pp. 484–497). New York: Macmillan.

Ladson-Billings, G. (1994). *The dreamkeepers: Successful teachers of African American children.* San Francisco: Jossey-Bass.

———. (1998). Teaching in dangerous times. *Journal of Negro Education*, 67(3), 255–267. Washington, DC: Howard University.

———. (2002). I ain't writin' nuttin:' Permission to fail and demands to succeed in urban education. In L. Delpit & J. K. Dowdy (Eds.), *The skin that we speak: Thoughts on language and culture in the classroom* (pp. 107–120). New York: The New Press.

Manning, M. L., & Baruth, L. G. (2000). *Multicultural education of children and adolescents* (3rd ed.). Boston: Allyn & Bacon.

McLaughlin, B., & McLeod, B. (1996). *Educating all our students: Improving education for children from culturally and linguistically diverse backgrounds.* Final Report of the National Center for Research on Cultural Diversity and Second Language Learning, Vol. 1. Washington, DC: NCELA. Retrieved May 22, 2005, from www.Ncela.gwu.edu/pubs/ncrcdsll/edall.htm.

Ogbu, J. (1988). Cultural diversity and human development. In D. Slaughter (Ed.), *Black children and poverty: A developmental perspective* (pp. 11–28). San Francisco: Jossey-Bass.

Porter, R. E., & Samovar, L. A. (1991). Basic principles of intercultural communication. In L. A. Samovar & R.E. Porter (Eds.), *Intercultural communication: A reader* (6th ed., pp. 5–22). Belmont, CA: Wadsworth.

Shade, B. J. (Ed.). (1989). *Culture, style and the educative process.* Springfield, IL: Charles C Thomas.

Shade, B., Kelly, C., & Oberg, M. (1997). *Creating culturally responsive classrooms.* Washington, DC: American Psychological Association.

Sheets, R. (1999). Relating competence in an urban classroom to ethnic identity development. In R. Sheets (Ed.), *Racial and ethnic identity in school practices: Aspects of human development.* Mahwah, NJ: Lawrence Erlbaum Associates.

Taylor, O. (1990). Cross cultural communication: An essential dimension of effective education [Electronic version]. Chevy Chase, MD: Mid Atlantic Equity Consortium. Retrieved May 22, 2005, from www.maec.org/cross/index.html#return.

U.S. Bureau of the Census. (1999). *Statistical abstract of the United States* (SAUS) (119th ed.). Washington, DC: Author.

Weinstein, C. S., Tomlinson-Clarke, S., & Curran, M. (2004). Toward a conception of culturally responsive classroom management. *Journal of Teacher Education*, 55(1), 25–38.

Young, B. (2002). *Characteristics of the 100 largest public and elementary and secondary school districts in the United States: 2000-01* (NCES No. 2002-351). Washington, DC: U.S. Department of Education, National Center for Educational Statistics.

II

MUSIC TEACHER STORIES

5

The Challenges of Urban Teaching: Young Urban Music Educators at Work

Janice Smith

After a 30-year career as a public school music teacher, I am now a college music educator in New York City. The problems the educators face here are numerous and could be overwhelming, yet many find their teaching experiences intensely rewarding. The purpose of this chapter is to capture and share the experiences of novice music teachers in some of these urban settings. When this book was announced by MENC, two of my graduate students approached me to ask whether I would write a chapter discussing their opinions and teaching experiences. They wanted to be sure that a book about urban music education contained the voices of practicing urban music teachers—people like them. As a faculty member at an urban university, I was interested in the professional experiences of my students and so I agreed to try to capture their thoughts. Six individuals eventually participated in semi-structured interviews about the rewards and challenges of teaching music in urban schools.

By its very design (exploratory case study), this chapter can only draw conclusions from in-depth interviews of a very small number of teachers. Thus, these results may not be generalizable to larger populations of urban music educators. They can, however, be used to better understand the experiences and perspectives of these novice teachers in their particular contexts.

DESCRIPTION OF THE STUDY

The study consisted of open-ended interviews with six novice music teachers from in or around the New York City area. The same teachers who requested that I do the study suggested the interview topics. The interview began by asking participants to describe the best and the most challenging aspects of teaching in urban schools.

Method

Each of the participants volunteered to be interviewed for this chapter, and as a result have the sense that they are communicating with a broad range of colleagues across the country. All of the participants are either enrolled in, or are recent graduates of, an urban university master's degree program in music education. Each of them spent about an hour answering interview questions. The interviews were recorded on an iPod digital music player and transferred to a Macintosh G4 computer. A CD was burned from those recordings and copies of the CDs were offered to the participants. These audio recordings were then partially transcribed by the author for this chapter. All names and locations are aliases to provide some anonymity for the teachers. Several interviewees also contributed further information after the interviews via email to the author.

Participants

All six of these teachers teach or have recently taught in a large metropolitan area on the East Coast of the United States. Kris, Holli, Melissa, and Robert all attended urban schools when they were growing up (all names are pseudonyms). Joy and Kathy came to the urban schools from other areas of the country. A former professional singer, Joy currently teaches elementary general music. She made a midlife career change and has been teaching music for seven years. It was Joy that originally suggested creating this chapter. Kathy has just taken a position in a suburban public school after teaching instrumental and general music in three different cities over the course of three years. Although she is Italian American, she grew up in the Midwest and graduated from a large midwestern university. Her passion is marching band.

Kris has been teaching secondary general music at a large public high school for three years. He also coaches percussion ensembles. He has a master's degree in music education from an urban public university. Holli has just finished her first year of teaching. She teaches secondary band and chorus in a private religious high school, the same high school she attended as a teenager. She also plays guitar and sings in pop music bands. She graduated summa cum laude with a degree in music education from an urban public university.

Melissa teaches middle level instrumental music and has just finished her second year of teaching. She is a city native, but attended college at a large midwestern university. She is passionate about teaching and helping students. Robert is Haitian American and teaches secondary chorus and orchestra in an urban public high school. He has been teaching four years. Both Melissa and Robert are active at their places of worship and view their teaching careers as a spiritual calling.

Data Analysis

These data were analyzed systematically by arranging the interview transcripts by teacher and also by interview question. The interviews were limited to participants' self-perceptions and did not include observations or site visits. The themes that emerged from the data formed the organizational basis of the analysis. Once an initial analysis was completed, the teachers read the draft and made suggestions for improvements. This helped to establish the credibility of the analysis and the trustworthiness of what was being written.

An effort was made to find the positives in the teaching situations of these young professionals and to describe their successes and motivations. We will also examine how they are confronting and solving some of the problems they encounter. Themes that emerged from the interviews include rationales for teaching in urban schools, benefits of cultural diversity, ups and downs of administrative support, and challenges in classroom management.

WHY TEACH IN URBAN SCHOOLS?

It's All about the Students

It may surprise those who view urban students as difficult to work with that it is the students who motivate these teachers to keep working in urban schools. Each of the participants described a special affinity for the students they work with. In Kris's words: "I love them because they're sassy. They'll tell you what they're thinking. They tell you exactly like it is. There is just something special about being here and having a good rapport with a kid."

The teachers who grew up in the city feel that they understand the needs of their communities better than their colleagues from outside the city. As Holli noted: "If I was not teaching at my current school, I most likely would still teach in the city, because that is where I grew up, and I feel more qualified to teach students to which I can personally relate." Melissa's perspective is that "These children represent a wealth of diversity, language groups, and cultural differences that just bring so much into education, particularly into music." Several participants in the study believe that teachers who do not teach in urban areas have misperceptions about their students. Kathy put it this way: "For people who haven't taught in the city, it's like: 'How can you teach the kids in that environment and the cursing and everything like that?' I say: 'It's not the kids. I love the kids.'"

Deserving Students

These city-born and bred teachers also feel a need to correct the deficiencies of their own educations. They feel strongly that urban students deserve well-trained, certified professional teachers who want to teach (as opposed to temporarily certified music teachers who are teaching, but would rather be full-time performers). As Melissa said:

> These kids have had three teachers in three years. Some of the nicest kids I've ever met are in my classroom. They deserve good teachers. They deserve people like us—the core of college-trained music teachers that are in the city. They deserve to have us to stay—we young teachers that are professional, that are getting our master's, that are actually certified to teach music. They need people like us.

Holli added:

> I jumped at the idea of teaching at my alma mater because I knew the music program was in a sad state when I was a student there, and I wanted, even back then, to do something about it. I find that the kids have never really been cultivated [musically] because they never really had the opportunity in grammar school, so it's just really exciting to see. They're really just bursting—they want this education really badly and that's such a cool thing to work with!

Their appreciation of the needs and diversity of their students may be a defining feature of these successful urban music educators. It is a disposition worth cultivating in prospective music educators considering careers in urban schools. Teacher preparation programs might encourage students with this kind of attitude toward diversity to consider teaching in urban settings. Administrators might want to look for this attitude when hiring new music educators to develop the musicianship of the wide variety of students in their schools.

Cultural Diversity Is a Benefit

Cultural diversity is a fact of life in most urban schools. The teachers who grew up in the city and attended urban schools expect to teach ethnically diverse populations. It was clear that all the teachers in this study consider this diversity a benefit for urban teaching. They value the vibrant culture of their schools and their surroundings; they are learning to cope with occasional ethnic tensions; and they are finding ways of overcoming language barriers.

Capitalizing on the Vibrant Culture

Melissa has created a project that she does each year with her seventh-grade band. She gives them a week away from their instruments to study the music of the world. Each student is responsible for sharing information about the music of his or her own culture. Melissa describes it this way:

> I usually start that project by sharing my own culture. I play shofar at the temple and I'm trained in all the calls and what they mean and the spiritual side of it all. So I bring it in and explain what the Hebrew terminology is and I play for the kids. [. . .] The kids are just wild about it. So I do the project and I present my culture, and then I tell them: "This is what you are going to do with your music."
>
> The kids do reports. They bring in the music. We listen to each other's music and kids discover that bongra sounds a lot like rap and that Chinese people rap too and we listen to Chinese rap (and I'm thinking, "I hope they're not cursing"). They bring in instruments and play them. They taught me a little bit about how to read their notation [South Indian].

Coping with Ethnic Tensions

The participants have had mixed experiences in regards to cultural tensions in their schools. Several of them indicated that they had very few issues related to cultural differences in their classrooms. Robert put it this way:

> I think kids today have less racism because they are already in a mixed bag. Their neighbors are of different cultures. For a while there was a rift between a couple of ethnic groups in our school, but for the most part there are very few issues, if any. There are definitely sects of people that keep to themselves—that are very ethnocentric. I find that especially true among whomever the newest immigrants are. They tend to remain with their own groups for a while until they get used to things here.

Kathy, who has taught in three different urban areas, has experienced more cultural issues than the other teachers who were interviewed.

> What was really hard, which I hadn't experienced in Chicago, were the Hispanic splits. In Chicago the Hispanics in my area were almost all Mexican. But here there are the Dominicans and the Puerto Ricans. There are serious rivalries with that. And that I didn't realize. It took me a while to see that they would segregate themselves seating-wise. And even if I would move them, they were like "Miss, you can't be mixing. Some things you just can't mix."

It may be that issues of racial or ethnic tension arise more frequently in some schools than they do in the schools of the teachers that participated in this study. However, it is important to note that racial or ethnic tensions are not ubiquitous in urban schools. There are settings where diversity is valued by teachers and administrators, and where students are allowed and encouraged to flourish regardless of their cultural origins. The educators in this chapter teach in those kinds of schools.

Language

Students who are English-language learners (ELL) are present in almost all urban public schools. Most of the teachers had found ways of helping these students learn music. Joy talked about how she made sure everyone learned when ELL students were placed in her elementary music classes.

> I like teaching them because they can't speak English. The other children tell me they can't speak English. So I give them an instrument and I tell the class that they don't have to speak any language at all to learn how to do music. I like being able to include them in something that they don't usually get to do. And the new children love it too, because it doesn't require any words.

Melissa also has a successful way of dealing with ELL students in her middle school instrumental classes. She has created a "buddy" system where experienced students that speak the new student's language can introduce them to the new instrument.

> Just as an example, I had this student that came the day before President's Week (February) from Korea to America and said he wanted to be in band. Didn't speak a word of English. So I pulled up one of my Korean kids and he translated. I asked, "Have you ever read music?" "No. Nothing. Don't even know the first thing about music." So I spoke to a Korean student after class, who is a clarinet player—and clarinet is not too hard to learn if you come in late. So I asked: "Would you mind working together?" and he agreed to teach him. They practiced in the back room for about a month. The new student is playing as well as anyone in the class now.

She has used the same system with other students:

> If you saw this class you'd be amazed 'cause you have one girl translating stuff into Chinese for another girl. You have a boy translating for a boy and a girl into Korean. I occasionally pitch in with Spanish to one of the kids. And then you have a bunch of students with special needs working in pairs. I mean, it's a lot louder than any class you can imagine. You'd walk in and wonder what was going on in my room, but then you'd realize that learning is taking place. And then the kids all pick up their instruments and they play.

More accommodations are needed with older students because so much instruction is language based. Robert, who speaks Haitian (French) and

Spanish as well as English, described what usually happens in his secondary school:

> LS 1 [Language Services One] kids—they have very little English. Those kids usually have at least two English classes a day, so they don't have room for electives and as a result we don't get them in our classes. Same thing for the LS 2 kids. By the time we get them, they usually have some English. Anyway, with the ELL [English-language Learners] kids, I'm all right with them because I taught ESL [English as a second language] my first year.

Kris has a diversity of languages in his high school general music class, so he modifies instruction to help these students learn:

> They are from so many different areas—a lot of Russian and Asian. And they'll have problems with names. I tell them, "If you're going to write a paper, you better take it to someone first and get it proofread. You can give to me and I'll proofread it, but hand it in early to show me you did the work."
>
> Good students are good students and they say will to me, "Could you write that on the board?" They usually do fine. I always write the important stuff on the board anyway. A multiple choice test, it works for them. But if I have some fill-ins, a lot of them [ELL students] won't do the fill ins.
>
> I always say, "Hey look. If you need help, come see me. I'm nice. I don't bite. And I'll help you. And we'll do it." Some students take advantage of that, but some don't, and there's not much more I can do.

These young teachers appear to enjoy the challenges and the richness the ELL students provide. They seem to have evolved ways of coping with language barriers—including those of the students' parents.

Communicating with Parents: Do You Understand What I Said?

Parental involvement is a common concern in urban schools. This problem is obviously compounded when the parents have little or no command of the English language or understanding of how American schools operate (Barton et al., 2004). Like teachers everywhere, these teachers put a lot of effort into making contact with parents and improving school/home communication to benefit students. And like teachers everywhere, the amount of success they have with those contacts varies widely.

The levels of parental involvement at Robert's school are varied:

> They run the gamut. They absolutely run the gamut. Some parents are always involved with their students, what they do. They actually show up to PTA meetings and they are there at the parent–teacher nights and they see their kids perform and they call the school periodically just to see what's going on. And they're great. And some parents are more middle of the road. They're there

> once in a while. They still support their kids. They work with them. Some parents are involved as best as they can, because they can't really be there because they are working two and three jobs. And it's phone tag—leaving messages, stuff like that. And then, of course, there are the ones that you gotta feel for—the kids with addicts of one kind or another for parents.

The other issue involved with making parent contacts is whether the parent can understand what is being communicated. Melissa has come up with a positive approach to contacting parents:

> I contact parents for all sorts of reasons. If I see a student make a big improvement, I'll call a parent. If I see a student that I think is really, really advanced and might have natural talent, I might even call and say, "Hey, have you ever considered piano or private lessons or pursuing this? I think they've got something." I do it a lot for high school placements. "If your student wants to go to this high school, here's what they need to do." So there are many positive reasons. Any time there is a free opportunity, an audition, a festival, I contact students and parents and send letters home. Then, of course, there's discipline.
>
> When I get on the phone with someone who can't understand what I am saying, I go the guidance counselor because usually they know the families—there's only 1,500–1,600 kids in the school, so it's not huge, it's not overwhelming. And they'll usually say, "Oh here's a number. Their uncle speaks English." Or they will actually put one of the ESL teachers with me—we have one that speaks Chinese and one that speaks Korean—and they'll translate. We work it out.

Like good teachers everywhere, these young professionals work at communicating regularly with parents. They know that language barriers are not an excuse for not trying to involve parents in their children's education. They have schools and administrators who are actively seeking to facilitate teacher–parent communication by providing the resources necessary for this to occur.

CHALLENGES OF URBAN MUSIC TEACHING

Administrative Challenges

Understanding Music Education

A common challenge stated by these teachers is educating their administrators about what a balanced, comprehensive, sequential program of music instruction entails. This finding is a recurring one among studies of urban music educators (Frierson-Campbell, 2004; Fiese & DeCarbo, 1995). Not only are these young professionals faced with the challenges of developing a teaching style and building successful programs, but also they must constantly advocate for their music programs. Their immediate supervisors are often people from other curriculum areas with little or no understanding of music education.

Kris was the only one of the participants who felt his administrator understood the value of supporting the music program. He was also the only one who worked under a music coordinator. He spoke glowingly about the way the administrator allowed members of his music department to work together and focus on teaching:

> Our music coordinator has been teaching there for about 20 years. He's wonderful, he's brilliant, he's excellent on paperwork. [. . .] There's four of us and he's the leader. Each teacher in our department teaches a couple of general musics and a couple of ensembles. Everyone in this department teaches general music. He's a great department head and gives us a lot of freedom to come up with curriculum, and the freedom to teach what and when I want to.

General Support

Kris's comments were in marked contrast to those of the other participants. Most felt their administrators simply had no comprehension of what it takes to run an effective music program. This has been somewhat substantiated by a senior colleague of mine at our urban university. Thanks to an influx of money from the Annenberg Foundation and the VH1 Save the Music program, many schools are able to obtain musical instruments. The principals of these schools then call my colleague asking if he can recommend an instrumental music teacher. They are often taken aback when he asks about arrangements for such things as scheduling and teaching space; supplies such as music, reeds, and valve oil; and a budget for repairs to the new instruments. He tells these administrators he will be happy to recommend some fine candidates for their programs when he can be assured that they will not be placed in situations conducive to failure. Unfortunately, the teachers I interviewed did not have this person protecting their interests when they took their current positions. Most feel their administrators mean well, but that they are seriously uninformed. Holli put it this way:

> They want a marching band. But I'm staying up at night worrying about the day I tell them, "You know how much a marching band costs?" Ah, really they don't understand what it takes—how one music teacher doesn't cover it. They don't see the difference between a band teacher and a chorus teacher and what that entails. All the work that goes into preparing for an ensemble.

Almost all of the participants are supervised by an assistant principal whose area of expertise is something other than visual and performing arts. One is part of the physical education department, one is part of foreign languages, and Robert is part of something called Communication Arts, which consists of mostly the English Department. His immediate supervisor stated to her music faculty that her goal for the music department was that music should be "fun." (One has to wonder if she felt the same way about grammar or poetry!)

Scheduling

The single most challenging aspect of working in their schools for most of these teachers is scheduling. There seems to be a widespread administrative assumption at the secondary level that it is appropriate to place any student into any music class regardless of his previous experience level, skill level, or interest in being in the class. This is consistent with the findings of Frierson-Campbell (2004) who found that "those who create music teachers' schedules and are supposed to advocate for them actually have little understanding of their needs" (p. 6). While all of these teachers had experienced this situation to some degree, perhaps Melissa's situation is the most extreme. In her middle school, beginners are started in sixth grade. Some students who come from other schools, however, have had lessons before that. Only students placed into certain homerooms can fit instrumental music into their schedules—and then for only one semester during each year of middle school. Needless to say, this presents quite a few challenges for the instrumental music program. Additionally, since she can legally have up to 50 students at once in her classes, her ensembles have become a place to put students with exceptional needs who need an arts class. In spite of this, she feels her principal does support her program, but he is leaving at the end of this year and she worries about what the next year will bring.

Kathy, who no longer teaches in the city schools, is even more adamant about the problems with scheduling:

> Hands down, whether it was here or in the Midwest, it was scheduling. In my last city school, I saw them every day for two and a half months, and then never again. And they would schedule in ninth graders with kids who were twenty years old in their junior year. So it's scheduling, hands down. It's made me not take jobs. I could have had a full-time job at a school here, and then I saw what kind of schedule they had and said "No way!" I am not putting myself through this again. I can't do it.

Survival Techniques

Holli and Robert have had similar problems with scheduling but have found some innovative ways to solve them. Robert and his colleagues have discovered that if they can find out who is actually making the scheduling decisions, they can do the necessary paperwork and take suggestions to that person. The key is that their suggestions have been checked out and are ready to implement. Unfortunately, it does add to their workload, but the end result is less frustrating. When the school decided to implement a system of schools within a school (houses), a music house was created, but the scheduling was done in such a way that chaos ensued. Eventually, with the blessing of the scheduling chairperson, the music faculty took over the scheduling for the music house and solved the problems. They now do this every semester. The four music educators in this school have found that by working together, they can do most of their own administrative work on scheduling, budgets, and supplies.

Similarly, Holli hopes to have solved her scheduling issues for the coming year even though she is a department of one:

> It's all in the terminology. My beginning band—they call it the freshman band. So freshmen coming in, whether they have experience or not, would end up in freshman band. So I am trying to educate them a little bit more about that. I managed to get three bands for next year: beginning, intermediate, and advanced, and as far as I know I will have the say as to who goes where. Before I did that [this year], they just put anyone anywhere.

These teachers have decided that it is part of their professional responsibilities to educate their administrators about the needs of music education programs and to help them fulfill their responsibilities in ways that will improve the music programs in their schools. By taking a collaborative approach and coming to their administrators with solutions already in mind, these teachers are able to solve the problems that plague them. This is what Fiese and DeCarbo (1995) labeled as having all the participants involved in a dialogue (rather than parallel monologues) to advance music education in urban schools.

Classroom Management: Above All, Be Fair

Classroom management is often an issue for beginning urban music educators. While they did not list it as the most challenging aspect for their teaching careers, it was an issue they had all confronted. For the most part, each teacher had arrived at working solutions for their particular teaching situations.

Establishing Routines

For the secondary students, the primary discipline issue was establishing rules and routines on the very first day, being fair, and using proactive management techniques rather than responding to violations. The performing ensemble teachers use written contracts that the students and their parents sign. They create versions in several languages to hand out to students who need them. Here is Melissa's description of that first class each semester.

> Specifically, start off really firm the first day. Here is the contract; these are the rules. I don't waste time the first day because I know the kind of kids I deal with. This is what I expect. Most kids at the onset are excited. I go through the rules. I'm very clear. These are the rules, these are the consequences. Here's how it's going to happen. Your first homework? Bring in this contract signed by your parents.

Kris teaches secondary general music and has another approach to these first few days. He teaches classes of 50 students at a time in a large choral rehearsal room. He divides the space up into four quadrants that allow him to easily move about the room. Kris also emphasizes the importance of establishing routines and taking steps early on to prevent classroom disturbances:

> The first couple of days I wait for them out in the hall and watch them come into the room. I watch their habits. Who's gonna go sit in the back of the room. Who's gonna sit with who. Who's gonna deliberately act like a wise guy to get attention. So, of course, when I call roll I make my little notes. Then I make my seating plans and some of that is taken care of right away. Separate the friends. Put the ones always in the back in the front row.

Another preventive technique Kris uses is a very animated teaching style. He moves about the room constantly as he teaches, which keeps him in close proximity to his students. He feels that the close proximity and being entertaining and animated prevents many management issues. He has the respect of his students and control of the teaching environment. Both of these were found to be important by Fiese and DeCarbo (1995).

Fairness

Most teachers indicated the importance of letting students know that they are being treated fairly. This means that all students will be treated the same way if they choose to break the rules. When a problem occurs, the student involved first needs to have known beforehand that the behavior was unacceptable and that it would be unacceptable from any student, not just him or her. Here is Kris's description of what he does when something inappropriate happens.

> When they're disruptive, I give them a stern look first. The look says a thousand words. I never yell. I'll just stand there and be quiet and the rest of the class will quiet them. "Can't you see he's waiting. Be quiet!" and I didn't say it. And the look kills everything. It'll burn right through you. In the early days of school,

> you squash everything, you know what I am saying? Everybody's like "How come you were so mean in the beginning?" No, no, no. I wasn't mean. I was stern. You know, 'cause if I was like this, you would walk all over me, you know. In the beginning I am very "This is the way it is." Very mean, and stern and fair. Most importantly, fair.

Kathy also talked about the necessity of being fair. She creates a collaborative atmosphere in her classes and to make students part of the solutions to problems.

> The number one thing with inner-city kids, whether it's here or in the Midwest—it's being fair. I think that is why I was as successful as I was because they felt I was being fair. I would take advice from them. I would say, "What's gonna work for you? This is the information I need you to know." And I just explained it to them like they were real, not like they were idiots or anything. I'd say here's the deal and I'd just be truthful with them. And we would make a deal.

When students in one of her classes resisted sitting together because of their ethnic differences, she came up with an interesting collaborative solution:

> And I was like, "Well, all right how about this? When we do music activities, when we do singing or rhythm stuff, that's supposed to unite us. We're united and we're playing together. We get mixed, we mix it up. But when we're learning, when we're reading, when we're doing our own thing, then we can split. So how about we do a Monday, Wednesday, Friday we do your split and Tuesday and Thursday we mix it up?" And they said, "Okay, we can deal with that." And it worked for me.

New Students Midsemester

Many of these teachers have students added to their classes throughout the year. Robert integrates those newcomers in his classes without rehashing things with the entire group. His approach typifies what the other teachers reported doing:

> But what I don't like to do—like three weeks into the semester when there's like kind of a groove going, I don't want to go back to square one for too long because then you lose the kids who you already have going. So when a new kid comes in, it's "Okay, here's your information card, fill it out as best you can. And here are the rules [written handout]. Listen carefully. Sit down, do the best that you can today. Stay after class and I will answer any questions that you have—and good luck." If I can, I pair them up with someone to help them out. But that depends on the class and what's going on—whatever the situation is.

Crisis Situations

All of the participants' schools have a protocol in place for dealing with crisis situations. The participants could all describe the protocol in their building, often down to the exact language they were expected to use. All of them had working telephones in their rooms with which they could summon help in an emergency. Fortunately, this is not something they use very often. Fighting where there was bodily injury seemed to be the most common crisis, and that occurred only rarely in the classrooms of these teachers. Melissa spoke for the group when she said:

> In my school you call security and I have had to do that only once this year. A kid took apart the jingle bells and was throwing the pieces across the room and wouldn't stop. So I called security and they came and took out the whole back row of kids to write a statement. I just had everyone put their instruments away, because there is less chance of someone getting hurt if they don't have instruments in their hands.

Kathy, however, spoke of the futility of that same approach in the school where she was:

> I tried to do their A, B, and C protocol, and all it did was escalate a small fight into a bigger one. The kids just egged it on and it spread all over the school afterward.

She came up with quite a creative solution that worked for her in her teaching setting.

> The kids called what I did "singing down the fight." They would say: "Miss busted out the singing down the fight song again." I would just launch into "Kum Ba Ya" and clap and stamp a rhythm and the whole class joined in and it broke the mood. It took the concentration off from the fight, and usually the perpetrators stopped and calmed down as well. If someone was injured, I called immediately. However, whether or not someone came when I called depended on who the student was.

Inappropriate Spaces

Spaces designed for performance are not usually acoustically and physically appropriate for instruction. Like many elementary music teachers in this city, Joy teaches on a stage in an old auditorium. She can't close the curtains because the space is too small for the number of children. With some classes she has children seated in the auditorium seats so they can't run around and jump off the stage. She believes the combination of limited teaching time and having class on the stage makes classroom management more difficult. Joy says:

> It's not effective because I see them once a week. I have certain things that they do understand. It takes them about three months to start catching on to those things, and I can't wait to teach music that long. It's like I can't hold in place the classroom management aspect of it so long because I only see them once a week. They come in and they've forgotten and I start over. We would spend the whole class doing that.
>
> There are three classes this year I see twice a week, and you can see the difference. Those are the children that I can work with and they start to learn how to put things together. There are fewer discipline issues, and those children have respect for me. They respect me and they want to do what we are doing because it makes sense to them. Once a week it doesn't connect.

Clearly, seeing students only once a week presents many more problems for classroom music teachers beyond those of classroom discipline. Joy does solicit help from the classroom teachers to remind the students of the music classroom rules just before they appear in her auditorium. But the larger issue here is the lack of an appropriate space for music instruction. Joy indicates that colleagues walk through the auditorium talking while she is having class, not realizing how distracting that can be. Perhaps administrators could gently remind colleagues that classes are in session and interruptions by walking though or talking should be kept to a minimum as a matter of professional respect.

Professional Respect

Joy also indicated that the auditorium space is often co-opted for other activities and she has to be prepared at a moment's notice to abandon her plans and preside over a large group of children who are expected to watch a movie while their teachers have a preparation period. (This may be a movie the children have watched repeatedly in violation of copyright law.) So for Joy, the biggest challenge of teaching in an urban school is trying to go with the flow of events and not be too upset by the constant disruptions. Her role within the school seems to change with the wind. There is certainly a lack of respect for music education and her role as a music educator if she can be commandeered as a babysitter on a moment's notice in order to meet contractual requirements for other teachers' preparation periods.

The negotiation of mandatory preparation periods into teaching contracts required that specialists be hired to provide preparation time. While this may have put more music educators into schools, the end result in many schools is that music educators with advanced degrees and many years of professional training are regarded by their administrators and colleagues as somehow inferior to classroom teachers. They are viewed primarily as a time resource: someone to provide classroom teachers with preparation periods away from their students. Sadly, this finding, too, is consistent with those of Frierson-Campbell (2004) and Fiese and DeCarbo (1995).

Until music educators are valued as professionals by their administrators and colleagues, their professional lives will continue to be frustrating and less satisfying than they could be. Perhaps there should be contractual language to the effect that teachers cannot be required to substitute for other teachers in lieu of teaching their assigned content areas. Perhaps part of the solution is making substitute teaching more enticing. Whatever the solution, this type of program interruption makes it difficult to provide a music education. General music in this setting (and many similar ones) seems to have been relegated to simple exposure to music occasionally, or as mere entertainment with little interest in developing the sequential knowledge or skills over time that a true education in music requires. Without adequate time or appropriate spaces, music education for every urban child remains illusive in any school.

Preservice Preparation

All of these beginning teachers expressed a wish that they had had more field experiences in urban settings before student teaching and more class time devoted to classroom management. They also mentioned the need for more training in accommodating students with special needs in music classrooms. They were especially interested in preventive management techniques and how to keep small conflicts from escalating. All of these young teachers felt they had taught themselves much about these topics during their first few years of teaching, but they wished to learn more about how others were successfully managing urban classrooms and rehearsal rooms.

CONCLUSION

These young professionals are committed to music education in urban schools. Four of them grew up in the city in which they now teach. Along with their colleagues, they are determined to "overcome the challenges of the urban school, to take advantage of the unique rewards of such teaching and to provide a quality music education to the young people in their classes" (Fiese & DeCarbo, 1995). They regularly spend free time (and often money) learning more about their students and doing things with them outside of the school day. They study the cultures from which their students come in order to more effectively provide an appropriate music education. They are enthusiastic and interesting teachers. Finding ways to keep them teaching in the urban schools should be a priority of everyone involved in this profession. They are rare and precious human capital that must not be wasted.

Three of them, however, routinely confront issues that have caused many teachers to seek positions in the suburbs or leave the profession altogether. These issues are related to inconsistencies in what Frierson-Campbell (2004) has labeled as the role of the music teacher and the role of music in the school. These young teachers need support, respect, and help to change the role they play, and that music plays in their teaching situations, so that they will continue to find urban teaching rewarding.

Having noted the limitations of exploratory case studies at the beginning of this chapter, here are some suggestions for improving urban music education and for retaining quality music educators in urban settings:

1. The four participants who grew up in urban settings are more comfortable teaching there than their colleagues from other backgrounds. This suggests that we should do more to recruit prospective music educators from urban secondary schools.
2. The participants suggested that preprofessional onsite field experiences in urban settings might have helped them be better prepared for working with diverse student populations and students with exceptional needs. This is consistent with the findings of Fiese and DeCarbo (1995) whose respondents indicated that prospective teachers would benefit from more emphasis on student differences, differing lifestyles, and classroom and rehearsal management.
3. Participants stated a need to understand the basics of school law—especially as it pertains to children with special needs and the overcrowding of classrooms. This should be part of preservice teacher education and ongoing professional development.
4. The participants' building-level administrators do not seem to understand the goals of school-based music education or the role of professional music educators. Music teacher educators and policy makers must reach out to administrators to help them create music programs that meet the educational needs of urban students. They must help them to see that a music education can be so much more than simply release time for other educators.

The voices of practitioners need to be part of the ongoing conversation about music education in urban schools. The teachers who contributed to this chapter were concerned that members of the profession should hear the voices of practicing teachers in urban settings. This is essential if the profession wishes to develop quality music education programs in urban schools, to promote effective educational practices in urban settings, and to recruit and retain a committed group of teachers to work in urban environments.

REFERENCES

Barton, A. C., Drake, C., Perez, J. G., St. Louis, K., & George, M. (2004). Ecologies of parental engagement in urban education. *Educational Researcher*, 33(4), 3–12.

Fiese, R. K., & DeCarbo, N. J. (1995). Urban music education: The teachers' perspective. *Music Educators Journal*, 81(6), 27–32.

Frierson-Campbell, C. (2004). Professional need and the contexts of in-service music teacher identity. *Action, Criticism and Theory for Music Education*, 3(3). Retrieved August 15, 2005, from www.siue.edu/MUSIC/ACTPAPERS/v3/Frierson04.pdf

6

Teaching Music in Urban Landscapes: Three Perspectives

Carlos R. Abril

> Good teachers possess a capacity for connectedness. They are able to weave a complex web of connections among themselves, their subjects, and their students so that students can learn to weave a world for themselves. (Palmer, 1998)

INTRODUCTION: THE URBAN CONTEXT

Over the past 30 years, educators, researchers, and the media have focused on the plight of urban public schools. In so doing, they have painted a landscape in urgent need of restoration. This has resulted in a heightened awareness of the complex challenges of urban education and prompted efforts to increase funding and direct resources to these schools (Noguera, 2003). The public's collective consciousness of urban schools has been shaped by reports of dilapidated facilities, abysmal test scores, high dropout rates, low motivation, poor attendance, and high poverty (Kozol, 1991, 2000; Rose, 1995). These images have the capacity to breed apprehension and even fear in potential and practicing teachers, making it difficult to recruit and retain high-quality teachers.

Principals are limited by the small pools of candidates willing to work in urban schools. Candidates with the strongest credentials have a good chance of being hired in suburban schools, where greater funds and resources are available (Ayers & Ford, 1996; Knapp & Woolverton, 2004; Kozol, 1991). As a result, urban districts may be left with underqualified teachers or teachers who view the position as transitory (Nieto, 2003a). Approximately half of all new teachers in urban public schools leave within the first five years of teaching (Haycock, 1998). Many leave the profession altogether, while some transfer to other school districts. Despite these issues, many exemplary teachers choose to work in urban schools and do not permit obstacles to cloud their goals. These educators should serve as role models for the profession.

Teachers

Teachers serve as agents of change, affecting students and the educational system. Research has documented that urban teachers educate through and beyond their respective subjects, while challenging school policy (Noguera, 2003; Ramirez & Gallardo, 2001; Rose, 1995). Nieto (2003b) conducted a study of seven "highly respected high school teachers [working in urban schools] who had reputations for success with students of diverse backgrounds" (p. 14). Many of these teachers were angered by conditions and injustices their students endured yet refrained from focusing on their frustrations. Instead, they focused on meeting the educational and emotional needs of their students. The teachers in the inquiry group expressed passion for their subjects and their students. Similar research has described the ways teachers affect students' self-images through interactions and verbalizations (Nieto, 2003a). Hargreaves, Earl, and Ryan (1996) conducted interviews with high school dropouts who revealed they might have remained in school if there had been a school staff member who knew and cared about them. As Noguera notes, teachers can make the difference between "success or failure, school or jail, life or death" (2003, p. 41).

Music and the Arts

As a school subject, music holds a unique position in the school curriculum. Music ensembles facilitate the development of positive school cultures, where students create a home away from home (Adderley, Kennedy, & Berz, 2003; Morrison, 2001). Education through music serves to provide students with a better understanding of their culture and the cultures of others (Abril, 2003, 2005; Campbell, 1998). Music education facilitates the development of the musical domain of intelligence (Gardner, 1999). Finally, the human experience can be transformed through musical experiences such as listening, composing, performing, and improvising (Bowman, 2002; Reimer, 2003). The traditionally underserved populations of this country, the largest concentration of which reside in urban centers, might be the people in greatest need of quality arts education.

Research on the effects of arts instruction for at-risk students has yielded some promising results. Jenlink (1993) found that participation in an elementary school performing group served to improve at-risk students' self-esteem and build common bonds between home and school. However, factors related to students' homes and communities were found to have a detrimental effect on their self-esteem. A similar study was conducted with at-risk adolescents in a school situated in a large urban district (Shields, 2001). After participating in a 16-week musical performance program, students' perceptions of musical competence improved significantly. Interviews with students revealed that music was an important part of their lives and students enjoyed the opportunity to perform. The Center for Music Research (1990) reported that at-risk children in urban schools were on task in their arts courses more often than in their non-arts courses. Teachers, administrators, and students claimed that courses in music and the arts were the sole reasons many at-risk students remained in school. Various city schools throughout the country have had great success in using the arts to improve student achievement, morale, and motivation (various studies cited in Taylor, Barry, & Walls, 1997). Research supports the assertion that music and the arts are positive factors in the education and lives of at-risk students.

Music Teachers

Music education has the potential of exerting a positive effect on urban students, but many novice teachers hesitate to work in urban schools. Kindall-Smith (2004) reported that preservice music teachers, with little to no experience in city schools, expressed anxiety with the thought of working in these settings. Preservice teachers have been found to view student diversity as a problem instead of a resource and express discomfort in interacting with those of backgrounds that differ from their own (Nierman, Zeichner, & Hobbel, 2002). Some music educators have reported feeling unprepared to teach in urban schools upon graduation from a teacher education program. They thought college courses were too focused on teaching music in ideal circumstances (Fiese & DeCarbo, 1995).

Despite these realities, many teachers thrive in urban schools. Outstanding urban music teachers connect with at-risk students by remaining compassionate about the students' world outside of school and maintaining high expectations (Robinson, 2004). Fiese and DeCarbo (1995) reported that outstanding urban music teachers throughout the United States attributed their success to support systems, continued professional development, and strong parental relations. In an effort to improve the condition of music education for those in greatest need, we must learn from the examples of others.

The images of urban schools portrayed by the media only tell part of the story. This chapter seeks to bring them into focus by exploring the ways three music teachers have successfully met the challenge of teaching in urban schools. Each teacher has built a well-respected music program in an urban school setting by meeting problems with viable solutions, thus impacting the lives of hundreds of students over the course of many years. Their stories can serve to guide beginning or struggling music teachers in urban schools, or inspire those who might consider working with underserved children. They can provide music teacher educators with ideas to better prepare their students to teach in urban schools. They also bring to light unique problems, which might be alleviated or prevented through improved policy.

PROCEDURES

I asked a local school music supervisor and a music education professor to create a list of outstanding music teachers from area urban schools. Teachers who appeared on both lists were then narrowed to individuals who: (a) were currently teaching music in urban schools; (b) had taught over five years in urban schools; (c) worked in high-poverty schools (over 75% free and reduced lunch); and (d) were willing to participate. The first three teachers who met the criteria and agreed to participate were chosen for the study.

I conducted one to two formal interviews with each teacher and observed them in their teaching setting for four to eight hours. During my campus visits, I spent time exploring each school and its surrounding community. Prior to the visits, I developed a series of interview questions to examine the reasons teachers decided to work in urban schools, the obstacles they have faced in urban schools, and the ways they have negotiated solutions to those problems. The questions were informed by the literature, my personal experience teaching in urban schools, and conversation with urban music educators.

Questions were intended to guide rather than dictate the interview process. In an effort to permit interviews to unfold like conversations, questions varied for each participant in terms of order, construction, and content. Some teachers expounded upon certain topics more than others, and a few propelled the conversation in unexpected directions. Nonetheless, the interviews remained centered around the original questions. After transcribing the recorded interviews, I coded data according to predetermined categories yet remained open to emerging themes.

Landscape

The three teachers taught in different schools within one of the largest school systems in the United States. Their schools were located in different parts of the city, and while each school was unique, they shared common traits. An overwhelming majority of students—88% to 98% in each school—

qualified for free or reduced-price lunch. Although most students were Hispanic, the overall student body was ethnically diverse. Each school was situated in a surrounding community that was alive with the din of traffic and the sight of people moving past storefronts. Neighborhoods reflected the diversity of their residents. A brightly colored mural depicting Mexican migrants in an outdoor market marked one community; a street, host to a Turkish grocery store, an Ethiopian restaurant, and a Swedish bakery marked another; a boarded-up brick building, check-cashing store, and auto repair shop the third. Each of the schools stood inextricably bound within its respective urban landscape. My visits invariably began with a greeting from security personnel who served as gatekeepers protecting the school community from the outside. They generally requested identification, an explanation for my visit, and a signature in a logbook.

Conditions varied inside each school. One had a newly renovated interior, with polished terrazzo floors, bright lighting, and fresh paint. Another suffered from dim hallways, chipping paint, and leaky ceilings. The third school consisted of an original early-20th-century brick edifice, juxtaposed against a recently completed modern building. Despite the physical condition of the schools, each of the music rooms I visited stood as beacons of light. They were places where students purposefully engaged in learning through the music experience.

In front of the band room, trophies proudly stood alongside a bulletin board displaying results of solo and ensemble evaluations. Students moved in and out of practice rooms with a seriousness of purpose, while the band could be heard polishing a march. In the hallway, outside a general music classroom, small groups of students were gathered, perfecting rhythmic patterns on tubano drums; on other occasions they could be found inventing verses to traditional rhymes. Inside another music room, bulletin boards displayed students' percussion compositions, writings about composers, and pictures of smiling students dancing with scarves. Despite the obstacles that could have stood in the way, the teachers remained focused on making the connection between students and music their top priority.

The case studies presented in this chapter illustrate the challenges, joys, disappointments, negotiations, and triumphs of teaching in urban schools, from the teacher's perspective. The data were organized around three main areas: the teacher-self, students/community, and the subject. Although these areas are not mutually exclusive, they serve as a framework for presenting each teacher's story. Within each of these broad themes, differing categories emerged for each teacher. Just as the chapter began with Palmer's note about the connections woven by good teachers, the stories of these three teachers demonstrate how they make connections with their selves, with music, and with the people in their school communities. Pseudonyms have been used for all teachers, children, and schools described in this chapter.

MICHAEL RHODES

In 1928, Dominion High School first opened its doors to 1,500 students. Today, the original brick edifice and a recently constructed wing accommodate almost double that number. Michael, a 27-year veteran who exudes the enthusiasm and energy you might expect from a graduating college student, proudly calls this predominantly Hispanic school his "second home." Like many successful music teachers, he wears many hats, and each suits him well. During my visit I observed him counsel a student, rehearse several bands, repair a euphonium valve, lend a student lunch money, and negotiate a class conflict with a colleague.

Self

As a college student, majoring in music education, Michael knew he wanted to teach music in an urban school. Having attended urban schools as a student, he often felt disadvantaged. He says, "We [his high school band] were always the underdogs. We were never as good as those in the suburbs because they always had more then we did . . . private lessons and all those other things, but we never took that stuff for granted." Despite recognizing the advantages that teaching in a more affluent area might have afforded him, he also recognized the potential rewards of teaching in an urban school. One of the things he preferred was the cultural diversity found in urban schools, which he said is "not like that in the suburbs . . . where it's pretty much one setting and one culture."

Michael describes how other music teachers he knows, who are unfamiliar with urban educational settings, react to his teaching situation. He says, "They are in awe of the things I face but I want them to know there is nothing wrong with this . . . the kids are great! People, that's all we are. We act different because of our cultures . . . and that's what makes things interesting. It's rougher at times. . . . we don't have all those luxuries . . . but there is something *real* about working here." Michael's commitment to teaching in urban schools stems from his understanding of and comfort in the landscape.

Connecting with Students

Michael's past has shaped his views and actions as a teacher. His father was a postman who befriended many coworkers of cultures different from his own: "When I was growing up we'd have guys from the post office coming over to the house . . . friends from all ethnic backgrounds. And it helps me now; it helps a lot. I know where my kids are coming from." He attributes his success in working in an urban school to his ability to understand people of different cultures: "I've always been in multicultural communities . . . with

Bohemians, Poles, Slovaks, Mexicans, African Americans. Each culture acted different but they got together and they worked together. I got to know how people work and talk with one another—how they worked through the bad times." His past experiences have undoubtedly informed his present approach to dealing with students.

Michael recognizes that conflicts may arise between families and school. Many of his students, especially those from Mexican families, are expected to earn money as soon as they are legally eligible for employment. They work part-time and full-time jobs to supplement family incomes. Long hours on the job make it difficult to keep up with the demands of school. He says, "Over time I figured out it was all that outside work. I understand their families expect it." Michael gives the example of José, a talented student who hopes to become a band director someday. Even though he hopes to major in music in college, José "has to go to school today and to work tomorrow at four o'clock which means he can't participate in jazz band rehearsals every day." Michael has learned to negotiate around these kinds of situation with students and families, to keep students in the band program. He says, "Flexibility is key."

I had the opportunity to talk with José. He explained that his parents "see more of the work side of the things [than the education side of things]: 'You're gonna work' they say. '*I know*,' I tell them, 'I'm gonna work the rest of my life!'" He says he is often tired at work and school because of the long hours but work is going well. He proudly states that his supervisor at the hardware store has offered to promote him to assistant manager. José says, "I want to be a music teacher, so I'll go to [a local college of music] . . . but right now I will work to save up money and keep practicing. . . . it's hard 'cuz I got to go to work every day. It's a lot—it's a lot. [He pauses.] But [Mr. Rhodes] understands." Because José has many demands placed on him both in and out of school, he and Michael have negotiated a plan. Michael allows him to miss rehearsals with the understanding that José will make an effort to create his work schedule so it conflicts as little as possible with rehearsals. Michael stresses the importance of understanding students, treating them with respect, and being flexible. He adds, "You have to. Otherwise they leave the program altogether and lose interest."

Behavior

Michael admits that managing student behavior can be a challenge: "One of the things I have to do is teach them how to behave. . . . I do it, no matter what it takes . . . they know I do it for their good but I have to balance it with teaching music." He explains the importance of connecting with the most challenging students: "Once you win him over, you got the class licked . . . everything will fall in place after that because a lot of kids will follow his lead. I will do what it takes because I want the students to have music . . . it's called doing your job." He believes in treating high school students with respect and getting to know them as people. He avoids reprimanding students for every single infraction of the rules; instead choosing his battles wisely. When students break rules he says: "I let them know I know. I usually give them a break. I always give you that one break, but don't mess up again. They know not to mess with me again because they will pay the next time." Michael claims to follow through on his threats and promises.

Over the years, Michael has had students who others dismissed as failures. He talks about one student, Daryl, who was a local gang leader and "school troublemaker." Michael found him to be "a real talented, musical guy," and hoped the music culture might steer Daryl in a more positive direction. Michael explains, "[T]he principal would say 'why are you letting him in school? Why did you let him play in the concert?'" Michael believed his actions were in the best interest of the student and was willing to confront the administration if need be. According to Michael, Daryl was a focused musician: "He got to play in the spring concert . . . and boy he had style . . . [*he pauses, nods, and looks upward*] he had style. He could play. *Man* . . . what talent. I thought music might be his way out." Unfortunately the story does not end well. Daryl was in and out of jail for a few years and was murdered during a robbery. In spite of witnessing the incarceration and death of some of his students, Michael continues to have hope: "I know I can't reach everyone all the time . . . but there are many I do . . . and that's what it's all about."

Staying in School

Michael believes that the music program has kept many students from dropping out of school: "There have been a lot of kids who tell me, 'if it wasn't for band I would have dropped out. I couldn't miss because you relied on me.' Some of the kids tell me when I bump into them as adults. The other day I met José [not the José mentioned earlier], one of my former students, who's now a sergeant in the police department. One of the first things he says to me, 'you know, you saved me from dropping out of high school. I loved playing in band so much!' That's what it's all about."

Connecting with Music

Most students arrive at Dominion High with no school music experience because music was cut from the elementary and middle school curriculum 10 years prior. While many programs in the nearby suburban schools begin instrumentalists in fourth or fifth grade, students in his school start in ninth grade. Despite this disadvantage, he is able to recruit large numbers of students (there are currently 630 beginners in his program!) and prepare them to successfully perform grade-five concert band music by the time they enroll in the advanced ensemble (where they have consistently received "superior" ratings over the years). He believes students remain motivated and engaged in music because of the challenges he places before them in the form of quality music, performances, and evaluations.

Many of Michael's students end up pursuing careers in music and music education. Three are "currently working on music education degrees [at a local college] and two at [the state university]. . . . One of my students is a renowned percussionist who tours around the world . . . a few are local band directors . . . others just enjoy making music." He gets joy from watching his students improve: "At first they think they can't do it. Sometimes they will sit here working on something and I've been listening to 'em and they'll be working on it, over and over, and then they get it and say 'I can finally do it, come here and listen to me' and I say 'I *have been* listening to you.' This is what it's about. In their lives other people put them down. That's why I push them. I want them to know they have to work and push to get better in life."

I asked him to describe how students' cultural backgrounds inform his curricular decisions. He says, "We play some Hispanic music. . . . I feel that they would like to play a little more but there's nothing written out there." He mentions a few arrangements he has played (i.e., Cuban composer Ernesto Lecuona's *Malaguena*) but admits he could do more. He claims that audiences are quite enthusiastic when he does program Hispanic music. Michael strives to connect with students and the greater school community through music.

Final Thoughts

I ask Michael for words of advice to share with someone planning to teach music in urban schools. He says, "Get to know the children . . . talk to them. If you notice a change, find out what's wrong. Don't be like, 'I'm the teacher, that's it! I don't want to hear nothing' because that puts you on the other end—these guys won't respond to you." He stresses the importance of being well prepared as a musician and a music pedagogue. He continues, "I look at it this way: you have to wanna do it and it's got to come from here [*he touches his heart*]. Music must speak to you . . . you've got to love the kids."

For those with less experience in urban schools, he suggests beginning with younger children. He feels that you can come to understand students best when you work with them at a young age. (His first teaching job was as an elementary school instrumental teacher.) He says, "You gotta know them and see things from their perspective"—he has mentioned this on several occasions. He feels the problems lies in administrative policies: "The problem is that new teachers are often put in the worst schools [administrators] can find. . . . I tell them that's why you scare so many people out of the system. We need to put them in more manageable places first." He feels this is one of the more serious problems in retaining teachers in the urban schools.

Someone once asked Michael when he was going to retire: "I said 'Why? I'm enjoying what I'm doing right now. When I can't communicate with students anymore, that's when I'll know to step down.'" Though he has a passion for music, he sees teaching as transcendent of the discipline. He says, "I want to inspire them in life. This is life, the good times and the bad times. Life is right here—that's why I have an ulcer [*he laughs*]. They have a good time, and I have one too. It's been an interesting profession. I wouldn't change it!"

MARY THOMAS

The dimly lit hallways of Belle Meade School proudly display exemplars of student work, plaques recognizing school and teacher accomplishments, and murals painted by students. These cheerful artifacts seem to make up for the lack of lighting. Visitors to the music room are greeted with photographs of the chorus, inspirational posters, colorfully painted chairs, books, and musical instruments. Mary teaches elective choirs and general music classes to students from elementary through middle school.

Self

Mary always wanted to teach in an urban school but initially settled for a suburban Catholic school. She recalls, "When I was in college I only considered working in urban schools, but when I graduated, the city schools had a job freeze for arts teachers so I got a job at a private school instead." She describes her impressions of that position: "[St. Peter and Paul] was in an affluent community where many of the students took private lessons on an instrument . . . a lot of them owned their own instruments and probably attended concerts and listened to music at home. I liked working there but I just didn't feel as fulfilled as I might be working with students who really needed exposure [to music]." Mary's desire to teach in the city schools never faded. Ten years after taking her first job Mary got wind that city schools were hiring arts teachers again. She was soon hired at Belle Meade School, a public school in an urban neighborhood not far from where she grew up, and does not regret the move.

Mary seems pleased to be teaching in an urban school. She says, "I'm getting back as much as I'm giving. In my other school [private suburban] I gave but didn't get back as much. . . . More than once, problems in [Belle Meade] have turned out to be good for me. For instance, because of tight budgets I've had to learn how to write grants. When the grants were awarded [two grants for a full set of African-style drums], I was invited to go to events where I met funders and other people who support the arts . . . and I got to meet other teachers like me. We get a lot of ideas and inspiration from each other. I don't think that would have happened to me in a private school because I had no need to write grants. . . . I think I'm a better teacher because of it." She views this and other challenges she has faced as positive opportunities.

Connecting with Students

Students are central to Mary's teaching practices. She constructs lesson plans, chooses music, and develops teaching strategies around them. She is also aware of the environment she creates: "my classroom needs to be comfortable [for my students] to take musical risks . . . and a safe haven from the issues and pressures that they encounter on a daily basis. . . . I want them to experience the joy of music making in here." Her passion for working with students is evident from observing her teach and our interviews.

Special-Needs Students

I asked Mary to describe some of the challenges she has faced in working with her students. She said, "Support. We don't get nearly enough support for working with students who have special needs. Many are mainstreamed into all special area classes without a classroom aide. Others need to be tested to find the right educational programs but we can't do it . . . there's not enough staff . . . plus we [teachers] don't get the training we need." She feels that her undergraduate teacher training did nothing to prepare her for this challenge. However, that did not prevent her from researching the matter herself. She says she enrolled in a course at a local university and researched relevant topics. As a result she felt better able to connect with special-needs students, and also prepared her to contribute to their "Individualized Education Programs."

English-Language Learners

The number of students with limited English proficiency at Belle Meade has increased significantly over the years. Mary has modified her teaching style in response to this change. She says, "many [of the Spanish-speaking students] must learn things visually. You can teach them the concepts through talking . . . but until they see it in some visual representation, it just doesn't click for them." On several occasions I observed Mary use charts with abstract symbols, brightly colored pictures, or words to emphasize a particular idea. Mary has learned to refrain from making too many assumptions: "When I first taught 'Jingle Bells' at this school I was surprised because some hadn't heard it before, and most did not know what a *sleigh* was." She has come to understand that certain terms and concepts are not part of students' lives.

Children are in bilingual programs throughout the day, but district regulations stipulate that music, art, and physical education classes immerse children in English. Nonetheless, Mary found it beneficial to learn basic words in Spanish to facilitate her students' learning. She also strives to connect students with their cultural heritage by singing Spanish-language songs from the Hispanic tradition. Mary says, "Active involvement is key and keeps them engaged even when they don't speak the language [English]. . . . You have to connect with them somehow."

Poverty

Belle Meade has one of the highest poverty rates in the city. Most of the students are unable to pay for school supplies, recorders, or even lunch. In 2003, 98% of students qualified for free or reduced-price meals (many currently receive three meals a day at the school). Mary is aware of the financial hardships most families endure, but she strives to provide students with first-rate musical experiences. She has sought and received financial support from local and national funding agencies including Target, State Farm, and the Oppenheimer Family Foundation. The money subsidizes or fully funds music field trips, artist residencies, choir uniforms, musical instruments, risers, and music. As the recipient of a prestigious regional teaching award, Mary was provided with computer hardware and software for use in the classroom. All the materials and programs she acquires contribute to the improvement of music education for her students.

Change Agent

Mary is an advocate for the rights of her students and their families: "Whenever policies are instituted at school [from either the school or district level], I think about its effect on two levels: what's best for the student and what's best for the entire school." She says, "I don't hesitate to talk to the administration about problems if I see they might be able to help improve the situation. If it is at a higher level, I will get involved by informing parents about the situation."

Mary stresses the importance of developing positive relationships with building administrators, who will then advocate for you and your students beyond the school level. She says, "I'm in charge of music in my school so I have to look out for students' rights in receiving a quality education. I'll speak out for them or their parents because many don't do it for themselves—some of them don't know their rights—others don't know English." Many of the parents at Belle Meade are recent immigrants and speak little to no English.

Connecting with Music

Mary feels greatly rewarded from teaching something she loves so much. She says the greatest rewards of teaching are "interacting with my students and watching them grow musically [throughout the years] . . . and participating with music for a living." Her students experience great joy as well, she notes: "Many times, I've seen students walk into the music room and smile because all the instruments were set up for them to play that day. I think the music and the instruments help them forget worries or bad moods." Her passion for the subject is infectious.

She also strives to provide her students with musical experiences that stretch beyond the musical styles and cultures with which they are most familiar. None of her students take private lessons and few can afford to attend a concert or buy an instrument; therefore most, if not all, of their formal musical education will occur in school. Mary thus strives to provide multiple opportunities for performance. She says, "Performing is a part of being a musician . . . and their performance is a natural outgrowth of something they have learned in class [chorus or general music]. I want them to perform something that really has become a part of them."

Final Thoughts

I ask her what words of advice she has for beginning teachers working in urban schools. She says, "Be prepared and know your lessons well before you teach . . . that way you can deal with other issues—special learners or discipline problems—during the lesson. It is also important to establish a relationship with the kids so that you're on the same page. Know their names, and get to know their families if possible . . . also develop good relationships with those who can support you the most, like your principal, colleagues, and parents." She notes that music teachers must think beyond the four walls of their classrooms and become a part of the school community.

Mary sums up her role as a music teacher in an urban school: "My focus is to provide students with a safe and comfortable place where they can experience the joy of music. [My classroom] might be a place for them to forget their troubles . . . for them to grow musically . . . or better understand their musical culture. Hopefully they gain sensitivity to the beauty of music."

SARAH RIVERS

Self

After graduating with a degree in vocal performance, Sarah went on to study vocal pedagogy where she first recognized her affinity for teaching. She says, "I realized I was really good at transferring my love of music to somebody else, even those who were having trouble. I made them enjoy it too." Not long after she decided to complete courses required for teaching certification. At the time she aspired to teach choir in a high school.

Today Sarah teaches general and choral music to students from prekindergarten through eighth grade at Optima International School. Nestled in an ethnically diverse community, the newly renovated building stands proudly, with its expansive three-story brick façade and spring flower garden. Sarah's classroom, which she refers to as "the Taj Mahal," is in the newest wing of the building. Assorted instruments, books, recordings, computers, sound equipment, and bulletin boards brighten her room and encourage musical discovery. It is not what one might expect from a poverty-stricken urban public school, but things were quite different when Sarah started teaching seven years ago.

Connecting with Music

When Sarah began teaching at Optima, she had no room or equipment to call her own. She moved among classrooms, teaching music from a cart and buying materials with her own money. She felt this arrangement relegated music to a third-class status. Sarah says, "I don't believe in teaching music if it is not a music class and that was the feeling that was out there. . . . I set out on a mission to make people see music as a core academic subject."

Knowing the limitations of school funding in her district, she capitalized on community resources to improve the music program. She describes some of these efforts: "We developed a four-year partnership [with the local symphony orchestra] where they worked in training faculty in music methods and provided the school with Orff instruments and many computers chock-full of music software." She also learned to write grants, which led to the acquisition of more instruments, costumes for performances, and teaching materials. (A sign on her classroom door celebrates the fact that she is a "Foundation for Education Grant Winner.") With all the instruments, computers, and other materials trickling in, administrators recognized she needed a place to house them, and she was soon assigned her own classroom.

Since music programs are often seen as a luxury in urban schools, Sarah feels music teachers have a responsibility to provide "students with stellar music educations, or else we can't say that music is important in our schools. Those in affluent communities often recognize the value of music education because they know what it should be like; those in the urban areas might have less experience. Since our [urban school] music programs here are always being held under scrutiny, a bad music program is not okay." Music programs in urban schools must work harder to maintain their place in the school curriculum because of the constant financial struggles they encounter.

Sarah is one of a handful of teachers at her school who have received National Board certification. She says, "I see it as one way to set the bar higher for teachers . . . and improve education for the kids—it's all about the kids." It also supports her goal of elevating the status of music education in her school: "It goes to show that music teachers are important and take their jobs seriously," she smiles, adding, "it's also a little harder to get rid of a board-certified teacher when push comes to shove." Overall, she feels it is important to make a music program indispensable, especially in urban school districts where the threat of budget cuts loom larger than in the suburbs. She attributes strong support from colleagues and administrators to her efforts that go above and beyond expectations.

Curricular Responsibilities and Compromise

When I ask Sarah about the challenges of teaching in an urban setting, she hesitates. She does not like to "dwell on those matters." After taking a moment to think, she confesses time is her worst enemy. There are not enough hours in the week for one person to teach over 1,000 students. She says, "When I go to Orff meetings and hear about the suburban teachers who see their kids two and three times a week, I realize the situation here is so different. I have to be realistic . . . there is [only] so much I can do." She claims it is logistically impossible for her to teach all the students every week and the school system will not provide funding for a part-time music teacher to assist with the teaching load. Currently, her salary is only partially paid by the school district; the rest of the funding comes from federal Title I funding. The decision to use Title I money to subsidize the position was made by the principal and a school council, comprised of teachers and parents.

As it is, her schedule leaves minimal time for planning and preparation. She and her principal negotiated a plan where seventh- and eighth-grade students only receive music part of the year, and first-grade students are excluded the entire year. This choice stems from Sarah's evaluation of her overall music curriculum, from pre-K through eighth grade. Students have music class once per week for 40 minutes. This has forced Sarah to reevaluate some of her curricular goals. "Ideally I would like my students to go away really musically literate. . . . They do learn some reading and notation, especially when playing recorders . . . but it's limited. I've come to realize other things are more important. I prefer for them to have great musical experiences singing, playing, and dancing." Sarah speculates that her curriculum might move at a faster pace if she were teaching in a school where she could see her students more than once per week. Despite the limitations, she says, "Kids are the most important things to remain focused on . . . and we must move them up from wherever they're at."

Connecting with Community

Sarah recognizes the importance of being part of her school community. She says, "I make it my business to understand how the school works." She is one of two teachers on the school council and is also the chair of the professional development committee. In addition, she started an afterschool program for teachers in the community called "Education through Music." It focuses on ways teachers can use music to develop students' cognitive skills and conceptual understanding in other subjects. (Over the years I have received emails from Sarah inviting my students and me to participate in these workshops.) She has collaborated with colleagues to write grants and produce school programs. Sarah believes music is important and recognizes that it is one piece of the larger puzzle. Every year she works with grade-level teachers to design a curricular project focused on the Renaissance. The cross-curricular unit culminates with a school performance that incorporates language arts, history, visual art, dance, and music. (On one of my visits, she was putting the finishing touches on a grant application to fund Renaissance costumes for the performance.)

Connecting with Students

When she started applying for teaching positions, Sarah was willing to work in most any setting. She says, "I had experiences in both . . . and felt comfortable in either but I probably did have a preference more toward an urban setting." Asked why she had a preference for the urban, she says, "It's a parent issue. Although there are kids in an urban setting that have good support at home, I knew many would not. That doesn't mean that parents don't want to, but there's a lot who are single parents, and work two or three jobs and can't be home. I thought I'd rather be with kids who needed somebody extra in their life."

I ask her to describe the challenges of teaching children at her school and how those might differ from children in more affluent areas. She says, "There are some problems that are universal . . . but I think that when you are more economically disadvantaged there is an anger that you are not fully able to participate in the world around you." She believes her students must learn to attribute their efforts to self-improvement. Sarah says, "I want them to know they do have choices to make and it is up to them to make the right ones." She feels that suburban children have their own problems, but awareness that their actions are directly related to their accomplishments is not one of them.

English-Language Learners

The majority of students at Optima are native Spanish-speakers. The younger students and those who have recently arrived in the United States are often unable to speak or understand English. While some teachers might see this as a major challenge, Sarah does not. She pairs those students with a bilingual student who serves as a translator when needed. She avoids giving excessive written work. She says, "It frustrates them . . . and it's not in the spirit of music anyway." She demonstrates how she might teach something nonverbally: "I ask them to copy what I'm doing on an instrument [*Sarah moves her hands demonstrating appropriate mallet technique*] or performing a particular rhythm pattern [*she taps out a rhythm*]." She has learned a few terms in Spanish to facilitate communication and on one of my visits fourth-grade students were exploring the music of Puerto Rico.

Behavior

Although classroom behavior is considered a serious problem in urban schools, Sarah claims to have few behavioral issues with which to contend. During several observations of her teaching, I never observed a behavioral issue arise. She attributes this to consistent rules and consequences that are enforced throughout the school. When she does have a problem with a student she attempts to understand: "I know there has to be a reason why this child is acting this way so if I can get through it that way . . . then I can get to the point a lot quicker. . . . I'll modify my teaching to accommodate that kid. . . . You have to know what's going on with these kids in order to be successful." If she observes a consistent pattern of misbehavior in a particular student she researches the matter. She reads the student's "Individualized Educational Program," and talks to their parents and grade-level teachers sooner rather than later. She claims the struggle is to "know the issues while remaining unbiased in your actions with that child." These issues are relevant to teaching in any school setting.

Final Thoughts

Sarah hesitates to wallow in the problems at her schools; instead she acts to solve them. That philosophy was evident in all my observations of her work with children. It also arose as a theme throughout our interview and written communications. During the interview she said, "I don't bitch and moan about how many hours I work (I don't count), and I don't get upset about how little we get paid. This is the job I took. . . . I made the choice . . . and I wouldn't change it."

CONCLUSION

A cursory reading of these stories might lead some to conclude that teaching in urban schools is like teaching anywhere else. There is some truth to that; teachers in any school are bound to face obstacles they strive to overcome. A more in-depth reading, however, reveals substantial differences. Urban schools face staggering teacher attrition rates (Haycock, 1998) and insufficient funding (Ayers & Ford, 1996), as well as large percentages of economically disadvantaged students (Kozol, 1991; Rose, 1995), students of limited English proficiency (Abril, 2003; Noguera, 2003), and high dropout rates (Kozol, 1991). In an attempt to improve the condition of urban education, generally, and music education, specifically, the various stakeholders of the profession—administrators, policy makers, teachers, and teacher trainers—must learn from those who have successfully traversed the urban landscape. Mary, Michael, and Sarah addressed many of the above issues through their perspectives.

Throughout his 27 years teaching in urban schools, Michael witnessed many music teachers fleeing urban schools because they worked in "the worst schools." Michael suggests that teachers who are unfamiliar with urban schools and students begin at the elementary level—as he did—so they can come to understand students from the ground up. Teacher educators should provide students with multiple opportunities to work with individual students and groups of students in urban schools so they can become better attuned to their emotional and educational needs. Administrators and policy makers might work to ensure novice music teachers are placed in schools where they are more likely to succeed and assign an experienced mentor to shepherd them through the first years of teaching.

Mary and Sarah both recognized that funds at their schools were limited and responded by seeking funds from local and national sources. They were both awarded multiple grants to fund artist residencies, musical instruments, computers, field trips, choir uniforms, and curricular projects. Sarah felt that grant awards not only provided needed funding but also elevated the status of music education in her school. Since funding may be quite limited in urban schools, teachers should be prepared to seek alternative sources of funding in their teacher education courses or through in-service workshops.

One of the characteristics most evident in all three teachers was the ability to understand and respond to their students' needs. All three teachers stressed the importance of approaching students by seeing issues through their lenses. Instead of giving up on a student whose work schedule often conflicted with afterschool band rehearsals, Michael understood the familial pressures (financial and cultural) José faced, negotiated a solution, and remained flexible to scheduling alternatives. Recognizing that many of her students were of limited-English proficiency, Sarah sought to connect with them directly through active music-making experiences—moving, playing, and singing. She understood that too much talking or writing about music is going to "frustrate them" and is "not in the spirit of music anyway." Feeling unprepared to work with students of various exceptionalities, Mary sought additional training and conducted her own research. As a result, she felt better prepared to plan and implement musical instruction for those individuals. These teachers' commitment to their students' educational and emotional needs corroborates with Nieto's (2003b) study of highly successful teachers working in urban schools.

The case studies in this chapter provide a view into the perceptions and experiences of Michael, Sarah, and Mary. They describe the less-than-ideal conditions in which they began and the ways they improved their situations. These teachers exemplify the ways in which teachers can remain focused on connecting themselves to the subject and students they teach, despite the static that clouds the system. While they were honest—expressing frustrations, fears, and anger—they focused on the joy they felt in working with children and music. It seems that their vision, initiative, and drive were capable of carrying them through the obstacles.

Thriving as an urban music educator may not mean having a collection of brand-new instruments, unlimited financial support, or state-of-the-art facilities. Those who thrive find satisfaction in helping students "move up from wherever they're at" (Sarah); "find a voice with music" (Michael); or "grow musically and develop of love of making music" (Mary). The journey through the urban landscape is a challenging yet fulfilling one. A bright and committed teaching force can weave connections among themselves, music, and students. This process will serve to improve the education of students of tomorrow.

REFERENCES

Abril, C. R. (2003). No hablo inglés: Breaking the language barrier in music instruction. *Music Educators Journal*, 89(5), 38–43.

———. (2005). Multicultural dimensions and their effect on children's responses to pop songs performed in various languages. *Bulletin of the Council for Research in Music Education*, 165, 37–52.

Adderley, C., Kennedy, M., & Berz, W. (2003). "A home away from home": The world of the high school music classroom. *Journal of Research in Music Education*, 51(3), 190–205.

Ayers, W., & Ford, P. (Eds.). (1996). *City kids, city teachers: Reports from the front row*. New York: The New Press.

Bowman, W. (2002). Educating musically. In R. Colwell and C. Richardson (Eds.), *The new handbook of research on music teaching and learning* (pp. 63–84). New York: Oxford University Press.

Campbell, P. S. (1998). *Songs in their heads: Music and its meaning in children's lives*. New York: Oxford University Press.

Center for Music Research. (1990). The role of the fine and performing arts in high school drop out prevention. Tallahassee, FL (ERIC 354 168).

Fiese, R. K., & DeCarbo, N. J. (1995). Urban music education: The teachers' perspective. *Music Educators Journal*, 82(1), 32–35.

Gardner, H. (1999). *Frames of mind: The theory of multiple intelligences*. New York: Basic (p. 123).

Hargreaves, L., Earl, L., & Ryan, J. (1996). *The challenge to care in schools: An alternative approach to education*. New York: Teachers College Press.

Haycock, K. (1998). No more settling for less. *Thinking*, 4(1), 3–12.

Jenlink, C. L. (1993). The relational aspects of a school, a music program, and at-risk student self-esteem: A qualitative study (Doctoral dissertation, University of Oklahoma, 1993). *Dissertation Abstracts International*, 0524, 9418710.

Kindall-Smith, M. (2004). Teachers teaching teachers: Revitalization in an urban setting. *Music Educators Journal*, 91(2), 41–46.

Knapp, M. S., & Woolverton, S. (2004). Social class and schooling. In J. Banks and C. Banks (Eds.), *Handbook of Research in Multicultural Education* (pp. 656–681). San Francisco: Jossey-Bass.

Kozol, J. (1991). *Savage inequalities: Children in America's schools*. New York: Crown.

———. (2000). *Ordinary resurrections: Children in the years of hope*. New York: Crown.

Morrison, S. J. (2001). The school ensemble: A culture of our own. *Music Educators Journal*, 88(2), 24–28.

Nierman, G. E., Zeichner, K., & Hobbel, N. (2002). Changing concepts of teacher education. In R. C. Colwell & C. Richardson (Eds.), *The new handbook of research on music teaching and learning* (pp. 818–839). Oxford: Oxford University Press.

Nieto, S. (2003a). *What keeps teachers going?* New York: Teachers College Press.

———. (2003b). What keeps teachers going? *Educational Leadership*, 60(8), 14–18.

Noguera, P. (2003). *City schools and the American dream: Reclaiming the promise of public education*. New York: Teachers College Press.

Palmer, P. J. (1998). *The courage to teach*. San Francisco: Jossey-Bass.

Ramirez, L., & Gallardo, O. M. (2001). *Portraits of teachers in multicultural settings: A critical literary approach*. Boston: Allyn and Bacon.

Reimer, B. (2003). *A philosophy of music education: Advancing the vision* (3rd ed.). Upper Saddle River, NJ: Prentice Hall.

Robinson, N. R. (2004). Who is "at risk" in the music classroom. *Music Educators Journal*, 90(4), 38–43.

Rose, M. (1995). *Possible lives: The promise of public education in America*. New York: Penguin.

Shields, C. (2001). Music education and mentoring as intervention for at-risk urban adolescents: Their self-perceptions, opinions, and attitudes. *Journal of Research in Music Education*, 49(3), 273–286.

Taylor, J. A., Barry, N. H., & Walls, K. C. (1997). *Music and students at risk: Creative solutions for a national dilemma*. Reston, VA: Music Educators National Conference.

III

TEACHING STRATEGIES

7

Motivating Urban Music Students

Elizabeth Ann McAnally

Every teacher has seen it happen. A child walks into the classroom with a certain expression on his or her face. The expression that says: "I don't want to be here, and you can't make me do anything." There are many different reasons for this particular expression, but the result is the same. This student, no matter how intelligent or talented, could make it very difficult for us to do our job. Unless we find a way to connect with this student, and quickly, he or she will not learn a thing, and the rest of the class may not either.

Now, let's be honest—there are many challenges facing urban music educators. We cope with the advocacy issues of budget and personnel cuts, the administrative issue of finding time for the arts in a school day packed with test preparation, the educational issue of working with students with a variety of skill levels, and the cultural issue of working in a diverse population.

There is, however, one challenge that is central to the frontline urban educator—how to motivate students. We all agree that motivating students to work to their potential is absolutely critical; after all, we can lead children to the classroom, but we can't make them learn. But, for many reasons, motivating urban students can be very hard to do. Over the course of my career, I have come to the conclusion that urban students come to school with a different set of assumptions about school than I did as a student in a small town. Many urban children seem to view school in general and teachers in particular with a high level of skepticism. Urban educators seem to need to work very hard to convince students that school is worth their time and effort.

In addition, urban children (like all children) bring with them a wide variety of issues that can seriously interfere with learning and with the desire to learn. There are students with identified physical, emotional, and learning disabilities. There are students whose home language is different from the language spoken at school. There are students in foster care, students caring for younger siblings, students suffering from abuse and neglect. There are students whose families cannot afford school supplies. There are students who carry burdens we have yet to identify.

Yet, as educators, we must strongly believe that every child in our classroom can and should achieve success. Time and again, teachers have seen students with seemingly insurmountable challenges set and reach high expectations—a student who wants to learn will go to great lengths to do so. Therefore, our first and perhaps most important task is to help students discover that an innate desire to learn is already present within them. When we have proven to our students that they can learn, that they should learn, and that we will help them learn, there is virtually no limit to the learning that can be achieved.

Unfortunately, accountability rather than motivation is the topic that is favored in contemporary educational circles. In the current climate of high-stakes testing, urban schools and students have been hit particularly hard with the challenge of raising scores under difficult conditions. Urban districts have tried to meet proficiency goals with lengthened school days and years. They focus on test preparation at the expense of "untested subjects," implement various reform methods rather than focus on local priorities, and in some cities, hire outside contractors rather than employ local educators. Discussions about testing data and the achievement gap have become regular parts of faculty meetings and professional development. This makes me wonder if perhaps we are missing the point—maybe students are not reaching testing goals because we are failing to connect with them. Maybe our efforts to improve instruction and test scores are not leaving us enough time to view students as individuals rather than faceless consumers of curriculum. It is time that we have a discussion among all stakeholders about how to reach out to children and motivate them to reach their potentials.

Motivating students is a task that is easier to identify than it is to solve. How do we convince students that they should value school when they may feel strongly that school does not value them? Dale Carnegie, author of *How to Win Friends and Influence People*, sums up the issue like this: "There is only one way under high heaven to get anybody to do anything . . . by making the other person want to do it" (1981, p. 18). Teachers know this to be true—students who really want to do something will find a way to do it. To take this one step further, students who really want to learn something will find a way to learn it—think of the student who has trouble remembering the multiplication tables, but is able to memorize lengthy and intricate song lyrics. So how do we make students *want to learn*? Well, Carnegie goes on to say, "The only way I can get you to do anything is by giving you what you want. What do you want" (p. 18)?

What do students want? What does anyone want? Abraham Maslow, in his book *Motivation and Personality* (1954), proposes a hierarchy of human needs, in which each level must be met before the next level can be addressed. At the bottom of the pyramid are the basic survival needs for food, water, and shelter, and the need for physical and psychological safety. Next are the needs for belonging and self-esteem. Only after these needs are satisfied will students seek self-actualization, the fulfillment of their personal potential, at the highest level of the hierarchy. Although self-actualization is not synonymous with motivation, it can be argued that motivation is required to achieve self-actualization.

In other words, we cannot expect our students to be motivated to learn unless their basic needs have been met. In some American schools, teachers can be reasonably sure that the needs of most of their students have been met at home; not so in urban schools. Most parents of urban students are like most parents everywhere; they love and care for their children and want the best for them. However, for a wide variety of reasons, urban students remain among the neediest in our nation. Many come to school with unfulfilled needs for physical safety, emotional safety, self-esteem, and a sense of belonging. The teacher who creates a classroom in which these needs are met is a teacher whose students will be motivated to learn.

Let's begin with the need for physical safety. Music educators see students for a relatively short amount of time, and although we can safeguard students while they are in our care, we cannot follow them through the hallways or take them home after school. We must, however, be constantly on the lookout for physical and behavioral signs that something is wrong, and we must build relationships with students that allow them to talk to us when they need help. It is important to be knowledgeable about the services available for children in crisis, and how to enlist this support when it is needed. Most schools have a counselor on staff who also serves as a liaison with public health officials. Some schools offer counseling from outside agencies on site, as well as drug-prevention programs and peer mediation.

Another way to meet students' need for physical safety is to create a physical space that makes them feel comfortable. This can be a challenge in an urban school. Some schools have no space for a music room, and the music educator travels from room to room with a cart. Others must use a space that was not designed for teaching music, such as a cafeteria, auditorium, or storage space. Those teachers lucky enough to enjoy a classroom may cope with leaky ceilings, holes in the floor, malfunctioning heating and cooling systems, and perhaps a few residents of the four- or six-legged variety.

Creating a physical environment that is welcoming—especially in a challenging setting—takes planning and thought. Teachers might ask themselves these questions: Are the bulletin boards attractive, colorful, and culturally inclusive? Can the seating arrangement be easily adapted for singing, moving, playing instruments, and working in groups? Does the flow of traffic allow for safe movement into, out of, and within the classroom? There are many ways to find resources that meet these needs. Look in magazines and newspapers for pictures of world instruments to laminate and display. Befriend the custodial staff in your building, and ask for help in finding furniture in good repair. Experiment with different room arrangements until you find a setting that works, and then teach a few student helpers how to assist you in setting up for your lessons. When the physical space is safe, comfortable, and conducive to learning, it is more likely that students will be motivated to learn while they are there.

Students also need to feel emotionally safe in order to learn. Students who feel valued, feel safe to take risks, and feel confident about achieving success are students who will be motivated to do their best. This kind of emotional environment is very hard to build and maintain, yet when it has been achieved, both students and teacher will reap enormous benefits.

The most crucial component in creating an emotionally safe environment is the attitude and demeanor of the teacher. Simply put, we must lead by example. The effective urban music educator is constantly aware of the messages he or she conveys to the young musicians in the classroom. Emotional support (or lack thereof) is communicated by every word, gesture, facial expression, tone of voice, and action that takes place within the sight or sound of students. If we want students to be excited about learning, we must first show that we are excited about teaching. If we want students to show us respect, we must at all times show respect to them. If we want our students to work hard, we must let them see us working even harder. A positive attitude from a teacher not only helps students feel emotionally safe, but can also encourage them to try something new. As veteran educator LouAnne Johnson (2005) says, "I learned the hard way that I can't *make* students do anything, but I also learned that my own enthusiasm can be an irresistible magnet for students. If I truly believe something is important, my students tend to at least give me a good listen" (p. 231).

The next major task is to prove to students that they have the potential to be musical—in other words, to build their self-esteem and help them understand that they are capable of achieving success. Johnson says it like this: "When students believe that success is possible, they will try. So my first priority in any class is to help my students believe in themselves and their ability to learn" (p. xiii). Many children enter the classroom with preconceived notions about their abilities; a child who has been told that she "can't carry a tune in a bucket" is not likely to want to sing in music class. In an effort to protect herself from failure or ridicule, she will stop trying. These same students would rather leave a test question blank than risk a wrong answer. Those who struggle with self-confidence issues may be under the mistaken (or at least incomplete) assumption that musical talent is fixed at birth, rather than developed throughout life. Consider the following passage and substitute the word *musical* for *intelligent*, and *musicality* for *intelligence*:

> Students' conceptions of what it means to be *intelligent* can affect their performance. Students who think that *intelligence* is a fixed entity are more likely to be performance oriented as opposed to learning oriented; they want to look good rather than risk making mistakes while learning. These students are more likely to give up when tasks become difficult. In contrast, students who think that *intelligence* is malleable are more willing to struggle with challenging tasks and are more comfortable with risk. (Bridglall, 2001, p. 3)

Students who are afraid to make mistakes find comfort and freedom in a place where a variety of answers are valued. In order to help students feel confident in their own musicality, we must make sure that music class is different from other subjects. In math, for example, an answer is clearly right or clearly wrong—not so in music class. There is more than one way to solve a musical problem, and when students begin to understand that creativity is valued, they begin to feel motivated to participate.

For those moments when there is a "right" answer, teachers must handle errors very carefully. Most students have experienced firsthand or at the very least witnessed the ridicule from students, and sometimes even teachers, that can follow an incorrect response. To raise a hand and offer an answer means first overcoming the fear of that sort of situation. Dr. Haim G. Ginott (1972) stresses the importance of teaching children that mistakes are okay: "Teachers often ask psychologists how to motivate children to learn. The answer is 'Make it safe for them to risk failure.' The major obstacle to learning is fear: fear of failure, fear of criticism, fear of appearing stupid. An effective teacher makes it possible for each child to err with impunity. To remove fear is to invite attempt. To welcome mistakes is to encourage learning" (p. 187).

How can a teacher create this kind of atmosphere? First, by asking the right kinds of questions. Open-ended questions that can be answered in several ways are more motivating than narrow, one-answer questions. Calling on several students to answer makes more than one person responsible for participating. Similarly, telling all students to have an answer in mind and calling on students randomly (being sure not to neglect those that do not usually seek attention in class) provides another opportunity for everyone to participate. When an answer is given, find something valuable in it, and give specific feedback. Ensure that students know that answering a question counts as participation, even if the answer is incorrect or incomplete.

It is also helpful to explain to students repeatedly and explicitly that musical growth happens at different speeds for different people. Students who feel that their contributions to class do not compare favorably with those of their peers will be uncomfortable and unmotivated—we must make them aware that they will only be judged on their own progress, not by comparing them to other students. A student who fears embarrassment will not be motivated to participate.

Another way to encourage participation is to plan activities that require creativity. Try a call-and-response improvisation exercise, where the class claps a four-measure rhythm and then an individual student improvises a four-measure response. Allow students to work in groups to create a pentatonic melody that can be played on resonator bells. In activities such as these, there are no wrong answers, and students who feel successful will be more motivated to participate in the next activity.

It is important to remember that urban students may demonstrate their comfort level in ways that teachers who are not from urban areas do not expect. A child who does not understand an activity may try to distract the class and teacher with poor behavior or a disrespectful attitude. Challenging such a student in front of his or her peers may not help the situation; showing weakness or backing down in front of the class is not an option many students are willing to consider. Students lacking in material possessions or family support may take comfort in their pride. Educators must find ways to help their students take risks in the classroom without sacrificing their sense of pride.

This brings about another important part of student motivation—managing student behavior. The urban educator who handles student behavior in ways that meet students' needs for acceptance and emotional safety will be much more likely to motivate students to learn. A complete discussion of effective classroom management is outside the scope of this chapter; the pages of this entire book could be filled with strategies for this topic. There are, however, some important points to be made. Teachers in urban classrooms should not ever assume that students know what behavior is expected of them. Urban students come from very diverse backgrounds, with diverse levels of educational experiences. I personally know students who did not receive any formal schooling at all until they entered the United States as teenagers. Students who are new to public education have no way to know what is expected of them. Therefore, music teachers must continually teach and reteach the desired behaviors, rather than just providing consequences when students fall below expectations.

Second, when behavior problems occur, and they will occur, teachers must think very carefully about how to handle the situation. We have amazing power to escalate or de-escalate any behavior issue in the classroom. Whenever possible, it is best to handle small problems in ways that prevent them from becoming large ones. For example, we want a student to throw away his gum or take off her hat. Consider whether it is necessary to yell and address the problem in front of the rest of the students, or whether the direction can be given quietly, in a neutral tone of voice. Remember that students do not want to give in to a teacher in front of their classmates; try not to put a student in the position of having to defy the teacher in order to maintain the sense of belonging to his or her peer group.

Third, carefully choose the situations to confront. It may be easier to handle small issues than to wait until they become large ones. Students who are not allowed to say "Shut up!" to each other (and who never hear it from the teacher) will not be as likely to say "Shut the **** up!" Similarly, students who are gently, yet consistently prevented from being verbally aggressive will be less apt to be physically aggressive.

Lastly, one of the most important classroom management rules: At all costs avoid losing your temper. Admittedly, teachers are human beings, and sometimes we lose control, especially in the pressure-cooker environment of urban education. So let's rephrase: At all costs, maintain your composure, and when you do choose to raise your voice, be sure it is for an issue about which you feel very, very strongly. Students often stop listening when teachers raise their voices, and the more often you do so, the less often they pay attention to it. Raising your voice frequently is not seen by students as a sign of respect, and children are more likely to be motivated when they feel respected by their teacher.

No discussion of motivation could be complete without at least mentioning rewards. Rewards can be very useful tools in the classroom, but when used incorrectly they can become a crutch. Once we get started, we must constantly look for bigger and better rewards in order to keep our students' attention. Whenever possible, choose intangible rewards over material ones, and intrinsic rewards over extrinsic. A favorite musical activity chosen by students at the end of a lesson or unit meets more educational objectives than a popcorn party. A positive phone call home will have more lasting results than the bribe of a piece of candy. Remember that the goal is to motivate students to be musical, not merely to do the bare minimum needed to earn a nonmusical reward, reverting to previous behavior as soon as the reward period is concluded. Ideally, lessons should be infused with opportunities to reward students. Well-planned lessons that encourage active participation, provide specific praise, and allow students to demonstrate their accomplishments are rewarding experiences.

One tool that has the power to be both a reward and a consequence is grading—a nonmusical construct if ever there was one. In the current educational climate, assessing and being accountable for student learning is serious business. How do we go about assigning a number or letter grade that fairly represents progress in music without damaging a student's self-esteem or sense of belonging? One way is to be sure that there is more than one path to a positive evaluation. Some students do not test well; perhaps those students could be allowed to demonstrate their learning in another way. Others may enjoy completing creative projects at home for extra credit. Music teachers must be sure that grades reflect a variety of skills and assessment methods, so that each child has a chance to be graded on his/her strengths. It is also important that students and parents know where they stand—if there is a problem that may cause a student to earn a lower grade, notification must be made with enough time to correct it.

Regardless of the tools employed, the real purpose of a music grade must be to motivate students. Grades are an opportunity for teachers to inform instruction and make improvements in student learning, not to gain satisfaction from the number of students receiving a failing grade. Students who feel their teacher wants them to fail will not be motivated to learn, while those who feel their teacher wants them to succeed will rise to those expectations.

This chapter has focused on creating a classroom environment that motivates students by first meeting their needs for physical and emotional safety, a sense of belonging, and confidence in their ability to succeed. The teacher who creates such an environment has set the stage for learning to take place. Ultimately, this is really only the beginning. All of the myriad tasks for which a music educator is responsible—planning lessons, choosing activities, selecting repertoire, and conducting student and parent conferences—contribute to motivating students. But these efforts are wasted unless teachers understand this reality: urban music students can and will achieve great things when their teachers know how to motivate them to do so.

I would like to see a conversation about student motivation begin among all of us who care so deeply about urban education. All stakeholders, from frontline educators, to administrators, researchers, and elected officials, need to consider motivation to be a crucial component in the school reform process. Let's see if we can learn how to more effectively connect with students and motivate them to do their best. Higher test scores will be only part of the exciting results of such efforts.

In preparation for this chapter, I took the time to consult the real experts—the students. What follows are excerpts from an informal survey of two hundred urban music students from a large, diverse middle school in a northeastern city. The students represent many ethnicities, native languages, and a wide range of musical backgrounds. Their comments have a great deal of relevance to this discussion. These students indicated that teachers have an amazing amount of influence on their attitudes about learning. Students reported that fairness, honesty, patience, and dedication were important attributes in their favorite teachers. Students also expressed that they feel more motivated when teachers are respectful to them and are creative in planning lessons. Responses have been edited only for grammar and spelling.

Think of your favorite class in school. Why did you like this class more than any other?

- I like that class because the teacher there is very nice to everyone, and not just one or two people.
- The class was different and had an atmosphere that was made for learning.
- Because it is exciting and we learn without even noticing that we are.
- This is my favorite class because you can be yourself. Also you can be creative. I like this class because we're always learning something new.
- Because the teacher is always honest to us.
- I like this class more than any other class because no one yells at you and you get to sing.

Think of your favorite teacher in school. Why do you like this teacher more than any other?

- This is my favorite teacher because he always makes me smile when I'm sad. He's not all in my business, but he knows what he needs to know to find out what is wrong with me.
- She works so hard for me even though I have a hard time.
- She makes learning fun.
- I like her more than any other teacher because she was sweet and polite. She treated us with so much respect and we showed it back.
- This teacher is a hard worker.
- I like this teacher more than any other because she teaches us in a different way.
- I like this teacher because she never yells at us. She makes learning fun.

What makes you want to learn?

- Having fun learning without pressure is what makes me want to learn.
- I want to learn when I am able to utilize my abilities.
- Coming to school with a teacher who has a smile on their face and makes learning fun.
- Teachers inspire me to learn.

The best-trained, most talented teacher in the world will not be successful without first motivating students to learn. After all, that is the ultimate goal of music education, in any environment.

REFERENCES

Bridglall, B. L. (2001, March). Research and practice on how people learn. *Pedagogical inquiry and praxis, 1*. New York: Columbia University, Teachers College, Institute for Urban and Minority Education (ED 452 305).

Carnegie, D. (1981). *How to win friends and influence people,* revised edition. New York: Pocket Books.
Ginott, H. G. (1972). *Teacher and child.* New York: Avon.
Johnson, L. (2005). *Teaching outside the box.* San Francisco: Jossey-Bass.
Maslow, A. (1954). *Motivation and personality.* New York: Harper.

8

Differentiating Instruction in the Choral Rehearsal: Strategies for Choral Conductors in Urban Schools

Daniel Abrahams

For the past century, educators have questioned how best to engage students in meaningful and lasting learning (Cuban, 1993). At the forefront of the debate is the notion that students learn best when teachers offer activities that develop high-level thinking and present content in ways that meet individual student learning needs (Gardner, 1995; Elliott, 1995; Miller, 2002). Recently, educational psychologists have developed teaching models to address student learning styles, claiming that lasting learning occurs when information is presented in ways that are consistent with how students perceive and process information. One model, which is popular in general education, is differentiated instruction (Tomlinson, 1999).

Simply stated, to differentiate instruction means to address the needs of all learners (Wormeli, 2001). Six constructs provide the foundation. They are:

1. The learner must make meaning of the information.
2. Meaning making is influenced by the student's prior understandings, interests, beliefs, how the student learns best, and the student's attitudes about self and school.
3. Knowledge must be clearly and powerfully organized.
4. Students should be highly active in the learning process.
5. Assessment should be rich and varied.
6. Students should feel a sense of safety and connection (Tomlinson, 2001, p. 8).

Bass (2005) notes that "a guiding principle of Differentiated Instruction is focusing on what the learners should be able to recall, understand, and do in a given domain. Instruction," she continues, "is centered around the concepts, principles, and skills of the subject. It provides a way for the learner to understand and retrieve information, to construct meaning and to see the relationship of the parts to the whole" (p. 3).

In general education, teachers use differentiated instruction in elementary and secondary classrooms to create an environment where all students can be successful. Results have been positive (Tomlinson, 1999). Teachers in urban schools, struggling to meet the mandates of No Child Left Behind find that differentiating instruction helps to decrease the achievement gap among students by maximizing the talents of all learners (Baltimore County Public Schools, 2003).

While differentiated instruction is common in many subjects, music teachers have embraced it with mixed emotions. Some claim that they have always been differentiating instruction since a typical general music class includes many activities and a variety of teaching strategies to address the learning needs of all students. Ensemble conductors may claim that using many different rehearsal techniques to hone a musical composition to a level of acceptable performance is a kind of differentiated instruction. Unfortunately, other music teachers reject the idea outright, claiming that they have too many students to teach and too little time to individualize instruction. Further, the pressures of readying students for performances overwhelm music teachers to the point where they could not imagine how they might meet individual needs since their focus is and has always been on the group as a whole.

In urban districts, the challenges facing choral conductors to engage students in meaningful musical experiences are significant. They must find repertoire that is suitable and acceptable to both singer and conductor and build the kind of community within the choral ensemble that is necessary to achieve a high level of performance. Students are sometimes reluctant to join ensembles where the conductor is of a different ethnicity or race. Singers find it difficult to connect to the Western art music that is such a mainstay and staple of many school choral programs. Conductors for whom the gospel repertoire is not part of their own personal traditions find it difficult to teach appropriate style or to find a middle ground between the vocal styles required in such music and vocal technique that is more appropriate for art music. The music of the street is not suited to choral singing, and the motivation to sing in school choirs is not always attractive to urban youngsters. In addition, conductors of urban school choral ensembles, like their colleagues teaching other subjects in urban settings, must address issues of social norms prevalent in urban culture.

Nevertheless, a model that differentiates instruction for students who develop at different rates, and learn in different styles, can easily be a routine part of a choral director's plan. Robert Marzano, Gaddy, and Dean (2000), Rachel Billmeyer (2004), Carol Ann Tomlinson (1999), and others have suggested techniques that, when applied to choir, are effective ways to meet individual learning needs. The purpose of this chapter is to focus on three such strategies and show how they might be integrated into a typical choral ensemble rehearsal.

GRAPHIC ORGANIZERS

Just as musical notation is a graphic representation of melody, rhythm, and harmony, graphic organizers use symbols to convey the meaning of musical ideas and concepts. Specifically, they depict the relationship of one musical idea or one musical term with another. Musical ideas such as the shape of a phrase or the difference between *andante* and *allegro* are typical of the types of concepts represented graphically and connect to the process of an ensemble learning to sing a particular piece. Sometimes, ensemble conductors use graphic organizers when they want their singers to "map out" ideas and use graphic organizers as visual aids or pictorials to show choristers the information as patterns that form relationships. Graphic organizers activate prior knowledge, summarize information, and provide a tool whereby the conductor can easily assess student learning. To use a graphic organizer, students must prioritize the information and determine what is important, and where the information should be placed on the map. Figure 8.1 shows a graphic organizer suggested by Frayer, Frederick, and Klausmeier (1969) for the tempo *andante*. Here the graphic organizer is divided into four areas to record information related to the concept. Concepts are presented in a relational manner so that students see the components in the learning process.

To use the Frayer model, the conductor suggests a concept or word for the singers to study. This could be a vocabulary word, such as our example of *andante*, selected from the literature being performed. The conductor explains all of the sections of the model that the students need to complete and provides an example using something that is familiar. Next, the students, alone or with partners, use their prior knowledge and experiences in order to complete the map (Billmeyer, 2004). Once the diagram is complete, the students share their work with the ensemble and submit it to the conductor for assessment.

THINK-PAIR-SHARE

Borrowed from the literature on cooperative learning (Kaplan & Stauffer, 1994), think-pair-share is a strategy whereby the conductor presents a ques-

Figure 8.1. Frayer Model

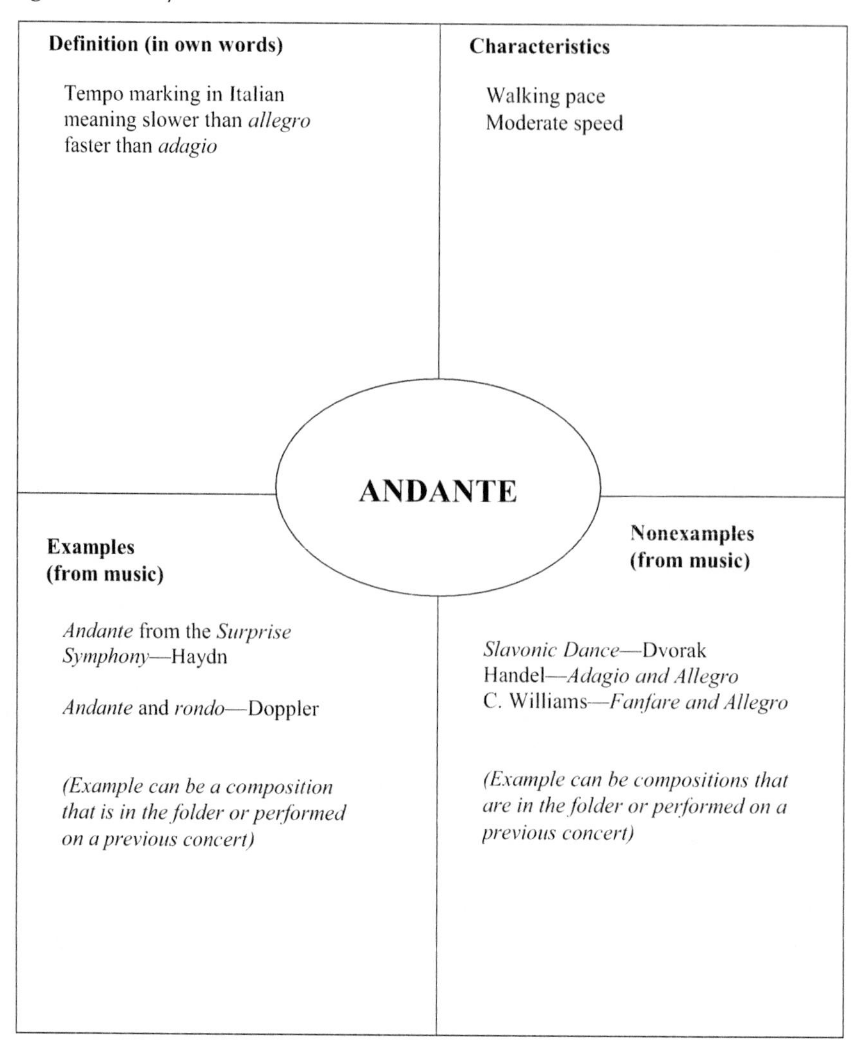

Source: Frayer, Frederick, and Klausmeier (1969).

tion to the choir and allows the students to have a few minutes of "wait time" to formulate an answer. Then, each student is paired with a buddy. The singers discuss the question and their answers, share their ideas, and formulate one answer by working together. Students in the choir are able to see the problem from another point of view and may discover information that they may not have known. Think-pair-share provides an opportunity for high-functioning students to be paired with low-functioning students. Deliberate thinkers have time to organize and test their thoughts, while "blurters" have a relief valve to share their ideas with a partner, restraining their impulse to respond. Singers are able to formulate their own thoughts without being influenced by peers. When finished, the ensemble regroups and the singers share their answers. They may write their answers on note cards and turn them in to the conductor at the end to be used for assessment. The strategy allows all students to express their ideas orally when working with their partner. Because the students have time to think and discuss, they are forced to use prior knowledge to form new ideas and present more precise answers. This process helps them to understand the concept, filter information, and draw conclusions. Students also are encouraged to consider and respect other points of view, and are engaged in reflective conversations based on active listening, restating, and inquiry. The conductor facilitates learning by providing opportunities for students to problem solve before making decisions. All of these outcomes are desirable in urban classrooms.

In a choral rehearsal, think-pair-share may be used when the conductor feels the ensemble is not singing in tune. For example, the conductor may ask the students to find two ways in which they can improve their intonation. The conductor gives the students a few moments to think about solutions and then pairs each student with a partner. The students brainstorm with their partners and share their solutions. The ensemble regroups and each pair demonstrates their solution to improve the choir's intonation.

In addition to the values for the students, think-pair-share provides many benefits for the conductor. For example, as with students, conductors need "wait time" in order to regroup and develop follow-up questions. Teachers are more likely to ask higher-order questions, developing critical thinking in their students, if time to gather thoughts is provided. During the "pair" time, conductors have an opportunity to monitor student responses and guide the learning process.

KINESTHETIC

Dalcroze (1930), Orff (Wheeler & Raebeck, 1977), Weikart (1989), and others acknowledge the importance of interpreting music through movement when students need to understand abstract concepts or to internalize information. While movement is regularly included in show choir or gospel choir, it is less frequently used as a teaching strategy in a large concert choir. As a strategy to differentiate instruction, physical experiences create pathways to the brain. According to Bloom, Nelson, and Lazerson (2001), when students participate in movement, both hemispheres of the brain are actively engaged and new information is stored in long-term memory. Having students create actions to represent musical concepts helps reinforce what is being performed in the literature. Students can represent sound through movement by using body awareness (different ways they move in isolation), spatial awareness (the use of a space by a mover), and effort (how the energy of a movement is expended). Through movement, students become more aware of their canvas to create expression.

Although one does not need to do all three strategies in the same lesson, the following rehearsal plan (figure 8.2) incorporates a graphic organizer,

Figure 8.2. Rehearsal Plan for *Elijah Rock* Arranged by Roger Emerson (Hal Leonard # 08551274)

TITLE: Understanding and internalizing the concept of phrase in *Elijah Rock* arranged by Roger Emerson (Hal Leonard # 08551274)

OBJECTIVE

Students will understand the concept of *phrase* through visual, auditory, and kinesthetic activities that differentiate instruction.

PROCEDURES to DIFFERENTIATE INSTRUCTION

1. *Graphic Organizer*—After students sing the piece, the conductor explains the graphic organizing activity as follows: On a sheet of paper, draw a circle in the center. Inside the circle, write the word *phrase*. In the upper left corner, students write (in their own words) a *definition* for phrase. In the upper right corner, students write the *characteristics* of a phrase. In the lower left corner, have students provide *examples* of phrase from their own life (*examples* can be from music in their folder). In the lower right corner, students provide *non-examples* of phrase (this can also be from music in their folder). The students perform their *examples* of phrase and share them with the other members of the choir.
2. *Think-Pair-Share*—The teacher presents the students with a problem in the form of a question: "In the second section 'Satan's a liar and a conjurer too' where do the phrases begin and end?"
   - Students have a few moments of wait time to formulate ideas.
   - Students break into pairs and discuss their findings. They make decisions and then come back together.
   - The conductor initiates dialogue with the choir and share the results.
     - Discuss the choices made by the students. Come to consensus.
   - The students mark phrases into their music.
3. *Kinesthetic*—Students move their chairs to create an area for movement. By voice part, divide the students into groups and have them form several circles inside the rehearsal room. Ask students to create a movement for each phrase. Then, as the ensemble sings the entire piece each student, one by one, performs their movement: Student 1: Phrase 1; Student 2: Phrase 2; etc. until all students in the group have had the chance to show their phrase-related movement. They will move during phrase, but when the phrase ends the student will freeze. Their movement should accurately portray the style of the phrase. Each student represents a different phrase, giving every student an opportunity.

think-pair-share, and kinesthetic activity to differentiate instruction in a middle school choir rehearsal.

Snow and Apfelstadt (2002) write that musical thinking and learning in the choral context are maximized when the singers have multiple opportunities to make musical decisions and use musical judgment. Bass (2005) indicates that differentiated instruction ensures that all students have the opportunity to develop their possibilities and pursue both equity and excellence. Tomlinson (2001) adds that students work in an atmosphere of respect and appreciation for their peers and their differences. These are all desirable outcomes of urban education.

Differentiating instruction such as in the lesson above lifts the music learning beyond the context of the performance to a level that is internalized within each individual student. If a purpose of the choral ensemble is to enhance each individual student's abilities to be engaged as thinking and feeling musicians, then meeting individual learning needs is a high priority. Adapting strategies that differentiate instruction from the repertoire of teaching strategies in general education increases the level of involvement for every student by encouraging reflective learning, advanced critical thinking skills, problem solving, and creativity and is a viable option for choral conductors in urban settings and beyond.

REFERENCES

Baltimore County Public Schools. (2003, May). *Differentiated instruction*. Retrieved July 17, 2005, from www.bcps.org/offices/oit/Liaisons/DifferentiatedInstruction.doc

Bass, C. (2005). *The impact of differentiated instruction on students' comprehension of introductory music theory: An action research* (unpublished master's thesis, Rider University, Lawrenceville, NJ).

Billmeyer, R. (2004). *Strategic readings in the content area: Practical applications for creating a thinking environment*. Omaha, NE: Dayspring Publications.

Bloom, F., Nelson, C. A., & Lazerson, A. (2001). *Brain, mind, and behavior*. New York: Worth Publishers.

Cuban, L. (1993). *How teachers taught: Constancy and change in American classrooms 1890–1990* (2nd ed.). New York: Teachers College Press.

Dalcroze, E. J. (1930). *Eurhythmics, art and education*. London: Chatto & Windus.

Elliott, D. (1995). *Music matters*. New York: Oxford University Press.

Frayer, D. A., Frederick, W. C., & Klausmeier, H. J. (1969). *A schema for testing the level of concept mastery* (Technical Report No. 16). Madison: University of Wisconsin Research and Development Center for Cognitive Learning.

Gardner, H. (1995). *The unschooled mind: How children think and how schools should teach*. New York: Basic.

Kaplan, P. R., & Stauffer, S. R. (1994). *Cooperative learning in music*. Reston, VA: Music Educators National Conference.

Marzano, R. J., Gaddy, B. B., & Dean, C. (2000). *What works in classroom instruction.* Aurora, CO: McREL.

Miller, B. (2002). Structuring learning in a different kind of classroom. In E. Boardman (Ed.), *Dimensions of musical learning and teaching: A different kind of classroom* (pp. 69–104). Reston, VA: MENC, the National Association for Music Education.

Snow, S., & Apfelstadt, H. (2002). Musical thinking and learning in the choral context. In E. Boardman (Ed.), *Dimensions of musical learning and teaching: A different kind of classroom* (pp. 192–216). Reston, VA: MENC, the National Association for Music Education.

Tomlinson, C. A. (1999). *The differentiated classroom: Responding to the needs of all learners.* Alexandria, VA: Association for Supervision and Curriculum Development.

———. (2001). *How to differentiate instruction in mixed-ability classrooms.* Alexandria, VA: Association for Supervision and Curriculum Development.

Weikart, P. (1989). *Movement plus music.* Ypsilanti, MI: High/Scope.

Wheeler, L., & Raebeck, L. (1977). *Orff and Kodály adapted for the elementary school.* Dubuque, IA: W. C. Brown, CO.

Wormeli, R. (2001). *Meet me in the middle: Becoming an accomplished middle-level teacher.* Portland, OR: Stenhouse Publishers.

9

Building an Instrumental Music Program in an Urban School

Kevin Mixon

Few challenges in instrumental music programs are exclusive to urban schools; strategies to build quality programs are similar regardless of environment. The urban instrumental music teacher will, however, need to consider certain program-building and teaching strategies that may not need as much attention in other schools. In this chapter I have identified four aspects critical to the success of urban band programs and have provided strategies to address them: (1) an initial survey leading to realistic program goals, (2) recruiting and retention, (3) collegial and parental support, and (4) administrative support and funding.

TAKING INVENTORY

Making an initial survey of the existing program is the logical first step to setting realistic program goals. This survey should include an inventory of existing instruments as well as an assessment of the needs and resources of the school and surrounding community. Urban schools often provide instruments for students who could not otherwise afford to participate; thus, the inventory of school-owned instruments may dictate the ensemble size and instrumentation. Supplies and maintenance for those instruments will also need to be assessed as reeds, oils, method books, and other ancillary items are often also provided by the school. In the absence of a large instrument inventory, the director will need to be resourceful, perhaps by supplementing an instrumentation imbalance with keyboard instruments and even obtaining sequencing equipment to prerecord absent parts. After some experimentation, the results can be quite satisfactory.

Available instruments and the makeup of the community may suggest that the director consider offering ensembles other than the traditional band or orchestra. Specialized ensembles such as Afro-Cuban percussion, steel drum (aka "pan") band, rock, or mariachi may be a better option. Motivation derived from these culturally relevant ensembles cannot be overemphasized, particularly with middle and high school students. Directors with training primarily in traditional ensembles will find that the instruments used in specialized ensembles are familiar from their college methods courses, but the particular musical styles may still be unfamiliar. Several publications and recordings are available to provide information. Directors will also gain requisite skills and understanding by immersing themselves in the genre at conventions dedicated to the given style (Mixon, 2004).

Community resources may be available to aid instrumental music programs, particularly for culturally relevant ensembles and repertoire. Musicians skilled in the style of a specialized ensemble can be a great help to both director and players. Directors should also search for community events that can provide opportunities for the school ensemble to perform. School concerts can serve as celebrations of community and cultural identity and provide powerful support bridges to students' peers, families, and other community members. These bridges are especially important to schools that want to provide a positive outreach to parents.

As with instruments, many urban music programs will also have a limited inventory of printed music, and much of that music may have missing parts or require unavailable instruments. In the absence of a budget to purchase new music or new instruments, judicious, realistic selection of available music is the first step. Rescoring or arranging for available instruments is often a solution. Of course, arranging is more difficult with advanced ensembles. But arrangements do not have to be complex, and the basic theory and orchestration knowledge acquired from undergraduate classes along with some study of scores written in the given style will provide the director with the tools to arrange music for their student groups.

Recruiting and Retention

Social relationships are of primary importance in cultures and environments that lack material wealth (Hale, 2001; Kuykendall, 1992; Kunjufu, 2002; Payne, 2001). This may mean "that there can be no significant learning until there is a significant relationship" (Kunjufu, 2002, p. 47). With respect to recruiting, a director who is highly visible as well as friendly, enthusiastic, and generally interested in all students will have access to a larger pool of potential ensemble members. Participating in other music teaching duties such as vocal ensembles and general music classes, as well as activities outside the music room, will help instrumental ensemble directors get to know potential students.

As mentioned above, the types of ensemble will often provide the cultural relevance or "salience" (Hale, 2001, p. 130) that will help both recruit and retain students. Unfortunately, in some urban schools these ensembles are extracurricular, often taught by volunteers, and structured more as a recreational activity. However, if a qualified music teacher is employed, the quality of these ensembles should be as high as that of more traditional band and orchestras to maintain student interest as well as provide meaningful music experiences. Further, these groups should be aligned with national, state, and district standards for music. MENC, the National Association for Music Education, has even published a resource to aid directors in such cases (see Cutietta, 1999). Directors should also account for student interest in traditional band and orchestras by programming jazz, mariachi, or other culturally relevant musical styles.

Regardless of ensemble style, students are motivated by caring directors with high performance expectations and the necessary persistence to help students meet those expectations. While I have found these to be necessary qualities for teaching urban students in general, several scholars specifically recommend these attributes for educating the African American (Hale, 2001; Kunjufu, 1999, 2002; Kuykendall, 1992) and Hispanic (Kuykendall, 1992) students that are often represented in urban schools.

These same scholars further describe motivating African American and Hispanic learning experiences—and again, in my experiences with most urban students—as "vervistic" (Hale, 2001, p. 114), meaning relevant, purposeful, and offering high degrees of stimulation. In other words, urban directors must plan rehearsals and lessons carefully. They must have prior knowledge of the score, be experts at lesson planning, and have acute listening skills. Score study will reveal doublings and similar passages that should be noted in lesson plans, and directors should hone their "rehearsal ears" so that errors can be detected while listening to larger groups of students to keep all participants as engaged as possible. For example, students may question the relevance of their attendance when there are long periods of inactivity for their section. To remedy this, directors might have all the instruments that are doubling play their parts, even though the problem section is the trumpets. Students who fear peer scrutiny may not understand the purpose of "calling out" individuals to fix parts. Therefore, it is imperative to have multiple students play through a problem part, rather than calling on one individual. Many urban students have developed defense mechanisms that disguise feelings of low self-esteem and fear of failure as anger, hostility, and defiance. These defensive emotions are often the root cause of conflict with teachers and peers. This is another reason why it is important to address sections of players rather than individuals when discussing performance errors and solutions.

Rehearsal and lesson tasks contextualized as noncompetitive games are particularly motivating because they are perceived as fun and also foster immediate purposefulness. This is especially important if rehearsals are scheduled at the end of the school day or—even less optimally but unfortunately increasingly more common—before or after school when students are less inclined to attend. Once goals and objectives are identified, activities to accomplish them can be planned as "play" instead of work. *Teaching Techniques and Insights for Instrumental Music Educators* (Casey, 1993) and *Band Rehearsal Techniques: A Handbook for New Directors* (Dalby, 1993) are two resources that provide a number of games to accomplish several common instrumental music objectives in group settings. Directors can also adapt just about any game of their own choosing, but, to keep rehearsals and lessons moving, it is best to keep games simple with minimal accessories and procedures.

To account for the social learning style and replace peer conflicts with espirit de corps, the director must consistently reinforce the importance of working together as a team to fix errors and improve performances for the good of the whole group. Directors may replace low self-esteem with confidence by rewarding individual and group achievement whenever possible. Verbal praise is motivating and effective to all students if it is specific and distributed equitably. Additionally, all positive comments directors receive about ensemble progress from school employees and parents should also be shared with ensemble members.

Playing an instrument is challenging work that requires long-term commitment, and celebrating small achievements along the way will help to motivate and retain students. Students who live in poverty or have a history of failure at school often attribute success merely to luck or fate rather than individual action (i.e., external versus internal locus of control) and may have difficulty mediating behavior that will affect outcomes occurring in coming weeks or even days or hours (Payne, 2001). Therefore, setting clear short-term goals that are modified so that all members are successful will help in retaining students. Public recognition such as "Band/Orchestra Student(s) of the Week" during school announcements or achievement posters with student signatures displayed in highly visible locations in the school are other examples of recognition that are motivating to students. Making sure students realize the goals they have achieved will help with esteem building and foster a sense of the internal locus of control necessary for long-term ensemble participation.

Delaying gratification by performing only two or three concerts will likely not be sufficiently motivating for many urban students for the mediation difficulties mentioned above. Performing early and often is an effective solution. Performances do not have to be formal. Audiences may consist of a single class, teacher, or administrator listening to a segment, or an entire piece performed by the full ensemble during rehearsals, or even a smaller group or individual during lessons. Although formal performances are every bit as rewarding and motivating in urban schools as in others, motivating urban students between these major events is equally important.

Some students will move during the school year or quit for various other reasons despite the director's best efforts at retaining them. Staying in contact with interested students and maintaining an active waiting list will help fill vacancies. This means starting new students throughout the school year. Directors can begin students later in the year by having them play only easier selections or simplified parts until they are caught up. When it is past a point in the year that new students can catch up to the ensemble, individual lessons may be given in preparation for the following year.

COLLEGIAL AND PARENTAL SUPPORT

Districtwide or even schoolwide support for instrumental music programs is rare in urban schools. Time is at a premium in these settings, especially with the growing pressures of legislative mandates that are often associated with low scores on mandatory tests. The challenge for directors is that successful instrumental programs, especially those that require pullout schedules for group lessons or even ensembles, need the support of several teachers. This support often begins with the director getting involved in school activities outside the music department. Teachers, like students, will support instrumental music ensembles directed by people they like and respect. As a way to build personal bridges to colleagues, music teachers can volunteer to chaperone a field trip or supervise a class while another teacher attends to a pressing matter. In a professional sense, ensemble directors are often viewed more as music performers than legitimate teachers; and volunteering for a curriculum committee or team-teaching an integrated unit are ways to help build respect for the "teacher" component of the musician-teacher.

Parental support is another crucial component of a successful urban music program. Because urban family structures are often a result of long-term poverty (Payne, 2001), they may engender home environments and relationships that are different from those of middle-class families (Hale, 2001). However, as Kuykendall (1992) points out, African American and Hispanic support networks are strong, particularly within extended families. Urban parents love their children as much as middle- and upper-class parents and want their children to be successful in school—and this includes instrumental music study. Because of this desire for success of their children, establishing contact with families from the very beginning of student participation will prove beneficial. However, as Kuykendall (1992) writes, "many Black and Hispanic parents are dealing with the day-to-day reality of their own survival. Some will avoid contact with the school if such brings only more 'bad news'" (p. 101). I have found this to be the case with many urban families regardless of ethnicity. The director that makes frequent, positive communication that tempers areas of concern with recognition of students' strengths will be more successful than one who only calls students' homes with complaints. As Wilson and Corbett have noted, urban students recognize and respond favorably to a positive teacher–family partnership (2001).

Communication with some families may be hampered by language barriers. School personnel, community members, and students themselves can help translate when directors communicate with parents. With very young students, older siblings can help. Software is available for written communication in the more common languages, though someone fluent in the particular language (such as an interested parent) will need to proofread before notices are distributed.

Traditional methods to garner parental support require knowledge of students' home situations. Some urban parents, often single mothers, spend much more time earning their lower wages than middle- or upper-class parents spend working (see Hale, 2001, for an African American perspective). Others have limited education and are intimidated by the school environment. For these families, home-based activities that typically require parental supervision, such as practicing a musical instrument and participation in evening activities such as concerts and fund-raising may not be possibilities. Although it is not ideal, there are ways that directors can help in such instances. Allowing students to practice at school is one solution, particularly with large instruments that are not easily transported or in neighborhoods where instrument theft is a concern. Setting up carpools well in advance of evening concerts is a way to ensure greater student and parent attendance. Directors who realize that raising children in urban centers is demanding, and account for these demands by providing as much school-based support as possible, will build more successful programs with less attrition. Most parents will also recognize and appreciate these efforts by directors and respond with as much support as they can.

ADMINISTRATIVE SUPPORT AND FUNDING

Urban administrators are under even more pressure than grade-level teachers because of mandates stemming from various issues such as testing and government funding. Building principals may be further bound by low status in a top-down administrative bureaucracy (Weiner, 1999). With the advent of site-based management initiatives that afford principals more autonomy, they do usually have the power to provide assistance with scheduling or rehearsal time and space. These types of space and scheduling issues are often addressed on a priority basis, so directors will need to convince administrators of the priority of instrumental music ensembles. Keeping administrators informed about program events and achievements will help. These achievements can include individual student successes; news about interdisciplinary activities with other teachers; and alignment of the instrumental music program with national, state, or district curricula. While not every administrator will personally agree with the importance of instrumental music in school, they will nonetheless support programs that are clearly fostering student achievement and drawing support from parents and the greater community. Directors who cultivate and report their successes will, in time, usually garner the endorsement of administrators.

Steering committees for scheduling and other building and district issues are usually facilitated by administrators, particularly within site-based management models. Directors can advocate for program needs through these committees, and it is essential that they volunteer to serve on them. Instrumental music program needs can then be addressed in a forum where administrators and colleagues view ensemble directors as team players.

Urban districts are constantly plagued with inadequate funding, so securing funds for instrumental music programs through building administrators may not be possible. Because of the impoverished environment in many urban areas, fund-raising through booster organizations and other parent groups may also not be an option. However, larger urban districts often have a music or fine arts administrator that might be a source of support via district funds or grants. There are also external grant sources that music teachers can pursue themselves. If grant writing appears too daunting, directors can team with colleagues to complete the applications. This team approach may even increase chances of winning grants as the proposal is strengthened through collaboration and the involvement of larger numbers of students.

Directors can also search for donations of instruments and equipment. Colleagues, local civic organizations, and businesses are potential sources for donations, which can provide a tax write-off for the donor. Directors who know a bit about instrument repair are better equipped to put these donations to use.

The committed, tenacious director who strives to effectively reach and teach urban students while building bridges to colleagues, administrators, parents, and the greater community will have success in building quality instrumental music programs. However, this achievement will usually come only after overcoming some daunting challenges. Given the benefits that a high-quality instrumental music program can offer to the many bright, talented, deserving children in urban schools, the rewards are truly worth the effort.

REFERENCES

Casey, J. L. (1993). *Teaching techniques and insights for instrumental music educators* (Rev. ed.). Chicago: GIA Publications.

Cutietta, R. A. (Ed.). (1999). *Strategies for teaching specialized ensembles*. Reston, VA: MENC: The National Association for Music Education.

Dalby, M. F. (1993). *Band rehearsal techniques: A handbook for new directors*. Northfield, IL: The Instrumentalist Publishing Co.

Hale, J. E. (2001). *Learning while Black: Creating educational excellence for African American children*. Baltimore: Johns Hopkins University Press.

Kunjufu, J. (1999). *Countering the conspiracy to destroy black boys* (Vol. III). Chicago: African American Images.

———. (2002). *Black students. Middle class teachers*. Chicago: African American Images.

Kuykendall, C. (1992). *From rage to hope: Strategies for reclaiming Black and Hispanic students*. Bloomington, IN: National Education Service.

Mixon, K. A. (2004). Building your instrumental music program in an urban school. *Music Educators Journal*, 91(3), 15–23.

Payne, R. K. (2001). *A framework for understanding poverty* (New Rev. ed.). Highlands, TX: aha! Process, Inc.

Weiner, L. (1999). *Urban teaching: The essentials*. New York: Teachers College Press.

Wilson, B. L., & Corbett, H. D. (2001). *Listening to urban kids: School reform and the teachers they want*. Albany: State University of New York.

10

The String Chorale Concept

Jeanne Porcino Dolamore

AN URBAN VISION

The String Chorale Concept is an approach that provides a foundation for successful string programs in urban music education settings. It begins with students making music, focuses on maintaining high musical standards and captivating audiences, and requires a community-wide effort. This approach motivates students to learn and encourages families and communities to participate. Its community-wide scope enlists politicians, businesses, colleges, and musicians into the process. It is a vision that will keep school teachers, district administrators, and policy makers energized to develop and sustain urban music programs.

A Brief History

The String Chorale Concept began in approximately 1951, when my father, Chet Porcino, began his 50-year career as a string specialist. His firsthand experiences teaching string music and his wealth of ideas and teaching strategies can be traced to many sources. These include the simple wisdom borrowed from many inspiring colleagues and the practical lessons learned from his string students, who span three generations. In 1962, Chet Porcino was among the first group of American teachers to study with Shinichi Suzuki, and he adapted much of the Suzuki method into his teaching long before it became popular. In later years, he studied with the renowned violin pedagogue Kato Havas and incorporated many of her ideas into his public school string classes.

My subsequent work, since 1981, led me to create the String Chorale Concept, a unique string teaching strategy in urban string music classrooms or any music classroom where a dynamic, growth-oriented program is desired; where commitment to developing an innovative, student-centered learning environment is required; and where community outreach is desired. Its focus rests firmly on investing in our youth through music and giving back to our communities.

The fundamental strategies used to incorporate the String Chorale Concept into urban string music programs are centered around five core values:

1. Strive to meet high musical standards
2. Embrace diversity of culture and economic level
3. Develop a student-centered music curriculum
4. Captivate the audience
5. Enlist a community-wide effort

The fundamental teaching strategies used to incorporate the String Chorale Concept into urban string music programs vary significantly from those used in traditional string orchestra programs. Students taught with String Chorale strategies learn repertoire through a standard choral approach, perform by memory, and stand when they perform. Lessons and rehearsals often take on a workshop format, where students explore string technique, hone music reading skills, and receive group ensemble and performance preparation in a noncompetitive environment. The specific strategies described below can be incorporated into all or any part of your string music education program. This chapter describes this unique string teaching approach and the solutions it offers for many of the most critical challenges in string teaching and community building in urban music teaching settings.

CORE VALUES AND FUNDAMENTAL STRATEGIES

Strive to Meet High Musical Standards

In all music endeavors, we should strive to meet *high musical standards*. It is especially critical that we demand the same high levels of technique and performance proficiency in urban locales that we would in any other educational setting. Pride in achievement is the greatest asset in the struggle to recruit, retain, and inspire students to remain involved in string music programs. The following strategies enforce this value.

Prioritize and Organize Lesson Materials

Excellent methods are plentiful for teaching note reading, scales, harmony, theory, and improvisation. Nonetheless, it is very important to personalize, prioritize, and organize instructional interventions including posture, the mechanics of playing, sound, intonation, rhythmic structure, and style (Culver, 1999). Likewise, educators should seek out supplemental materials that offer a variety of technical information including a variety of musical images, explanations, and solutions to both technical and artistic challenges.

Encourage Students to Internalize Music

Help students to internalize music through singing and clapping rhythm, dynamics, note names, and artistic style. Exaggerate technique, dramatize notes and dynamics, and teach your string players to truly comprehend their music inside and out (Havas, 1998).

Help Students to Memorize Music

Encourage both excellent note- and sight-reading of lesson and rehearsal music and memorization of performance music; the two are not mutually exclusive. In a String Chorale, most works are learned primarily through note reading, but performed by memory. Students have an infinite capacity to memorize music, including arrangements that are quite complicated (Starr, 1976). Memorization is freedom for string players: freedom from music stands and searching for parts, freedom to focus on the audience as they discover the unlimited potential for making music with string instruments.

Establish Written Goals

Establish written goals and work with students individually and collectively to achieve them. Use challenges, evaluation forms, and student prizes. When students feel ownership they will give their best efforts and take pride in the results. If you expect dependability and loyalty from all players you just might get it!

Use Assessments

Evaluate student progress with regularly scheduled individual and group assessments using published and/or original evaluation forms.

Replace Discipline with Intervention

Intervention is crucial to success in the urban music class. Communicate honestly and directly with your students and expect them to be accountable and responsible. Do not allow students to play the instruments until they understand the structure of rehearsing (including unpacking and tuning) and know your guidelines for respect and behavior. Beseech, cajole, and push when necessary and communicate with parents and teachers every step of the way.

Embrace Diversity of Culture and Economic Level

If we want string programs to survive and flourish in urban communities, we must work harder to recruit and retain an *economically and culturally diverse group* among string students, teachers (Gillespie & Hamann, 1997), and the often overlooked audience base as well. The String Chorale approach is designed to address the diversity in urban string classrooms: not simply ethnic diversity, but diversity of cultures, income levels, abilities, and musical styles. Its intent is also to ensure that string students are able to access instruments, and to actively participate in string music lessons and string ensembles, regardless of ability to pay. The following strategies enforce this value.

Choose an Eclectic Mix of Ensemble Repertoire

Ensemble repertoire should reflect the reality of each teaching environment, which may include students of diverse cultures, any combination and number of string instruments, and students of varied ability levels performing together in one ensemble. Select artistic repertoire that reaches across the spectrum from classical music to jazz, fiddle, folk, and contemporary, and perform it all within the same ensemble.

String players sometimes label *serious* music as that which is played by sit-down orchestras, and *alternative* music as that which is heard in special clubs. It is *all* serious music. Explore each style for its musical and performance potential and try not to label any musical style as *alternative*. (Remember that many classical composers were considered alternative in their time.) Students will appreciate each new musical genre introduced to them once they understand the value of performing it.

Take Best Musical Advantage of the Group You Have Now

Change, adapt, and/or transpose parts to complement your current group, while maintaining the intended integrity of any arrangement. If you have no strong cellists one year, feature your violists. Teach the viola part to the cellists or the bass part to the violinists. Consider making each part available for treble, bass, and/or tenor instruments.

Adapt scores and arrange music (Olah, 2002) to enable students of varied technical levels to play within the same performing ensemble. Offer music that addresses each new technical challenge, expanding or reducing the notes on the page when necessary. Arrange simple open string accompaniments, or simple harmonies to include beginners in your ensembles from the start. Music arrangements of a piece of music are an exclusive right of the copyright owner, but under the legal compromises surrounding the law, some things are considered to be reasonable exceptions:

- Music teachers can edit or simplify purchased, printed copies, provided that the fundamental character of the work is not distorted, and
- Music teachers who get a compulsory license for recording can make a musical arrangement of a work "to conform it to the style or manner of interpretation of the performance involved" (National Association for Music Education, 2003). This arrangement cannot, however, change the basic melody or fundamental character of the work.

Be Creative!

Be innovative and imaginative. This does not distract from the music, but rather enhances the enjoyment of both player and listener. It's time that string ensembles got serious about *having fun* with music!

Develop a Student-Centered Music Curriculum

Teachers must *center the string music curriculum on students*, so that both can joyfully explore the newest trends in string education within a dynamic, resourceful learning environment. Urban string education programs must be designed to give string students the tools, skills, and information they need to succeed at music, the desire to continue with music, and the ability to transfer some of their learned skills to all parts of their lives. The following strategies enforce this value.

Think Choir, Teach Strings

Although "chorale" usually brings singing voices to mind, a *choir* or *chorale* can also be defined as a group of instruments or a family of musical instruments playing together. Choirs are usually categorized by the voices they include, based on soprano, alto, tenor, and bass (SATB) voices used in any combination (The American Heritage Dictionary, 2000).

Introduce ensemble string parts based on a choir model, adding parts gradually and when appropriate as the ensemble progresses. Begin with unison string voices, rounds, and partner songs. Add the SB (violin/cello or melody/bass) voices next. Present additional harmonies and inner voices (alto/tenor or obligato parts) one at a time, so every student in the group can understand both the beauty of harmony and the value of dissonance, which is very different from struggling to play the notes in the second violin section.

Begin with Simple Melody and Rhythm

Begin with rounds and partner songs, move on to two-part arrangements, and grow into complex/multileveled harmonies when students are ready. Avoid distributing parts that are too difficult, while simply hoping for the best! When you eliminate first and second violin parts distributed by level, you'll find that students request to play the harmony, rather than aspiring only to first violin and/or melody sections. Otherwise, in elementary orchestras, children are playing parts that do not yet make sense to them musically.

Challenge Advanced Players

Challenge outstanding players with advanced harmony or obligato parts. Feature them as soloists or in highlighted soli groups within an arrangement. Introduce new finger patterns, intervals, and positions when a challenge is needed. This approach lets you use your advanced players to their fullest capacity, rather than as section leaders in orchestras that select repertoire based on the average student level of a group.

Solicit Student Input

Solicit student input whenever possible; make changes when necessary.

Recruiting: Early and Often

Recruitment begins with a listening audience of diverse ages and backgrounds. There is nothing like a delighted audience member (be it a perspective student, grandparent, or board member) to encourage instrument selection, motivate long-term participation, and promote your program.

Highlight String Instruments

Use performances, workshops, and exploratory programs to highlight string instruments. Students must be able to hear and touch stringed instruments to imagine themselves on stage playing one. Some students have been listening to string music from a young age, and others will hear a violin for the first time in your program.

Recruit an Audience

Make sure every child has someone in each audience (a relative, teacher, friend) who is there especially for him or her, to cheer and admire their hard work.

Compliment Sincerely

Deliver compliments as passionately as you deliver expectations and demands. Accept compliments with grace, and share the compliments with your students. Keep a journal of listener comments.

Eliminate Competition

Competition evaporates when each student has a *part to play* in the ensemble that he/she can feel good about. Teachers and students should be so busy making music together and calculating which arrangements work best that there is no energy or time for competition.

Model Your Love for Mistakes

Ensemble members can't give a gift to the audience if they are afraid that something is going to go wrong. Fear limits our creativity, and makes us stay in safe areas, instead of taking the musical risks which are necessary in any thriving ensemble (Kooistra, 1990). To help students learn to take risks, model your love for mistakes in front of the audience. If a mistake occurs at a concert, be bold enough to start a piece again. I often joke with the audience that if the entire group breaks into a big smile all at once, it's probably because of a really big mistake I made.

Acknowledge Stage Fright

When students understand the nature of their fears and strategies for diminishing stage fright, both concert attendance and student morale improve. When students play in the present, know their music incredibly well, and are totally involved in making music in the moment, there is little time left for nerves (Havas, 1978).

Initiate Field Trips

Augment your curriculum with educational programming that takes place both inside and outside of the schools. Initiate field trips, exchange, concerts, and performance tours statewide. Consider bringing a performing group or facilitating a workshop at a state or national music conference.

Attend Concerts

Attend live concerts free or with reduced tickets that are often provided by local chamber groups and community theaters. An eclectic mix of performing artists and outstanding string ensembles are plentiful in our urban communities.

Remember the Audience

When students play, they give a gift of themselves and of their talent. Students live for the glow of audience response, as all musicians do. Every time students perform they make a human connection. Audiences come to concerts not just to hear good music, but to experience this connection.

Expand the Audience's Image of a String Ensemble

String orchestra listener comments often focus on the difficulty of the music, not the enjoyment they receive. Peter Schickele (P. D. Q. Bach) of WAMC NY radio's *Schickele Mix* says regularly, "If it Sounds Good, It is Good!" and I go a bit further: If it sounds bad, it's too hard! Your audience is truly not comforted at the end of a long concert to know that it didn't "sound good" because it was a difficult, complex piece.

Enchant the Audience

Enchant the audience by delighting them with your ensembles' technical proficiency and artistic interpretation and by keeping them engaged and interested throughout your performance. When we share music often within the community, we create enthusiasm, pride in achievement, and a sense of delight in all givers and receivers of music.

Rotate Concert Times

Rotate concert times and days so that so that those with nontraditional work hours or family and friends living at a distance can attend.

Perform at All Stages of Development

Have students perform at every stage in their musical development from taking the instruments out of the case to performing their first concerto. Practice presentation almost as much as playing. Include lining up, entrances and exits, resting positions, performing stance, choreography, speaking, stagehand responsibilities, and more. When we ensure musical achievement and combine it with the thrill of communicating with an audience, students will want to practice. The processes by which students learn to love their instruments and appreciate their intrinsic musicianship are practice and performance. These are amazing motivators.

Let Every Student Shine

Give every child a chance to shine with individual and small group solos throughout every concert. Don't restrict solos to your advanced players. Create solo parts to reflect the ability of any child in your ensemble.

Talk to the Audience

Talk to your audience about both the music and the students. Introduce, explain, describe, tell stories. Try it, and you'll never be a silent professional again!

Use Every Physical Space to Your Performance Advantage

Stand on choral risers, on the stage, on a stairwell. Surround your audience when you play. Stroll down an aisle, through a door, around tables. Pop up from scattered seats or enter from several directions.

Add Narration

Add narration to compliment the historical or cultural background of any piece or poetry that enhances the mood, season, or theme of your repertoire.

Add Choreography and Costumes When Appropriate

Incorporate simple steps, or full dance movements into a musical arrangement. Have students wear ethnic costumes; use hats of every description. Dress your instruments with holiday ribbons; hang small props from the violin scroll or try a hat on your bass.

Experiment with Nontraditional Sounds

Try producing new pizzicato or percussive sounds with string instruments. Retune the strings to play authentic folk music, or ask students to create new string sounds of their own within a controlled environment.

Seek Out Joint Performances

Seek out joint performances and festivals with area music teachers and community ensembles. Be diverse here as well. Highlight your strings not only by performing with other string ensembles, but by performing with choirs, jazz bands, percussion ensembles, and dance ensembles as well.

Perform with a Variety of Artists

Your communities are filled with classical, jazz, and folk musicians who love working with their area schools and give generously of their time and talents. Develop an Artist in Residence Program to highlight a specialty area such as jazz or fiddle music with a local professional musician.

Enlist a Community-wide Effort

If we want to promote music and secure support for urban music education programs, we must maintain high visibility throughout school districts and local communities. Performers should be viewed as student ambassadors who serve their communities through music making. When we enlist a community-wide effort through performance, partnership, and collaboration, we will discover that urban communities, already rich in culture, will embrace both our music and our goals.

High visibility helps to connect students with the community and secure support for urban music education programs. Community connections are key to addressing what seems to be an ever-growing musical achievement gap between communities whose school students can afford private lessons and participate in community orchestras and the many equally talented school students whose families cannot afford these extracurricular music programs.

Be of Service to the Community

Perform for school boards, school administration, community leaders, service organizations, business associations, senior residences, and hospitals. Perform at community festivals, in museums, historic homes, and more. Perform with and for not-for-profits in your area or collaborate with them to raise funds for both programs.

Encourage Long-Term Participation

Encourage participation in or start your own community string ensemble. Help students obtain scholarships for ensemble participation and instruments as required. Send students off when it's time for them to move on to new performing opportunities, yet promote their further involvement in music education through peer practice programs, internships, and further education. The current shortage of string teachers in our nation is a challenge requiring initiative and innovative programming in all string music settings in order to attract young musicians to careers in the field of string music education (Hamann, 2002).

Develop Internships

Start an internship or peer tutoring program with your district high school. High school students can become practice partners for younger students in carefully planned afterschool, summer, and weekend internship programs. Offer a student internship to a recent graduate of your performing ensemble. Graduate interns can assist with ensembles or music libraries, and can be recognized by performing a concerto or special solo with your group.

Initiate College Mentor Programs

Many colleges have music programs, and almost all have excellent student musicians who are willing to give of their time to an organized mentor program. Our School-to-College Mentoring program includes private music lessons, chamber music coaching, and music theory classes coached by college students in afterschool and Saturday morning programs.

Join Community Partners

Create and sustain partnerships with YMCAs, arts organizations, education groups, civic groups, local business sponsors, individual supporters.

Encourage Parent Participation

If you have nourished your audiences and reached out to urban families through performance and direct communication, you will find that the desire to participate among urban families is high. Tap in to the resources among families and their community networks. Encourage parent participation by initiating parent booster clubs or associations. Create cooperative projects from fund-raisers to festivals, and delegate tasks from baking to website design (Schwarthoff, 2004).

Maintain Ties with Colleagues

Maintain close ties with colleagues on districtwide, citywide, and statewide levels. Initiate interdisciplinary projects with classroom teachers. As educators strive for new heights in urban string music settings, we should be able to demonstrate shared values with action in music classrooms.

Compile Statistics

Publish enrollment figures and program benefits to students. Chart concert logs, honors or grants awarded, scholarships, tributes, and accolades received. Display information about your program and relevant press clippings at performances and presentations (Kendall, 1997).

Publicize, Publicize, Publicize!

Publicize your successes, upcoming performances, and student profiles in school newsletters, local newspapers, and magazines. Request publicity or perform live on local TV and radio.

Seek Funding

A combination of subsidized school rental and purchase programs and district/community alliances with commercial and wholesale retailers and competent repair centers, as well as funding from local, state, and national grant programs, will ensure that the resources are available to make access to string instruments and extracurricular string programs a reality for students in every community.

With this in mind, seek out funding for instruments, extracurricular programs, and mentor stipends through traditional fundraising activities and a variety of grants sponsored by school districts, teachers associations, professional associations, and local businesses. Request donations from local politicians, supporters, and businesses. Most are available both for public school music programs and not-for-profit community ensembles.

The String Chorale Concept provides a model for urban string teachers, a set of ideas for urban music teachers and school administrators, and a catalyst for observation and discussion among all who would like to see music in our urban schools profoundly impact urban students and communities. It has been remarkable to participate in the development of several cohesive, talented, and vibrant corps of young musicians who have done much more that engage audiences through their performances, but have become worthy, contributing members of their communities.

REFERENCES

American String Teachers Association. (1998–2001). National string teacher standards. Retrieved June 29, 2005, from www.astaweb.com/advocacy/stringstandards.html

Choir. (2000). *The American heritage dictionary of the English language.* Boston: Houghton Mifflin. Retrieved August 5, 2005, from www.answers.com/topic/choir.html.

Culver, R. (1999). How to develop community-wide support for string study. *American String Teacher*, 49(1), 48–54.

Gillespie, R., & Hamann, D. (1977). Survey on the status of orchestra instruction in the public schools. *American String Teacher*, 47(4), 45–49.

Hamann, D. (2002). Wanted: 5,000 future string teachers. *American String Teacher*, 52(1), 72–78.

Havas, K. (1978). *Stage fright: Its causes and cures.* London: Bosworth and Co.

———. (1998). Editorial. *Kato Havas Association for the New Approach*, 13(2), 1–3.

Kendall, S. (1997). Securing our string programs. *American String Teacher*, 47(2), 47–51.

Kooistra, N. (1990). The habit of fear. *Kato Havas Association for the New Approach*, 6(1), 5–6.

National Association for Music Education. (2003). A guide for music educators for use in preparing derivative works (Rev. ed.). *The United States Copyright Law.* Retrieved June 29, 2005, from www.menc.org/information/copyright/copyr.html#school.

Olah, D. (2002). Why not write music for string orchestra? *Teaching Music*, 10(3), 49–53.

Starr, W. (1976). *The Suzuki violinist: A guide for teachers and parents.* Knoxville, TN: Kingston Ellis Press.

Schwarthoff, P. (2004). Making the most of parental involvement. *American String Teacher*, 54(3), 51.

SUPPLEMENTAL RESOURCES

National Standards

American String Teachers Association (ASTA). (copyright 1998–2001). National string teacher standards. Retrieved June 29, 2005, from www.astaweb.com/advocacy/stringstandards.html.

Music Educators National Conference (MENC). (n.d.). Standards for arts education. Retrieved June 29, 2005, from www.educationworld.com/standards/national/arts/music.

Swarthoff, P. (2004). Making the most of parental involvement. *American String Teacher*, 4(3), 51.

Community Resources

Art Education Advocacy Guide. (2000). Davis Publications, Inc.

Bobstsky, V. (2003). Turn parents into partners. *Teaching Music*, 11(1), 38–41.

Fredricks, J. (2002). There is more than one way to write a grant. *Teaching Music*, 9(5), 50–53.

Kindall-Smith, M. (2004). Teachers teaching teachers: Revitalization in an urban setting. *Music Educators Journal*, 91(2), 41–46.

Mixon, K. (2005). Building your instrumental music program in an urban school. *Music Educators Journal*, 91(3), 15–23.

Sheldon, D. (2001). Peer and cross-age tutoring in music. *Music Educators Journal*, 87(6), 33–38.

Classroom Resources

Bakhshayesh, G. (1985). *Ringing strings and dancing bows: String tutorials.* London: David Bentley Pub.

Blankenship, G. (1988). Implementing Kato Havas ideas in heterogeneous string classes. *HANA*, 4(2), 4–5.

Dabczynski, A., & Phillips, B. (1999). *Fiddlers philharmonic encore.* Van Nuys, CA: Alfred Publishing Co., Inc.

DePorter, B. (2000). *The 8 keys of excellence: Principles to live by.* Oceanside, CA: Learning Forum Publications.

Feigelson, S. (1998). *Energizing your meetings with laughter.* Alexandria, VA: Association for Supervision and Curriculum Development.

Jeannotte, K. (2000). *Bows and chords: Children's lessons on string instruments.* Shokan, NY: Bows and Chords Pub.

Kobena A. (1997). *Let your voice be heard: Songs from Ghana and Zimbabwe*. Danbury, CT: World Music Press.
Peterson, D. (1989). *Strollogisms: Ten fundamentals every stroller needs to know*. Monteco, CA: Don Peterson.
Porcino, C. (1985). *The Flying Fiddlers string series*. Commack, NY: New Strings Music Pub.
Rolland, P., & Mutschler, M. (2000). *The teaching of action in string playing*. Urbana, IL: University of Illinois String Research Project.
Starr, W. (1976). *The Suzuki violinist: A guide for teachers and parents*. Knoxville, TN: Kingston Ellis Press.

11

The Small, Big City in Music Education: The Impacts of Instrumental Music Education for Urban Students

Karen Iken

Music has always been a part of my life. My grandma would sing gospel songs and hymns to me as a small child. Hearing those same songs today brings back a feeling of warmth and security. My dream was to learn to play piano, and I was fortunate to begin those lessons at the age of nine. As I entered fifth grade, a neighbor let me borrow a saxophone in order to join our grade school band. I took music seriously in school. It was a necessity. There were parades and concerts, deep friendships and purpose.

Music was part of my growing and is now my life's work. That work has taken me from a small farming community in western Wisconsin to Green Bay, a city in eastern Wisconsin, with the fifth largest school district in the state. I spend my days with a diverse community of students, some who are very similar to me, and others who speak a different language at home, have special needs, or live in a blended family. Music has been so important in my life. Seeing myself in my students is the motivation that pushes me to advocate for them. I want to make the way for their stories.

This has already been a fabulous journey for me but there is another trip to speak of. As I completed my master's degree, I became a teacher-researcher. This adventure led me to discover a wealth of information about education and educators, students, parents, and finally, myself.

> This study, based on my master's thesis, taught me to view personal teaching practice by studying student and parent reactions. Grounding this study in issues traditionally considered "urban" enriched the trip. All my students are special, but growing up without much money myself gives me the incentive to do my best for them. It has motivated me to continue practices that I see working and look for input on what can be improved. I also found that a typical "urban" picture speaks for some of them, but not for others. Either way, the needs are still there.

Join me for an adventure. It is an adventure that requires research to find a direction for travel, a method for moving forward, stories about the sights we will see along the way, and a return trip home. I look at my students' faces, contemplate a direction for travel, and move forward.

BACKGROUND—DIRECTION OF TRAVEL

As we consider urban issues, an obvious question arises: How can Green Bay, a city of 106,000, be compared with the likes of Los Angeles, Milwaukee, or New York City? Renfro (2003) tells of Judy Svengalis, former music supervisor and current music teacher in Des Moines, Iowa, and founder of the Urban Music Leadership Conference. As Svengalis explains it, the challenges of big cities are seen on a large scale, and are much more visible. Chicago and New York engage greater obstacles than smaller cities such as Des Moines, Lincoln, or Green Bay. But smaller cities have the same problems on a "smaller scale." In Svengalis's words, "If you think you might be urban, you're urban" (Renfro, 2003, p. 36).

The differences within a single school district like Green Bay can be staggering. A music teacher can drive from a school with dairy cows in a nearby field and sailboats on the bay, to a school with a fenced-in playground where several languages are heard at recess and coded announcements for occasional security lockdowns occur more frequently.

The issues in urban education are often summarized by a list of challenges. As Englert (1993) notes, these include but are not limited to: schools that are too large, but not large enough to meet the needs of the student population; are very impersonal and unconnected to the outside; and have poorly motivated students with low expectations, terrible attendance, and an unsupportive environment. Flaxman, Schwartz, Weiler, and Lahey (1998) and Lapp, Block, Cooper, Flood, Roser, and Tinajero (2004) provide suggestions for topics that we will address, including family structure and involvement, poverty, and ethnicity and language.

A visible issue in urban areas is the inequality of education funding. Kozol's (1991) description of Morris High in the Bronx is telling: "The first things one senses in the building are the sweetness, the real innocence, of many of the children, the patience and determination of the teachers, and the shameful disrepair of the surroundings" (p. 100). New York is a long way from Green Bay, but even in Wisconsin students fully realize the differences. Low-income communities do not have the tax base to produce the funds needed to equip students with the resources and facilities required for a quality education. High-income communities have a much wealthier tax base and the personal resources to provide for any needs of their children that are not met at school. Middle-income communities seem to have adequate funding but not always the personal resources for unmet educational needs.

There are other inequities in urban education beyond the physical challenges. One challenge comes in the form of expectations. Some teachers do not believe that students of color can achieve. Others substitute language, disability, or family makeup as the cause. The challenge is to not be caught up in this misconception. The challenge is to be sure that all teachers believe that "We can whenever and wherever we choose, teach all children successfully whose education is of importance to us" (Lapp, et al., 2004, p. 15).

Take these expectations to another level—parent involvement. Corbett, Wilson, and Williams (2002) suggest that some urban parents have a negative concept of education based on their own experiences. Other urban families are very involved in their children's education, but in a way that is not always visible to educators. Parents may not be able to help with homework or read to their children, but they show support for effort, responsibility, and perseverance. There are also cultural factors at work. The perception that the teacher is the sole figure in a child's formal education can be culturally different than the one White middle-class educators expect. This forms a misconception between the two groups of adults. This is related to apprehension among potential band and orchestra parents. Many parents feel that if they did not play an instrument themselves, they will not be able to help their child.

With the groundwork and direction mapped out, let us move forward on the journey. How will we find the impacts of instrumental music education for urban students?

METHOD—MOVING FORWARD

Inspired by the voice and content of Vivian Gussin Paley's stories of education in Chicago with *Kwanzaa and Me* (1995) and *In Mrs. Tully's Room* (2003), my study took the form of a *portraiture*. The format of portraiture is explained by Sara Lawrence-Lightfoot and Jessica Hoffmann Davis in their book *The Art and Science of Portraiture*. Lawrence-Lightfoot (1997) says portraiture is, "a method of inquiry and documentation in the social sciences. With it, I seek to combine systematic, empirical description with aesthetic expression, blending art and science, humanistic sensibilities and scientific rigor" (p. 3). So, this study entails writing a story. The characters are the students, and the plot is their journey with their instruments. As their teacher, my own experiences and remembrances were part of this tale, a part of how I view the importance of my job. Lawrence-Lightfoot says this is appropriate and necessary.

The schools that form the backdrop for this study are both part of the Green Bay Area Public Schools (GBAPS). Nicolet Elementary is an inner-city K-5 school. Originally built in 1936, it has doubled in physical size in the last 15 years. From the outside it does not appear impoverished, with its old flagstone finish being matched with a similar color yellow brick during remodeling. A report to the GBAPS Board of Education, however, lists the school's population as 91% below the poverty level, 81.4% minorities, and 52.8% ESL (English as second language) or ELL (English-language learners). The many classrooms in this building house 576 students, but there is not a room for music classes. Music teachers deliver music on a cart or teach in whatever spaces are available.

The second school in this study is Aldo Leopold Community School (ALCS). With an enrollment of 407, ALCS is the district's only exclusively "choice" school, and is a K-8 building. The school is located in the historical part of downtown Green Bay, and its curriculum is based on individualized instruction with a noncompetitive, nontraditional grading philosophy. Students come from throughout the city with a wide variety of backgrounds and economic status. The school program has been moved four times in 25 years. ALCS is presently housed in an old parochial high school built in 1910 and purchased by the district. It sports an addition from the 1960s and another from 2002. Most rooms are small, with no water or sinks for the elementary classes. The middle school science lab is located in the back of the computer lab. The band room is the size of a high school classroom with no storage.

The student narratives were compiled from parent questionnaires, student questionnaires, and student interviews. These tools included open-ended questions about involvement on instrument, in school, and with music, and personal observation.

Interviews occurred during the second year of instruction (2003–2004) for the ALCS students. Interviews were audiotaped with parental permission and notes were taken from these tapes. All student names were changed to pseudonyms. Additional data were extracted from selected pages of the band and orchestra portfolio/journal used by the teacher for middle school age students. All student and parent quotes in the results were taken directly from data in this section.

As a researcher, I also kept a journal thoughout the period. Stories, portraits if you will, were compiled from these data sources. The voices of the students, parents, and myself, their teacher, are all heard. We have moved forward on our journey in research. What have we found?

RESULTS—STORIES ABOUT THE SIGHTS ON OUR JOURNEY

It is June; the spring weather has been unseasonably cool and wet. There is the anticipation of the final days of school for the year even without the toasty temperatures. Students are excited and downhearted at the same time. They long for the freedom of summer break but regret the lack of structured activities and daily meetings with friends. My own feelings are not much different. I look forward to sleeping later and reading more, but I also have concerns about my students. These are but a few of the thoughts that come to mind as I say my good-byes and go to clean my classroom.

As I put away the instruments and file the music, I look back at the journeys of these students. What have they really learned through the lessons and rehearsals? Where does this knowledge and ability take them? Is it important to them? What are the impacts of instrumental music education on these preadolescent urban students?

There are many studies in research journals and periodicals. Catterall, Chapleau, and Iwanaga (2000), Rarus (2000), and Weinberger (1999) show test score improvement; Campbell (1992) and Jensen (2000) discuss increased brain activity; Habermeyer (1999) emphasizes life skills; Hansen, Bernstorf, and Stuber (2004) connect music and literacy; and Weber, Spychiger, and Patry (1993) show the impact of music on school environment. The important factor is not that there are studies to support music. The important factor is that the benefits these studies report are not available unless a student is given the opportunity to take part in music programs. To start in a quality instrumental program at an appropriate age is vital for the student and crucial to the extent of the benefit. I cannot stress this point enough: *The beginning makes a difference.*

When we look back at these beginnings, we find many interesting stories. With the stories come growth and a reflection of the impacts. Let us look at the stories of four urban students from Wisconsin.

Maria

Maria attends Nicolet Elementary. It is classified as a Title I school, and with that comes many testing requirements and scheduling constraints. For that reason, Maria and her fellow string players come to school early for large group rehearsals. These rehearsals take place in the gymnasium. If the weather is inclement, students come into the building early, into the gymnasium. Then we rehearse in the hall between the cafeteria and the bathrooms. Students are only let out of class every other week for the 20-minute small group homogeneous lessons. Lessons are held in a room that is shared as an office by three teachers. The room is actually a custodian's supply closet with doors at each end, one opening into the gymnasium's physical education classes and the other into the cafeteria. A portion of one wall contains three power boxes (this area is off limits for instruction space), and the second wall has a sidewalk and four-lane street outside the cinder block. With these challenges, we work through the first year together and learn the basics of violin.

There are several Hispanic students in this school, and they teach me Spanish. There is a growing need for me to understand at least a basic amount of Spanish in this setting. I also learn to count and greet others in Hmong, the language of my students from rural Laos. We all laugh at my pronunciations and we form a bond. The students take on a special role as teacher. There is a unique relationship.

Maria is one student who gives me Spanish "lessons." She has dark eyes, long black hair, and a huge smile. Maria's family is from Peru, and part of her extended family is still there. Quiet and respectful, she works hard in school. Maria begins her journey on violin during 2003–2004. She says, "I chose my instrument because I always saw people playing it and it sounded so good. Then when I got to fifth grade I had a chance to an instrument and I said this is my big chance to play what I wanted . . . violin. Then after I did start playing violin and I really liked it a lot."

As Maria moves from fifth grade (elementary school) to sixth grade (middle school), her family chooses for her to attend ALCS. Maria does not immediately sign up for violin when she gets to her new school. However, with a familiar face, some coaxing, and reassurance of the availability of a school instrument (the district provides instruments for some students with financial need), she realizes that she is still excited about the violin and misses playing. The excitement for instrumental music is in that "I am learning new things." Maria's mother notes during the middle of sixth grade that Maria is "quiet and sometimes shy," and she has seen changes in her daughter since beginning violin. "She wants to learn more about music . . . she loves playing her instrument."

As our second year together ends, Maria says she plans to continue violin and maybe even try clarinet, too. She says, "I like the violin sounds" and "like learning new stuff." Maria reflects on what orchestra has taught her. After careful thought, she says violin practice gives her "time to spend with other violin students at school," and teaches "how to work together" and "how to help each other."

During the early summer of the 2004–2005 year, I have a chance to speak with Maria's mother. She tells me she has seen growth in Maria since she began violin. There is a responsibility seen in bringing the instrument to school, and excitement that is not always evident in the actions of this quiet student. Maria's mother and father are "happy that she is learning to play an instrument," and emphasize that they "will do whatever Maria needs to continue to learn." Most of all, they "will support her and give her time." They are proud of her and share her progress with family in Peru. Such a support system!

There has been change for Maria in recent school years with a move in schools. She continues to be positive and continues with activities and learning that help her to grow. Could music, such as violin lessons and orchestra, be part of those activities that aid students in adjusting to new situations? It is the one constant in Maria's move.

Almost two and a half miles from Nicolet, at Maria's new school, ALCS, are students who are part of the same study that actually began a year earlier in the 2002–2003 school year. These ALCS students do not have the same urban background as Maria, but they experience many of the same needs and adventures.

Lora

Lora is a quiet fifth-grade girl. She does not have the outward appearance of a student in need. If we search deeper, will we find the need? Lora's mother shares the following about her instrument choice: "When Lora was really young, we had a neat lift-the-flap book called *Trilby's Trumpet* and I've always wondered if that is what made her want a trumpet so much." Lora remembers how "Dad took me to a music store when I was four and I saw a trumpet. Ever since that day, the trumpet is all I ever wanted to play. I like the sound and I like how it looks. My mom and dad say it is OK with them, too."

Where has trumpet taken Lora? Her mother writes that after the first year of trumpet she is "less shy, more outgoing. Band would be her first school experience of veering off on her own path rather than being herded with the pack." This is an example of the impact of the social dimension on the student through an education in music. After the second year, the growth that Lora's mom sees is "accountability, more responsibility, perseverance." These qualities can be learned through other venues, "but especially in music it becomes readily apparent that practice goes a long way, and it is important to remember your instrument! The individual part to create the whole (song) and working together to achieve that, [benefits the child as well as] the importance of planning and practice. The joy that creating music can add to life."

Robert

Robert is a redhead with a toothy smile, and like Lora, chooses trumpet. In the first couple months of trumpet lessons, Robert forgets his instrument several times. While Robert says he enjoys school, and feels he does well, his organizational skills need work. When I approach his mother about the situation, I learn a lot more about this trumpet player. Robert is diagnosed with Asperger's syndrome (AS).

As I understand it, AS is a high-functioning form of autism. There are many more complexities to the syndrome than this simple statement. Forgetting to bring the trumpet to school is a factor of organization and routine in AS. There are also sensory issues for students with AS. Robert has a challenge dealing with sound and touch. His mother says, "I would think the vibration in his mouth would be a problem." As I think about that for a second, I respond, "But he doesn't have to put it [the mouthpiece] in his mouth. The trumpet mouthpiece is on his lips; granted there is a vibration, but it is on his lips. With clarinet or saxophone, that vibration would be on his teeth and in his mouth." That makes sense to his mom.

I follow up by saying, "On a survey, the question is 'why did you pick trumpet.' His answer: 'from what there was available, that was the one that worked the best.'"

"To give any sort of an explanation would be difficult for him."

"You mean I was looking for a 'how' and 'why' answer, and he is a 'what' answerer?"

"Not even 'what.' Yes, no, end of discussion kind of guy. Does he have any talent on the trumpet?" she asks. "The only time I hear him play is at the concert."

I respond, "Fingerings are great. I told him once that he needed to sit tall, no slouching. He will sit straight *every* time he comes in. Practice would help more."

"His brother said he would practice upstairs in his room before I got home."

"That makes sense. He couldn't get what he does by never practicing."

Then she tells me a very interesting story about Robert being in band and choir. "I found a note from school in his backpack recently. It was [from the classroom teacher] from the beginning of the school year. It said, 'If your child is going to be in band and choir, he will have more homework and you need to be aware that he will be out of the classroom that much more.' When we talked about it at home, Robert said, 'You don't understand. I have to do that!' Maybe it is something he gets; internally, and he needs it [music]. He feels some comfort there."

"Is it an issue of having a friend in choir?"

"I don't think so. He says he *needs* to do it."

Libby

A bubble-gum-chewing spunky girl, Libby is "playful, easy going, energetic and in charge!" Her stepfather sees her as "outgoing, loving, compassionate, stubborn at times, very intelligent." Her parents manage the blended family well. Her mother shares the following story: "Libby told us she would like to play violin. I believe she was influenced by the Dixie Chicks [current country-pop female group]. Marc [stepfather] urged her to consider a woodwind. Libby decided she would like to play violin. We honored her choice."

Libby has a different view of her decision. She says, "Well my mom thinks I like the Dixie Chicks but that's not right. I chose violin because it looked fun yet challenging, and it's cool to be able to tell someone that you can play violin. I'm glad I chose violin." Interesting views. The important part of this exchange is that Libby's mom allows her to choose what she truly wants to play. I believe that is an important factor in retention. It is her choice.

Family members notice a change in Libby during the first year of her violin playing. Her stepfather says, "She pays closer attention to some of the music around her." Mom says, "She seems more confident." After a second year of violin, Libby's mom sees "improved motor skills," and finds "increased self-esteem and confidence [have] enhanced personal growth." She believes "music performance enhances school spirit and brings the community together. Musical expression is a beautiful way to honor people in the community. Music as creative expression serves as a bridge to allow for emotional release and healing. I wish band/orchestra would be introduced at an earlier age in the school curriculum." Yes, I also believe the emotional release is big in urban America.

This journey is coming to an end. We have reminisced with the stories of our travels but what do they mean? What do we see when we examine the pictures from our trip?

CONCLUSION—THE RETURN HOME

The students in my schools teach me about life. Maria teaches me to work outside of my cultural comfort zone and to be accepting of culture and language differences. Her story also poses the issue of providing for students with financial need. Lora appears to have no unique needs, but what lies beneath the surface? Robert teaches me to work with students who live with educational, emotional, or physical challenges. Libby shows me that children growing up in urban settings are also positive, productive students. Students become better organized, make more friends, and learn to be positive about themselves through an education in music. They also work on being more outgoing, and, I am sure, much more.

Good teachers equal more learning. Corbett and Wilson (2002) describe what students see in a good teacher. One point addresses relationships. A good teacher "took the time to get to know the students and their circumstances" (p. 18). I agree with the students. We need to get to know each other.

I was able to allow myself extra time to get to know these four students. Because of the case studies required for this work, extra time was set aside and students were released from homerooms for extra sessions to talk with me. The time is invaluable. If I were to do the same with all my students, I would not have time for the instruments. That is unfortunate and I do whatever I can in the time available to find out about my young musicians.

I love getting to know my students, and I find the varied ways in which they grow. That is what we see through their stories. The student comment from Corbett and Wilson's research hits home. These students are individuals with unique personalities and needs. I need to get to know as many as possible. I owe them that.

Communication with parents is also important. I know the connections do not always work, but I need to try. A note from a parent with a personal response is one way to communicate and to discover their views. Personal meetings are even better. After the early data were collected for my study, I decided to offer parent informational meetings at Nicolet School. These are my most impoverished and culturally unique families. I feel a need to meet as many as I can to explain the program and my expectations. I invite them to meet with me. A dozen take me up on my offer. It is a start. I need to try to connect. I owe them that.

Music is important for all students to have as part of their education. It may be even more so for urban students. It gives a means to make dreams and realize them. There are subjects and activities that can impact urban students, but the richness of music makes so much sense. It provides an emotional release. Again, I owe them that.

I cannot help but notice that there are facility inequalities in this case, too. The inequalities do not come between high- and low-income districts but within the district and within individual buildings. The inequalities are there but on a smaller scale.

The comparisons between student stories affirm that what I do for students is important. As I search for the impacts of music education for urban students, I find the tables turned. I find how the students impact me, their teacher. I have discovered, by talking directly to students and parents, that my job is important. I have become a more passionate advocate for urban students. I find that "urban" does not necessarily reflect the pictures you see of big-city education in television documentaries. The small, big cities also experience urban issues but on a smaller scale. This is a topic that needs to be addressed. I am optimistic. Through my study, I find that orchestra is important. Band is important. Music is important.

REFERENCES

Campbell, D. G. (1992). *Introduction to the musical brain* (2nd ed.). St. Louis, MO: MMB Music.

Catterall, J. S., Chapleau, R., & Iwanaga, J. (2000). Involvement in the arts and human development: General involvement and intensive involvement in music and theatre arts. In MENC (Ed.), *Music makes the difference: Music, brain development, and learning* (pp. 74–101). Reston, VA: MENC.

Corbett, D., & Wilson, B. (2002). What urban students say about good teaching. *Educational Leadership*, 60(1), 18.

Corbett, D., Wilson, B., & Williams, B. (2002). *Effort and excellence in urban classrooms.* New York: Teachers College Press.

Englert, R. (1993). Understanding the urban context and conditions of practice of school administration. In P. Forsyth & M. Tallerico (Eds.), *City schools leading the way*. Newbury Park, CA: Corwin Press.

Flaxman, E., Schwartz, W., Weiler, J., & Lahey, M. (1998). Trends and issues in urban education (ERIC Document Reproduction Service No ED 425 247).

Habermeyer, S. (1999). *Good music brighter children: Simple and practical ideas to help transform your child's life through the power of music.* Roseville, CA: Prima Publishing.

Hansen, D., Bernstorf, E., & Stuber, G. (2004). *The music and literacy connection.* Reston VA: MENC.

Jensen, E. (2000). *Music with the brain in mind.* San Diego, CA: The Brain Store.

Kozol, J. (1991). *Savage inequalities.* New York: Crown.

Lapp, D., Block, C. B., Cooper, E. J., Flood, F., Roser, N., & Tinajero, J. V. (2004). *Teaching* all *the children.* New York: Guildford.

Lawrence-Lightfoot, S., & Davis, J. H. (1997). *The art and science of portraiture.* San Francisco: Jossey-Bass.

Paley, V. G. (1995). *Kwanzaa and me.* Cambridge, MA: Harvard University Press.

———. (2003). *In Mrs. Tully's room.* Cambridge, MA: Harvard University Press.

Rarus, S. (2000). SAT scores of students in the arts. In MENC (Ed.), *Music makes the difference: Music, brain development, and learning* (pp. 56–57). Reston, VA: MENC.

Renfro, L. (2003). The urban teacher struggle. *Teaching Music*, 11(2), 36.

Student learning and performance data, 2003-04 school year. Report to the board of education of the Green Bay Area Public School District. January 18, 2005.

Weber, E. W., Spychiger, M., & Patry, J. (1993). *Music makes the school* (abridged version). Essen, Germany: "Die blaue Euel."

Weinberger, N. M. (1999). Can music really improve the mind? The question of transfer effects. *MuSICA Research Notes*, VI(2) retrieved January 31, 2003, from www.musica.uci.edu/mrn/V612S99.html.

IV

ALTERNATIVE TEACHING MODELS

12

A New Sound for Urban Schools: Rethinking How We Plan

Frank Abrahams and Patrick K. Schmidt

A TRUE STORY

We were told that the school was in one of the most dangerous parts of the city. We were warned not to wear blue or red clothing, lest we might anger students who belonged to either of the gangs who ruled the neighborhood. We were prepared for the worst.

Williams Academy (not its real name) was an arts magnet middle school. We visited at the invitation of the music teacher, Tameka Johnson (not her real name). This was Tameka's first year at Williams Academy and she was having difficulty. When we entered her classroom it was easy to see why. First, there was no furniture. "I've asked for chairs," she told us, "but, they don't seem to have any for me." There was no piano and no sound equipment, although sometimes Tameka would bring a boom box from home if her lessons included listening. We did see a brand-new set of music series books complete with editions for both students and teachers, as well as the CDs that accompanied them. "Do you use these?" we asked. "No, I don't. First, the students cannot read the words. But, more importantly, they cannot relate to the songs or to the lesson materials. So the books stay in the closet."

While there was no furniture or equipment in the room, there was evidence that music lessons were taught there. Posters of Leontine Price and Kathleen Battle lined the bulletin board. On the chalkboard were facts about Mozart. "What's all this?" we asked. Tameka explained that today's lesson would be on Mozart. This seemed peculiar in that earlier she said that the students didn't relate to the music in the series books. How would they possibly relate to all these facts about Mozart? But, we never got to see. There was a fight in between classes and the music class never happened.

"It's hard to build any skills," Tameka explained, since she never knew from one class to the next who would show up. There was no continuity and so each lesson had to be an entity unto itself. Her students were tough, hardened by deplorable family situations, and had little hope for the future. Most would not attend high school and of those who did, many would not finish. And for Tameka, she confessed that she just could not seem to find a formula for music lessons that would engage her students and ensure meaningful learning experiences.

Music teachers in urban districts agree that many of the strategies that work in suburbia are not applicable in the urban classroom. And while Tameka is herself from a minority culture, she prefers the music of Price and Battle to that of the contemporary hip-hop scene. The question then becomes "What do we teach our students when we turn our backs on the vast majority of the musical experiences they find meaningful?" (Bowman, 2004).

CRITICAL PEDAGOGY FOR MUSIC EDUCATION

Music teachers at all levels and in all situations, but particularly in urban schools, are faced with the issue of making classroom music relevant. As trends come and go, music teachers find it difficult to keep up with the music of pop culture and often find what they hear to be distasteful. The challenge is to determine what formal music education can offer to students who are more familiar with the music outside the school. Such music represents the social, cultural, political, and economic issues that define them, and therefore it deserves a prominent place in the organization and conceptualization of music curriculum and the planning of instruction.

Critical Pedagogy for Music Education (CPME) is a way to address this issue. Coined by the authors, CPME describes a teaching model that seeks to empower children in urban districts to be musicians by breaking down the barriers that separate "school music" from the music that children listen to and enjoy outside school. Based on the idea that meaningful learning results from teaching that is conversational and dialogic, the model synthesizes research and practice from three domains. First, CPME is grounded in critical theory, a postmodern perspective interested in the nature of reason, truth, and beauty and concerned with social transformation. Embedded within critical theory is the process of self-conscious critique. It provides a basis to perceive the complex interactions that exist between the individual, the school, and society. These are issues of paramount importance to children in urban classrooms. Next, CPME looks to experiential learning where children learn by constructing meaning for themselves. Such a perspective addresses the diversity of learning styles presented by students in urban classrooms. Finally, CPME promotes classroom activities that are praxial and integrate theory with practice. For this, the model looks to teaching strategies that encourage critical and creative thinking, student-centered learning, differentiated instruction, and strategies that enhance children's abilities to read language (Billmeyer, 2003). Adapting these to music education offers music teachers in urban schools alternatives to the traditional teaching methods that they find so unsatisfactory, and better connects them to the global issues now facing schooling.

Critical Pedagogy for Music Education is not a "method" that music teachers recognize like Orff, Kodály, Dalcroze, Suzuki, or Gordon. Instead, the goal of CPME is to use the knowledge about music that students bring with them to the classroom as a bridge to new learning. This results in a change of perception for both the students and their teacher. Several key principles define CPME. They are:

1. Music education is a conversation where students and their teachers pose and solve problems together. In music classrooms this means composing and improvising music in styles consistent with who the students are and the contexts in which they live.
2. Music education broadens the student's view of reality. For CPME the goal of music teaching and music learning is to effect a change in the way that both students and their teachers perceive the world. In urban settings, students and their teachers view the world through the lens of the urban experience and the music that defines that experience.
3. Music education is empowering. When students and their teacher "know that they know," one can claim that the phenomenon of *conscientization* has occurred (Freire, 1970). Conscientization implies a deep knowing that goes beyond the recall of information. It combines understanding with the ability to *act on the learning* in such a way as to effect a change. In this view, music is conceived as a verb of power. It evokes critical action and critical feeling by engaging students in musical activities that are both significant and consistent with what musicians do when they are making music.
4. Music education is transformative. For those teaching a CPME approach, music learning takes place when both the teachers and the students can acknowledge a change in perception. It is this change or transformation that teachers can assess.
5. Music education is political. There are issues of power and control

> inside the music classroom, inside the school building, and inside the community. Those in power make decisions about what is taught, how often classes meet, how much money is allocated to each school subject, or program, and so forth. Those who teach the CPME model resist the constraints that those in power place on them. They do this first in their own classroom by acknowledging that children come to class with knowledge from the outside world and as such, that their knowledge needs to be honored and valued.

At the center of CPME is the notion that music teachers cultivate habits of mind (Greene, 1995; Gardner 1999). The teaching emphasizes problem posing and problem solving where students acquire a new perception of their role in the community, society, and culture. For inner-city children, music education serves as an intervention for a reality where failure is often present. In addition, CPME creates possibilities for validating new and varied ways of musical knowing. Most importantly for urban children, music education, when connected to their experiences and meanings, adds value to their lives. Such an approach to music education charges students to be creative, critical, and aware individuals who are committed to change.

Engaging in CPME means developing teaching episodes that are empowering. Students are involved in thinking musically, but also in feeling and acting musically, always situating such processes in the political realm in which their education and lives are experienced.

A CPME views music not as a noun, but as a verb of power. Such power is multifaceted and has a wide range of meanings. A music education that defines music as a verb of power becomes a serious learning enterprise. It enables teachers to teach skills and connect to other subject matters, and encourages thinking in different ways (Gardner, 1983). Music as a verb of power suggests a view of music education that creates a democratic relationship between knowledge and our own realities. Such a realization leads to the transformation of ideas and actions.

Just as CPME is concerned with making connections between students and their realities, a critical perspective allows teachers to view their roles inside the context of their own realities. Like those of their students, such realities include previous experiences, and their own conceptions of the political, cultural, and economic components of schooling. They can connect what they know with what their students bring to the classroom and as a result, move together from what Ouchi (1981) calls the *is* to the *ought*.

PLANNING INSTRUCTION

When planning instruction Critical Pedagogy for Music Education teachers ask four questions. They are: Who am I? Who are my students? What might they become? and What might we become together? (Abrahams & Head, 2005)

Question 1: Who Am I?

At the center of Critical Pedagogy for Music Education is the idea of teachers as intellectuals: individuals that cultivate habits of mind (Greene, 1995; Gardner 1995), and who develop habits of breaking habits. This interaction of thinking about teaching and learning as an interconnected process fosters a dialogical relationship between teachers and students. CPME envisions the act of teaching as a provisional way of looking at problems, emphasizing specific things at particular times and making judgments that consider the context in which problems occur or where new problems are developed.

Music teachers in urban schools, like music teachers in nearly all teaching situations, are often isolated from other music teachers and from their own building colleagues. In the same way, music programs are sometimes isolated from education in general, and do not connect with the current politics of high-stakes testing and back-to-basics rhetoric. CPME provides a context for teachers to interact with their students and to create the space for critical and engaged thinking about music teaching and learning. Such realities include previous experiences, and political, cultural, and economic contingencies. These also include prior knowledge and the life experiences music teachers and their students bring to the music classroom.

Question 2: Who Are My Students?

Critical Pedagogy for Music Education acknowledges ideas developed by Paulo Freire (1993, 1985, 1983, 1970), who spent much of his career in Third World countries teaching illiterate adults to read. He believed that learning takes place when it connects to the student's lives, including their social and cultural experiences inside and outside of formal schooling. Similarly, if students with their teachers are constantly involved with school musical activities that are significant and meaningful to them, those experiences impact not only their own sense of self, but also how they perceive themselves within the greater community, society, and culture. Understanding who the students are and how they situate themselves inside their own culture affects all instructional decisions. A CPME view of music education then, opens the door of possibility to engage students not as the custodians of their cultures, but as creative, critical, and aware individuals, committed to changing and creating their cultures anew.

Question 3: What Might They Become?

Urban students live and deal with realities that are often oppressive, restrictive, and particular to their own socioeconomic situations. Issues of retention, mobility, unstable learning environments, and isolation are often present. These issues apply to teachers as well. Music as an art form for self-expression and socialization is a way to understand, question, conform, resist, and transform their worlds. In CPME, music education assumes a role in the constitutions of students that is more significant and more telling than any other aspects of their school lives. Music as a vehicle for self-expression and socialization is important and true, but music is also a way for students to understand, question, conform, resist, and ultimately transform their worlds.

Question 4: What Might We Become Together?

A CPME planning model creates strong connections among students, their teachers, and their cultures. CPME lessons encourage students to produce and add to their cultures in addition to appreciating and consuming them. Engaging in CPME means developing music lessons that challenge students to center upon their places in the world and their own realities. Thus, teaching and learning start from contextual situations and knowings and address the cultural elements that permeate and inform them, to knowledge that is already present in the teacher and in the students. Such a creation of meaning leads to a new set of musical realities and cements new relationships between the music students hear in the classroom and music they listen to in their own worlds. CPME lessons encourage students and their teachers to think, feel, and act critically. By providing scenarios for children to learn to work cooperatively together and to develop and encourage their individual musical potentials, the music lessons create the possibility for students to engage in a democratic relationship between musical skills, understandings, knowledge, and their own realities. Such a change transforms their ideas and actions.

CRITICAL PEDAGOGY FOR MUSIC EDUCATION LESSONS

Unlike traditional instruction that begins with an objective or concept, CPME lesson plans emerge as the result of students and their teacher engaging in and with the musical content (see table 12.1.) This redefines the role of music teachers who in CPME are ready to seize teachable moments as they appear inside the classroom. A sample lesson plan is presented in table 12.2.

CPME lessons actually flow in the way that musicians think. That is, musicians think in terms of musical forms. They relate easily to sonata form, or rondo, or theme and variations. One objective for CPME is to present

Table 12.1. The Critical Pedagogy for Music Education Lesson Planning Model

Critical Pedagogy	*Empowering Musicians*	*Lesson Steps*	*National Standards*	*Lesson Form*
Who We Are	Engaging Musical Imagination	1 Honoring Their World *Teacher engages the students in problem solving by creating an experience that presents a need to know.*	Experiencing Music (6, 7)	Exposition
		2 Sharing the Experience *Students and their teacher process the experience. They share feelings and reflect.*		
Who They May Become	Engaging Musical Intellect	3 Connecting Their World to the Classroom *Teacher connects the experience using comparable concepts from the other arts, cultures, or student out-of-school experiences.*	Connecting Music (8, 9)	Development
		4 Dialoguing Together *Teacher presents the lesson content. Students gather the evidence they need to solve the problem.*		
		5 Practicing the Content *Teacher provides students with an opportunity to practice the content. A homework assignment or quiz might be included at this step.*		
Who We Might Become Together	Engaging Musical Creativity	6 Connecting School Music to the Students' World *Teacher invites students to find alternative solutions and new ways to use the information presented. Students have the opportunity to create something new.*	Creating Music (3, 4, 5)	Improvisation
		7 Assessing Transformation *Students and their teacher reflect and evaluate the work completed. An assessment rubric may be applied at this step.*		
	Engaging Musical Celebration through Performance	8 Acknowledging Transformation *Students and their teacher celebrate the new learning through presentation, exhibition, or other form of demonstration.*	Performing Music (1, 2)	Recapitulation

Table 12.2. Rapping the Chant, Chanting the Rap: A Lesson for Upper Elementary or Middle School Students

Critical Pedagogy	*Empowering Musicians*	*Lesson Steps*	*National Standards*	*Lesson Form*
Who We Are	Engaging Musical Imagination	1 Honoring Their World Teacher poses the following problem to the students: You have been hired by the Grammy committee to nominate a rap artist for a new award category called "Hip-Hop Artist Whose Rap Best Represents Who You Are." As a class, decide what the characteristics of such a rap might be. List them on the chalkboard. Teacher chooses three examples of raps to play for the class, and students vote by secret ballot rating them according to the criteria they developed.	Experiencing Music 6, 7	Exposition
		2 Sharing the Experience Votes are tabulated and the results are announced. The teacher plays the winning rap and students are invited to "rap" along. Together they list on the chalkboard the characteristics that define "who they are" and how the winning artist was the most appropriate choice. Then, students imagine ***they*** are the winning artist and are asked to write their acceptance speech to be delivered at the awards ceremony. In the speech they must identify and thank those who helped shape "who they are" and "who they have become." Then, they must explain how the music portrays or represents that. Students share their speeches in a mock "Awards" ceremony in class.		
Who They May Become	Engaging Musical Intellect	3 Connecting Their World to the Classroom With drawing paper and markers, students are asked to design a logo or symbol representing the winning rap, without using words. Teacher tapes the logos onto a classroom bulletin board or wall. As students draw, teacher plays a recording of Gregorian chant.	Connecting Music 8, 9	Development
		4 Dialoguing Together Teacher asks the students, "Is rap really music? Although there is pitch inflection, tone, and dynamic contrast in the way they present language, is it melody?" Together they discuss. Then, teacher plays another example of Gregorian chant and asks the question "Is this music since there is no recurring rhythm or beat?" Students discuss and then the teacher asks,"What are the similarities? What are the differences?" Teacher uses a Venn diagram to show similarity and differences. A discussion follows in which the teacher guides students to		

		discover that both rap and chant are representative musics that define a particular dominant culture. That is, rap is the voice of hip-hop urban youth while Gregorian chant is the voice of the monks in the medieval church. Both encompass clothing, language, music, style, belief system. The teacher then asks, "What would it take to turn chant into rap?" A discussion follows. The teacher scribes the thoughts on the board. In class, students write a "rap" about "chant."		
		5 Practicing the Content Students listen to several more examples of Gregorian chant. If appropriate, they learn to sing one. Then, they listen to several more examples of rap. If appropriate they perform one. The teacher suggests the following: "What if the award show we did earlier was to reward a chant instead of a rap?" They discuss, and then together, the class with their teacher develops a rubric that the awards committee might use to judge chants.		
Who We Might Become Together	Engaging Musical Creativity	6 Connecting School Music to the Students' World In cooperative groups, students share the raps they wrote in step 4. They assess them against the rubric they developed in step 5. Then, they take the best elements of each group member's rap and turn it into a group rap. One member of the group scribes the rap. Then, a member of the group is selected to perform the rap while the other members of the group accompany using body percussion and vocal sounds.	Creating Music 3, 4, 5	Improvisation
		7 Assessing Transformation Each group performs. The class critiques according to the rubric developed in step 5. After, the students regroup and make the necessary revisions.		
	Engaging Musical Celebration through Performance	8 Acknowledging Transformation The students create a video to accompany their rap and burn it onto a DVD to be played at a later date.	Performing Music 1, 2	Recapitulation

musical experiences in the classroom that encourage children to think musically. Therefore, the lessons flow in a modified sonata form. They begin with an exposition and move through development and improvisation to recapitulation. The lessons begin in the children's world and move into the world of the classroom and then back into the outside world. In the process the children's perceptions of that world are changed.

CPME lessons meet content and benchmarks of the National Standards for Music Education (Music Educators National Conference, 1994). The lesson planning model includes places for each of the nine content standards. In addition, the model provides opportunity to integrate reading strategies that support the literacy initiatives so prominent in urban districts. Then, instructional content and teaching strategies are sequenced such that they accommodate the variety of learning profiles students bring to the classroom. When students are happy and have high self-esteem, they learn. Finally, CPME lessons have the flexibility to include Orff, Kodály, Dalcroze, or Gordon strategies. Party songs, movement, folk music, and the development of audiation skills are easily integrated at the teacher's discretion and when appropriate.

These lessons are not time bound. That means that they may take more than one class period to teach. This is because the steps are not even. Some steps may take longer than others. If students are composing in step 6, this may take several lesson periods. The section of the lesson where there is dialogue or discussion may take only a few minutes.

FINAL THOUGHTS

Paulo Freire said that while education is not a lever for the transformation of society, it could be. Similarly, while music education, as it is traditionally taught, is not a lever for the transformation of children and their teachers, it could and should be. CPME is a pedagogy of resistance and as such is concerned with the issues of power, control, and alienation inside schools. This view is wider than those that are ensconced in methodologies. CPME challenges teachers to explore possibilities that are beyond the specifics of a particular lesson plan or lesson planning model to broader and more important discussions. Changing the realities of music education in urban schools requires teachers to connect the social, political, economic, and cultural issues of schooling in general to the specifics of music curricula. CPME can provide a venue where together, teacher and students can initiate musical and literary dialogue. Such a systemic change will yield a new agenda for music education that is relevant and significant for children and their teachers in music classrooms everywhere.

REFERENCES

Abrahams, F. (2004). The application of critical pedagogy to music teaching and learning. *Visions of research in music education*, special issue (online, www.rider.edu/~vrme/special_edition/index.htm).

———. (2005, Spring/Summer). The application of critical pedagogy to music teaching and learning: A literature review. *Update: Applications of research music teaching*. Reston, VA: MENC: The National Association for Music Education, 12–22.

———. (2005). Transforming classroom instruction with ideas from critical pedagogy. *Music educators journal*, 92 (1), 62–67.

Abrahams, F., & Head, P. D. (2005). *Case studies in music education* (2nd ed.). Chicago: GIA.

Billmeyer, R. (2003). *Strategies to engage the mind of the learner*. Omaha, NE: Dayspring Press.

Bowman, W. (2004). "Pop" goes . . . ? Taking popular music seriously. In C. X. Rodriguez (Ed.), *Bridging the gap: Popular music and music education* (pp. 29–49). Reston, VA: MENC: The National Association for Music Education.

Delpit, L. (1995). *Other peoples' children: Cultural conflict in the classroom*. New York: The New Press.

Freire, P. (1970). *Pedagogy of the oppressed*. New York: Continuum.

———. (1985). *The politics of education*. New York: Bergin & Garvey.

———. (1993). *Pedagogy of the city*. New York: Continuum.

Freirer, P., & D. Macedo. (1987). *Reading the word and the world*. New York: Bergin & Garvey.

Greene, M. (1995). *Releasing the imagination*. New York: Jossey-Bass.

Music Educators National Conference. (1994). *National standards for arts education: What every young American should know and be able to do in the arts*. Reston, VA: MENC.

Ouchi, W. G. (1981). *Theory Z: How American business can meet the Japanese challenge*. New York: Avon.

Regelski, T. A. (2004). *Teaching general music in grades 4-8: A musicianship approach*. New York: Oxford University Press.

Schmidt, P. (2004). Music education as transformative practice: Creating frameworks for music learning through a Freirian perspective. *Visions of research in music education*, special issue (online, www.rider.edu/~vrme/special_edition/index.htm).

Wink, J. (2004). *Critical pedagogy: Notes from the real world* (3rd ed.). Boston: Allyn & Bacon.

13

Music of Every Culture Has Something in Common and Can Teach Us about Ourselves: Using the Aesthetic Realism Teaching Method

Edward Green and Alan Shapiro

As we enter our classrooms, we meet young people of various cultures and backgrounds. The National Standards for Music (as well as common sense) suggest that we should include in our curricula not only works from the Western classical and American popular traditions, but also music from many parts of the world, including Asia, Africa, the Caribbean, Eastern Europe, and the Middle East. But in many cases neither our training nor personal experience has prepared us for this. How can we as music teachers honestly relate to such diverse cultural traditions? And how can we encourage our students to value—without any prejudice—music from traditions other than their own?

In nearly 50 years of combined experience in the classroom, we have seen that the Aesthetic Realism Teaching Method answers these questions. This method is based on the philosophy founded in 1941 by the American poet and educator Eli Siegel (1902–1978), who taught that the purpose of all education is to like the world through knowing it. And the biggest interference to learning—and to art—is contempt, "the lessening of what is different from oneself as a means of self increase as one sees it" (Siegel, 1976). Contempt can take such everyday forms as a student summing up all of classical music with the statement, "It's boring!" or a teacher scornfully declaring,

"These kids are impossible." And contempt, as Aesthetic Realism explains, is also the cause of all injustice, including racism and war.

Teachers using this method—in the field of music and across the curriculum—have enabled young people at all grade levels, even those hard-hit by economic injustice, to learn successfully. And *through the subject*, Aesthetic Realism encourages people of different backgrounds to see each other with respect and kindness. This has been documented in articles that have appeared in many professional journals and newspapers throughout the country and overseas, some of which are republished on the website of the Aesthetic Realism Foundation in New York City (www.AestheticRealism.org).

Our chapter will illustrate the Aesthetic Realism method in the teaching of music in two ways. First, we will show how it is an approach free of cultural bias, for it begins at a point deeper than any single culture: the fundamental aesthetics of reality and the human mind. Then we will describe a specific lesson about one of the elements of music—rhythm—taught by Alan Shapiro in a New York City public high school, and show how the Aesthetic Realism method opposes prejudice where it begins.

In an essay titled "Music Tells What the World Is Like," Eli Siegel wrote (1975):

> Music for a long time has been telling what the world is really like. What music has to say now, in a manner that has both logic and emotion in it, is that the world has a structure persons could like; be stronger by. At this time, when there is less belief in the good sense of the world than perhaps at any time before, . . . it is well to show that the permanent structure of the world is beautiful and the most sensible thing possible.

Today, more than 30 years later, it is perhaps even harder for young people to believe in the good sense of the world, with so many parents out of work or afraid of losing their jobs, with Americans having greater and greater difficulty paying for the things they need most, with racism still prevalent and war going on. Yet there is evidence in music, and every subject of the curriculum, that the "permanent structure" of reality is something we can honestly like. It is described in this core principle of Aesthetic Realism: "The world, art, and self explain each other: each is the aesthetic oneness of opposites" (Siegel, 1967). This is the basis of the lessons we teach.

MUSIC OF EVERY CULTURE PUTS OPPOSITES TOGETHER

Increasingly, music teachers find their own training has not included the kinds of music cared for by their students. This is especially true in the urban setting. A teacher may know jazz, but may not know the music of the Chilean *cueca*. He or she may know Bach, but feel at sea when it comes to hip-hop, let alone the traditional music of Pakistan. For music teachers to do our jobs well, we have to honor the individuality of each culture, yet not isolate it; we need to be fair to the phenomenal diversity of world music, and still see—and show our students—that every instance of music making has something in common. While it is clearly unjust to deny people their cultural uniqueness, it is equally wrong to act as if the differences between people are larger than the kinships.

Aesthetic Realism enables us to meet our students' hopes, because it shows what all music has in common: opposites working as one. We give now some examples ranging from jazz, Arabic music, and Mozart, through Indian and Chinese music and the rap of Tupac Shakur.

Freedom and Order

A valuable and exciting way to compare music of different cultures is to study the essay "Is Beauty the Making One of Opposites?" by Eli Siegel, published in 1955. It is a series of 15 questions about how particular pairs of opposites are together in art. Originally written with the visual arts in mind, these questions shed new light on music as well. Teachers at all grade levels can use it as a guide and, with older students, as a classroom text. For example, there is this question about freedom and order:

> Does every instance of beauty in nature and beauty as the artist presents it have something unrestricted, unexpected, uncontrolled?—and does this beautiful thing in nature or beautiful thing coming from the artist's mind have, too, something accurate, sensible, logically justifiable, which can be called order?

With this question in mind, a teacher can show a class that improvisation—wherever it happens in the world of music, from the ragas of Ravi Shankar to the New Orleans jazz of Louis Armstrong—is both free *and* orderly, unexpected *and* logical. Then, as students learn about Arabic music, they will see that these same opposites are put together there as well—for instance, in the *nawbah*, a suite, in which the first part, the *taqsim*, is metrically free, while the section that follows is always in strict dance rhythm. And freedom and order, personal expression and accuracy about the object are also the central matter when a performer—whether from Shanghai or Detroit—interprets a musical composition. We can hear this in the diversity of performances of the pi'pa masterpiece "Ambush from Ten Sides," or in the two versions of "I Heard It through the Grapevine": energetic and upbeat as recorded by Gladys Knight and the Pips, sinuous and ominous as recorded by Marvin Gaye.

As you can see, this approach enables teachers to prepare technically strict lessons that gracefully relate music from around the world. Our experience has been that this is far more effective than teaching about musical cultures separately.

All true musicians and composers have, in their unique, individual ways, put together freedom and order, the unexpected and the symmetrical. About two of the masters of the Western classical tradition, Sir Donald Francis Tovey wrote (1935–39/1989):

> From one moment to the next [Haydn] is always unexpected, and it is only at the end that we discover how perfect are his proportions. With Mozart, the expectation of symmetry is present all the time, and its realization is delayed no longer than serves the purposes of wit rather than humour. Both composers are so great that in the last resort we shall find Mozart as free as Haydn and Haydn as perfect in form as Mozart; but the fact remains that Haydn's forms display their freedom before their symmetry, while Mozart's immediately display their symmetry, and reveal their freedom only to intimate knowledge. (pp. 351–352)

Freedom without any order is chaos, disorganization. Order without freedom is dull predictability. When we hear freedom and order together in a piece of music—whether it is one we are familiar with or one we are meeting for the first time—we respond. Like people on any continent, we are trying to put together these opposites in our everyday lives, too. We have asked our classes, "Do you like to do as you please, to be spontaneous, let loose?" Yes; sure! "And do you also like to have routines and make plans?" Everyone wants both—and we don't want them one at a time. Music can give every person hope because it shows order and freedom don't have to fight: they can work beautifully together. Stated Eli Siegel: "All beauty is a making one of opposites, and the making one of opposites is what we are going after in ourselves" (1967).

Rest and Motion

Consider now the opposites of rest and motion, stability and change. Has there ever lived a human being who didn't want both? No; and these are opposites present everywhere in music. There is, for example, the relation of a melody to a drone that we find in the bagpipe, whether of Scotland, Ireland, or Bulgaria. And in India, so important is this relation of the changeable and the fixed that melody instrument players are reluctant to play without a drone. The ethnomusicologist A. H. Fox-Strangways (1914) observed this when he heard two musicians playing oboe-like instruments at Tanjore "They took it in turns to play chanter and drone. When the second was asked to surcease from droning, the first said he felt 'like a ship without a rudder'" (p. 46).

Leaving India, we hear stability and change in much contemporary rap and hip-hop music, with its underlying "bed track" remaining constant throughout a song, while the rhythms of the words change. These Indian and contemporary rap musicians are comrades, across centuries and continents, of J. S. Bach, who was a master of the passacaglia: a form that also features a fixed element below—the ground bass—and a changing one above. Discussing the ways these and other instances of music put together rest and motion, stability and change, makes for exciting music education. We have seen delight and amazement on students' faces as they see, for example, that the "Crucifixus" of Bach's *Mass in B Minor* (figure 13.1) actually has something in common with Tupac Shakur's "Keep Ya Head Up" (1998—see figure 13.2).

Of course, we need to be careful critics of each instance of music, and encourage our students to be as well. For it would be just as wrong for us to say all music is of equal value as it would be for us to say greatness in music is a matter of style, or worse, nationality. But the fact remains that whatever the music, whatever the style, whatever the century—the opposites are there.

The deepest hope of every person, Aesthetic Realism explains, is to like the world, and when we and our students like a particular instance of music, we can ask: Is it the structure of reality we are liking? We have asked our students, for example, where else they see rest and motion, stability and

Figure 13.1. Ground Bass of "Crucifixus" from *Mass in B Minor*, by J. S. Bach

Figure 13.2. Bed Track (without Drums) of "Keep Ya Head Up"

change together. They've described seeing these opposites in a tree that changes with the seasons, while it is still *that* tree; and in a basketball game, as the players run, dribble, and shoot, while the court and baskets stay where they are. Yet motion and rest are often tormentingly awry in young (and older) people. A student may be nervous, agitated, and unable to sit still one moment, and dull, lethargic, and unable to stay awake the next. What people seek is what we find in music: the oneness of rest and motion, stability and change. It's a central reason why, in fact, we *like* music. Quite literally, it's "like" how we want to be!

In various educational situations, including elementary and high school levels, highly technical conservatory education, and adult music appreciation classes, we have seen that the Aesthetic Realism method, in explaining that all music has reality's opposites in common, enables students and teachers to listen to any type of music more perceptively, to be stirred where they might have been puzzled or even scornful, to have deeply engaging discussions about the various kinds of music they care for, and so, to learn from each other.

STUDENTS LEARN ABOUT THE WORLD AND THEMSELVES THROUGH AN INTRODUCTORY LESSON ABOUT RHYTHM

We go now from a discussion of the overall principles of the Aesthetic Realism method to a description of a specific 40-minute classroom lesson to give readers an idea of how these principles can be applied. This is a lesson Alan Shapiro has taught to classes in several New York City public high schools. Students like this lesson very much because through it they see evidence that the world has a structure that makes sense. And they begin to see both the cause of and the opposition to one of the most troubling and dangerous concerns in America today: prejudice. They see that opposites that are so corrupted in prejudice—sameness and difference—are beautifully one in a fundamental aspect of music: rhythm.

The first time I, Alan Shapiro, taught this lesson it was to eleventh graders at a high school in the Crown Heights section of Brooklyn, New York. The way students responded impelled me to write down what occurred, including their comments. Their names have been changed for this publication.

When I met these students, who were from Jamaica, Trinidad, Barbados, Guyana, Panama, Haiti, and Puerto Rico, as well as the New York City boroughs of Brooklyn, Queens, and Staten Island, it was clear they had found many reasons to feel the world didn't make sense and was against them. They were subjected every day to injustice; their lives were horribly affected by the profit-driven economy. Many were from homes where a single parent was working while also trying to take care of small children. Some had experienced violence in their neighborhoods and even in their own families. Early in the fall, several students had been robbed as they walked between the school and the building where the gym was located, a few blocks away. And in this neighborhood that is well-known for the tensions between Black persons and Jewish persons, they were understandably very angry at the racial prejudice they had met. Often, they were looked at suspiciously as they went into a store or walked down the street. In an early class, Kevin LaPlanche said with anger, pain, and also a desire to understand, "Police are always looking at us, coming up in our face. They think we're up to something, like we're going to rob somebody." And they felt teachers judged them unfairly by the clothes they wore, the music they listened to, the ways they spoke.

Early in my career, I began to study in Aesthetic Realism consultations. (Consultations are one way people study Aesthetic Realism. They are given to individual men, women, and young people—including via telephone—by consultants on the faculty of the Aesthetic Realism Foundation, NYC.) One of the things I wanted to understand was the difficulty I was having in the classroom, and some of the questions I heard from my consultants were: "Do you think your students are asking: 'What kind of ethics do you have? What matters to you? Do you really care about my liking music—or are you trying to be superior?'" Hearing these and other questions has made it possible for me—a White, Jewish man—to be truly affected by my students, including those I speak of here, most of whom are young African American, Afro Caribbean, and Latino men and women, and to have a good effect on them.

A big danger for students, like all people, is to use injustices they've endured to feel justified in scorning and being angry with everything. These same young people who were furious at the way they were seen could themselves make disparaging, contemptuous comments about each other—the food they like, the way they talk or dress—and this contempt hurts a person, makes them ashamed.

I knew that by approaching music through the Aesthetic Realism method, my students would be able to see that the various techniques of music demonstrate that reality has a structure they can respect, and that this structure is also in people—including the person sitting next to them in the classroom. It was with this purpose that I prepared to teach the subject of rhythm very early in the semester. Later, we went on to learn about melody, harmony, instruments, and musical form—all in terms of the opposites.

To begin this lesson, I asked the class to listen to a recording of a drum ensemble from Tahiti performing a short piece called *Ahuru Ma Piti* (1992), and think about what opposites the music puts together. I said we would use this example to get to a definition of rhythm. "What do you hear?" "I hear a drum," Richard Lopez said. "Just one drum?" I asked. "A lot of drums," he added. "How would you describe the sounds of the different drums?" Ralph Joseph said, "There's tapping and hitting," and he demonstrated on his desk, making a clicking sound with his pen, and making a deeper sound with his fist. "Are the different drummers playing in the same way?" I asked. Students said they weren't; the deeper sound was steady, while the higher, clicking sound changed, going faster and slower.

Based on what they had just heard, I asked the class how they would define *rhythm*, explaining that it has been very difficult to define. Lajuan Johnson said, "There's a steady beat." Ralph agreed and said, "It makes you want to move." Many other students spoke about the beat, too. We read these definitions from *The American Heritage Dictionary of the English Language*:

> Rhythm: 1. Movement or variation characterized by the regular recurrence or alternation of different quantities or conditions. 2. The patterned, recurring alternations of contrasting elements of sound or speech.

The word *recurrence*, students pointed out, has to do with the same thing happening over and over again, while "contrasting elements" has to do with difference. I read a third definition, one Eli Siegel gave in a lecture titled "The Rhythms, They Are There" (1970), a class in which he discussed not only musical but poetic rhythms: "Rhythm is sameness in difference of sounds or of anything." I asked the class, "Do you think all those sounds made by the Tahitian drummers were not only different, that they also had something in common that brought them together?" The students felt that was true: The sounds of these drums were the same *and* different, and together they made a dynamic, coherent composition.

To illustrate how rhythm at its very beginning puts together sameness and difference, I asked the class, "What's the simplest rhythm you can think of?" Tanja Williams, Lajuan, and Monique Ekwensi all started tapping on their desks in a steady pulse. "Can you make a rhythm with just one sound?" I asked. They didn't think so. I showed the class a metronome, and turned it on so it made one click. Clearly, we couldn't feel rhythm. Then I set the metronome to click a steady beat, and everyone agreed that now we *could* feel rhythm. "How are sameness and difference here?" "There's the same sound over and over," Michael Wall said. "Are all the sounds *just* the same?" I asked. Many said they were. I played exactly five clicks on the metronome. "Are those five different sounds?" We saw that the clicks, while sounding the same, happened at different times; they were the same *and* different. "And what's in between the sounds?" "There's a pause," one student said; "It's silent," said another. "Are there any two things more different than sound and silence?" "No!" several called out. These young people had looks of wonder and were eager to clap this fundamental rhythm.

I asked, "Do the different things—the different sounds themselves and the silences in between—add to each other?" They felt they definitely did. "And we can ask: How do we see what is different from us, including people who may look or sound different from us? Have you ever not liked something or not welcomed something simply because it was different?" Marlin Jones, with a sense of simple factuality, and also surprise and self-criticism that I respected very much, said, "Yeah, White people." I told the students that I learned from Aesthetic Realism that racism begins with the desire to dislike and feel superior to what is different from us. "And do you think," I asked, "that attitude is very ordinary?" As an example, I described how once I saw a friend washing the dishes differently than I did and I automatically assumed that my way was much better. Prejudice can include mocking a person's shoes or insulting their accent or the kind of music they like. "Does this attitude, which is contempt, make a person stronger or weaker?" I asked. For example, if a newborn baby didn't welcome air or food coming from the world different from himself, he couldn't live and grow. If a little girl didn't welcome words coming from the world, she would never learn to speak or read. Students saw this was true; many nodded, while others said, "That's right."

As to rhythm, I continued: "What we just clapped is called the beat, which is the steady pulse of music. It has beauty, but we wouldn't call it music yet." I read this sentence from *Self and World*: "An aspect of rhythm, or form in time, is the feeling of speed in slowness, slowness in speed" (Siegel, 1981, p. 120). Slowness and speed are different, but if one is *in* the other, then there must be sameness, too. To demonstrate this, we divided the class into two groups. Group A clapped a slow, steady beat, while Group B clapped a beat exactly twice as fast (see figure 13.3).

"Do you like that?" "Yeah," many students answered, and everyone looked pleased and interested. "How are the two parts the same and different?" Students described how they all clap together, and then Group B claps by itself before the two groups come together again. "As you do this," I asked, "do you feel both the same as *and* different from other people?" "Yes!" they said. "That feeling," I said, "is the opposition to contempt and prejudice—it is the pleasure of respect!"

As the lesson continued, we demonstrated other examples of how same-

Figure 13.3. A Slow, Steady Beat with a Beat Twice as Fast

ness and difference, speed and slowness work together. First, Group B clapped three times as fast as Group A (see figure 13.4). Next, Group A clapped twice for every three claps by Group B—two against three (see figure 13.5).

I explained that this is called a polyrhythm, a common feature of African music that also occurs in classical music, particularly the music of Brahms. This was a challenge, and the class liked trying to do it very much.

Finally, one group clapped the steady beat, while the other clapped the clave rhythm, which students were familiar with from Latin American music and is closely related to certain rhythms from Africa, where it probably originated (figure 13.6).

All the students had pleasure clapping the various combinations, and they saw in each case that the two rhythms being clapped together were not just different, they were the same, too; and in their difference they added to each other, and together made something more beautiful than either alone.

Through this lesson and others, my students changed; they learned the subject with eagerness, and became much more at ease. Byron Martine, who at the beginning of the term sat at the back of the room, did almost no work, and often called out with comments like "This is boring!" moved his seat to

Figure 13.4. Group B Clapping Three Times as Fast as Group A

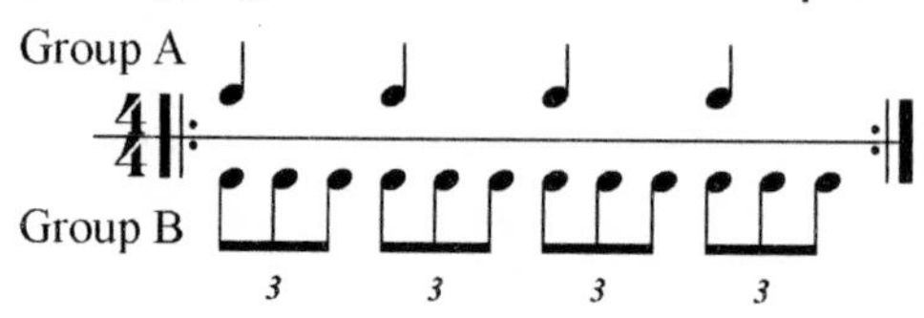

Figure 13.5. Group A Clapping Twice for Every Three Claps by Group B

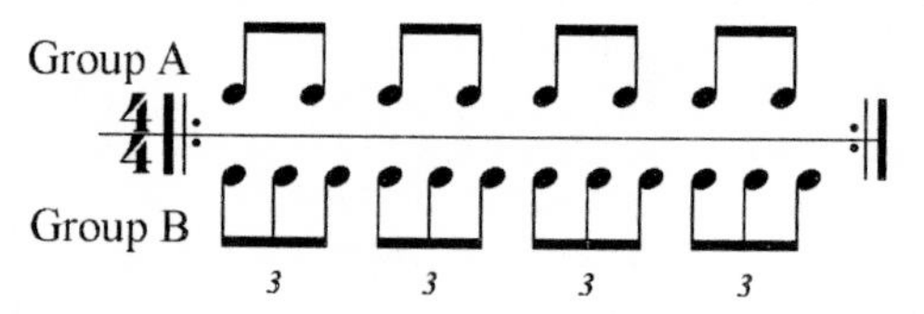

Figure 13.6. Group A Claps the Clave Rhythm while Group B Claps a Steady Beat

the front row, and did his work more seriously and with more pleasure. Olivia Reynolds, who early in the term said she saw herself as essentially different from the other students, wrote on a test that she liked learning about sameness and difference in rhythm "because it helped me to see things in ways I haven't seen before, about situations in everyday life, like how my peers can be the same as me and also different, [and] about how I should consider others' opinions and ideas, because they can be the same as mine or different, just as [mine] could be to someone else."

TEACHERS LEARN ABOUT CONTEMPT AND RESPECT

A teacher who doesn't want to see that students' feelings about music are as large as his or her own can make various pedagogical mistakes. We know this from personal experience. We may patronize our students and choose music we assume *they* will like, and not music that traditionally has been seen as great, like that of Beethoven or Mozart, feeling "they couldn't appreciate it." Or we may choose *only* the "classics," because we don't think anything popular could have real, lasting value. In "An Aesthetic Realism Manifesto about Education," there is this: "Teachers need to know they are more like their students than different. A tremendous mistake of teachers is not to see how like our students we are" (Perey et al., 1986). We need to ask: Do I have an unconscious stake in feeling superior to my students? As I look at other people, do I see them as fundamentally different from me, or as essentially the same? A large aspect of our personal gratitude to Aesthetic Realism is learning about the fight between contempt and respect, enabling us to become better critics of ourselves—and, in the process, better musicians and teachers.

Teachers of any subject or grade level can study the Aesthetic Realism method in a biweekly workshop, as well as in public seminars and individual consultations at the Foundation. Of particular interest to music teachers, there are: The Art of Singing: Technique and Feeling, taught by Carrie Wilson, and The Opposites in Music, a class in general music appreciation, taught by Barbara Allen, Anne Fielding, and Edward Green. More information, including how to study this method outside the New York area, can be found on the Foundation's website.

Most anyone who has taught in an urban school knows the great challenges there. Students often feel that the world as they've met it is unfriendly, and this can turn into the feeling: Why study anything? As music teachers we are in a unique position, and an advantageous one, because we are teaching a subject most students already like. When they are able to learn that what they are liking in music is the oneness of opposites, and that these same opposites are in the world they meet every day—at home with their families, on their neighborhood streets, in the events reported in the news—they come to see reality itself as more friendly and coherent, and are more ready to welcome learning the other subjects they study. And when students and teachers are able to learn that the same opposites that make for the beauty of music are in themselves and other people, near and far, we will be combating the contempt that causes racism, war, and economic exploitation. We will be approaching what Eli Siegel once called the culmination of all education: authentic good will. Aesthetic Realism therefore not only brings a new excitement to the study of music; it is also a means of having students—and teachers—be kinder to each other. It is a means of having music education be really useful!

REFERENCES

Ahuru Ma Piti. (1992). *Tambour du monde* [CD]. Playasound PS 66001.

American Heritage Dictionaries. (2000). *The American Heritage dictionary of the English language* (4th ed.). Boston: Houghton Mifflin.

Fox-Strangways, A. H. (1914). *The music of Hindostan*. Oxford: Oxford University Press.

Perey, A., Allen, B., Murphy, R., & Reiss, E. (1986). An Aesthetic Realism manifesto about education. *The right of Aesthetic Realism to Be known*, 703, 2.

Shakur, T., et al. (1998). *2Pac greatest hits*. Death Row records/Interscope records INTD2/90301.

Siegel, E. (1955). Is beauty the making one of opposites? New York: Terrain Gallery. Reprinted in *Journal of aesthetics and art criticism*, December 1955.

———. (1967). *Four statements of aesthetic realism*. New York: Aesthetic Realism Foundation.

———. (1970). The rhythms, they are there. Unpublished lecture. New York, Aesthetic Realism Foundation.

———. (1975). Music tells what the world is like. *The right of Aesthetic Realism to be known*, 93.

———. (1976). *An outline of Aesthetic Realism*. New York: Aesthetic Realism Foundation.

———. (1981). *Self and world: An explanation of Aesthetic Realism*. New York: Definition Press.

Tovey, D. F. (1989). *Concertos and choral works*. Oxford: Oxford University Press. (First published 1935–1939.)

14

Music Educators in the Urban School Reform Conversation

Carol Frierson-Campbell

MUSIC IN URBAN SCHOOL REFORM

Urban schools have been a critical part of the school reform conversation since the turn of the last century. Whether as the "crucible" to begin the process of assimilation, the training place for workers in the nation's industries and armies, or the last bastion of hope for the nation's impoverished children, schools in America's cities have long held the attention of educational policy makers and reformers. Since the beginning of this conversation, many have indicated that music is a worthwhile discipline for study in urban schools. If this were universally accepted, however, we would not need this chapter, or this book. Music teachers, who believe passionately in the power of music to change student lives, struggle daily to find a place in the school reform efforts that have, for better or worse, come to define *urban schooling* in the United States.

Part of this conversation concerns the role of teachers in the school reform process. Recent case studies of successful school reform efforts indicate that "reform-minded" teachers have a prominent role as

> the protagonists of change mindful of and responsive to the needs of their students and those conditions that create the best opportunities for the development of their students, classrooms, and school. As reforms evolve, their voices are heard, their choices recognized, their knowledge sought and interrogated, and their changes engaged and extended. (Thiessen & Barrett, 2002, p. 766)

Similarly, many school districts and educational administration programs are changing their emphasis from a traditional "top-down" management style to a collective kind of leadership in which all educational professionals, from paraprofessionals to grade-level teachers to special area teachers to building administrators, participate, with the principal serving as a "leader of leaders." This involves a commitment on the part of all to lead as experts in their subject area, their classrooms, and in the vision and mission of the school/district. "Teacher leadership" is a common label for this arrangement.

Wynne (2001) notes the following commonalities in the literature: Teacher leaders are expert teachers who "are consistently on a professional learning curve" (p. 5) and willingly share their knowledge with others. They are reflective practitioners who constantly seek what is best for children and use action research to test their own effectiveness. They "collaborate with their peers, parents, and communities, engaging them in dialogues of open inquiry/action/ assessment models of change" (p. 5). Finally, they are "risk-takers" who are active at the building level as leaders and mentors, and who work with colleges in the preparation of new teachers.

Spillane, Hallett, and Diamond, three researchers who study the ways teachers impact school reform efforts, have found that teacher-leaders are "fundamental in efforts to change instructional practices" (2003). Thiessen and Barrett (2002) apply this concept to "reform-minded music teachers," suggesting that they have "the capacity . . . to act as savvy, informed change agents" (p. 759). They assert that "right from the outset of and continuing throughout their careers, the professional work of teachers encompasses an intricate web of responsibilities" (p. 761) that includes music classrooms, the school corridors, and the community beyond the school. My research, however, indicates that music teachers may not have opportunities for this kind of leadership, particularly in urban settings.

THE SOUND WAYS OF LEARNING PARTNERSHIP

In 1999, the College of Education at William Paterson University joined two other New Jersey universities to form the New Jersey State Teacher Quality Enhancement Consortium. The coalition was created to implement a five-year Federal Teacher Quality Enhancement grant that was awarded to a number of university coalitions across the country to support efforts to develop school reform partnerships between Colleges of Education and high-needs, culturally diverse urban schools in the region served by each consortium. While our partnership was begun under the guise of developing a professional development school (PDS) relationship, these findings relate to music educators working in any kind of school reform effort.

Initially, our College of Education (COE) chose five schools from three city school districts in New Jersey as preliminary sites. COE faculty members were recruited to serve as liaisons between each PDS site and the university and to plan and coordinate partnership activities at their site. The grant required the involvement of arts and science faculty from the university but did not stipulate a specific role for their participation.

Pre-planning

The grant application process provided the initial direction for the partnership, as it required clear goals with measurable outcomes that had the capacity to impact urban education at the local, regional, and state level. This forced us to expand our vision from serving teachers at the local level to impacting the music education community on a broader level. It is impossible to overemphasize the importance of these goals to the overall project; they provided benchmarks throughout the duration of the project. In addition to the partnership goals, I established "navigational points" and "unacceptable rationales" for the project prior to getting involved.

Navigational Points

- Belief in importance of music as a discipline for students of all ages and cultures.
- Desire to become involved in urban music education as researcher and colleague.
- Belief in interdisciplinary education that is true to all disciplines, both in a discrete and a multidisciplinary sense.

Unacceptable Rationales

- The idea that music education is purely for "relaxation" or "enjoyment" without a disciplinary or skills base in the curriculum.
- The idea that the purpose of music education is to enrich other academic subjects without recognition of the academic nature of musical skill and knowledge.

Method

As the coordinator of the music partnership, I was determined to focus on the needs of the music teachers from the partner schools rather than those noted by their administrators, the grant directors, or even my own perceptions. For this reason I began to collect data related to the participants' needs from the outset of the project. The nature of the study evolved as the partnership developed. Eventually the data that comprise this study came from three types of interactions:

1. On-site interviews and observations of a small number of music teachers and administrators make up the first year's data.
2. Data from the second year consist of field notes from a series of meetings on the WPU campus with a somewhat larger group (n=9) of music teachers who became the advisory group for the fledgling music partnership.
3. The third year's data reflect the results of a formal needs assessment administered to all music teachers from the three districts served by the COE partnership (n=76). While it was not planned beforehand, our interactions fell naturally into stages marked by the school year.

Who Are You and What Do You Want?

The process of building the partnership began with a series of unstructured interviews and observations. This involved making "cold calls" to administrators and music teachers in each of the COE's partner schools. It took a few attempts before I realized the hierarchies in these districts. I learned to speak to building administrators in order to gain access to music teachers, and eventually I was able to visit the administrator and music teacher at each partner school. None of the music teachers was aware of their school's participation in the partnership.

I have previously referred to this stage of our relationship as the "who are you and what do you want?" stage (Frierson-Campbell, 2003). It is uncomfortable, particularly after committing to action and being provided with resources, but it seems to be a necessary part of any successful partnership. Robinson (2000) mentions similar stages in his review of the arts partnership literature. My journal during the first year of the partnership reflects a growing understanding that Title I schools that had also been designated "Abbott" (New Jersey's "failing school" designation) provided few opportunities for the music teachers to participate in the school reform efforts that each of their schools was required to undertake.

Forming the Core

Research indicates that activities rather than goals propel partnerships through their initial stages (Robinson, 2000). With this in mind we invited the PDS music teachers to come to the university to move the music partnership forward. Planning for this meeting began on September 11, 2001; the events of that sad day meant that it was not until February of 2002 that we actually met. Since the COE partnership had expanded to five schools by year two, a total of 11 teachers were invited to attend a professional development session at the university. The agenda consisted of explaining the basic goals of the partnership and leading participants to brainstorm about ways we could meet their instructional needs. The participants were enthusiastic, and the meeting concluded with an ambitious list of needs to be met, primarily related to materials, professional development, and recognition. While more concrete issues (materials and training) are the easiest to address in a partnership relationship, notes from the first meeting indicate the greatest interest in the area of professional recognition: *There is a strong sense among these attendees that they need a collective voice that has the power to speak about the needs of urban music teachers in a more public forum. . . .*

The group met a total of three times before the end of the school year. During the second meeting, based on a strong sense that conveying the importance of music in urban schools to state leaders would bring them more recognition in their day-to-day work, the group decided to focus most of their energy on the creation of a mission statement. A third meeting was called for that purpose, and at that meeting the group decided that involving all of their colleagues—all of the music teachers from the three urban districts in the partnership—would help them create a stronger mission statement. This idea propelled us into year three of our relationship.

The Formal Needs Assessment

Reaching out to all of the music teachers from the three partner districts changed the direction and scale of the music partnership. Instead of planning activities at individual schools to respond to the needs of specific music teachers, we began to analyze music teacher need from a broader perspective. Although we continue into the present to define our model as the Professional Development School, in many ways this activity launched our partnership into a more traditional "arts partnership" role, one with less interaction between partners, where the university provides content designed to meet the professional development needs of its partners.

Our needs assessment was scheduled in September of 2002 as a full-day in-service workshop for all music teachers from the three partnership districts. The president of the state MEA and members of its Multicultural Awareness Committee were also invited to speak and participate in the event. The formal needs assessment followed the three-phase model suggested by Altschuld and Witkin (1995). Briefly, during the *pre-assessment* stage a committee is formed to decide whether there are needs to be met. The advisory group from the second year served as this committee. The *assessment* stage involves formal assessment of a constituent group for the purpose of understanding and prioritizing the perceived needs of the participants. Our in-service day provided quantitative data for the needs assessment; qualitative data including observations and unstructured interviews were held with the advisory group. The *postassessment* stage involves identifying and selecting solution strategies; we began this stage in the spring of 2002 with a second full-scale event, this time focusing on the professional development needs that were indicated by the participating teachers.

The needs assessment was based on the question: "*What is needed to take urban music education from where it is now to where it could be?*" The day was structured to direct participants to construct and then prioritize their professional needs both as individuals and as a group, to give focus to our mission statement and to the partnership. Participants were organized by specialty (general music, band, or chorus) and then divided into focus-type groups of approximately nine people. Each focus group was facilitated by one of the coalition music teachers (CMTs). The process began with a dialoguing exercise that served to prepare the participants for the in-depth conversations that would comprise most of the day's activities. In the next activity, individual participants created "mind-maps" around the question of the day. They shared their maps with a partner and later with their groups. Each group then created a prioritized list of professional need based on the lists created by each individual. In a final presentation, each group presented their 8–10 priorities to all of the teachers in attendance. The priorities listed by two or more groups included the following:

- Facilities 8
- Supplies/Instruments 7
- Administrative/Collegial (nonmusic) support 5
- Funding 4
- Scheduling 4
- Discipline 3
- In-District Networking/Staff Development 2

Participants were also asked to complete an open-ended questionnaire to further define and strengthen the data related to their professional needs. The questionnaire, based on a survey by Fiese and Decarbo (1995), was returned by 52 out of the 76 music teachers in attendance at the workshop. Not every respondent answered every question. Still, answers provided by those who did respond provide interesting insights about music educators in these three districts' school reform efforts. Respondents' answers were categorized post hoc.

The first question had two parts: "Did your undergraduate/graduate education courses prepared you to teach in the urban setting? If yes, what specific areas in your education prepared you? If no, what areas would you suggest need to be included?" A majority of respondents (66.7%) indicated that their undergraduate preparation had not prepared them for teaching in an urban setting. Fifty-seven percent responded that *experience teaching in the urban environment* should be part of undergraduate training. *Navigating the school culture* (dealing with administrators, getting by with limited resources, understanding that the system breaks down sometimes) was mentioned by an additional 16%. *Discipline specific training, educational issues* (primarily having to do with overcoming language barriers), and *musical/cultural issues* (music for diverse cultures of students) rounded out the lot.

Fiese and DeCarbo (1995) surveyed 20 urban music teachers who were recognized by state-level MEA presidents as highly successful. Their responses to this question—published almost seven years before our survey—were almost identical. Responses to Fowler's 1970 interviews of music teachers from urban schools are also strikingly similar, stressing the need for teacher education programs to provide a realistic picture of urban education, use culturally relevant curricula, emphasize general music as well as performance, emphasize a broader spectrum of musical genres, and provide "in-depth cultural, sociological, and psychological understanding of the students" (p. 83).

The second question asked participants about their practice: "Can you describe one or two specific teaching techniques, strategies, or approaches that you have found to be particularly effective for teaching music in the urban situation?" Specific musical approaches (i.e., the Kodàly method) or teaching approaches (i.e., Gardner's Project Approach) were recommended by 11% of the respondents. Forty-one percent responded with either a *general teaching approach* (present content in small doses in an organized way) and another 41% with a *general musical approach* (use movement to keep students interested; relate concepts to music the students are familiar with).

The answers from the successful teachers surveyed by Fiese and DeCarbo were somewhat different, implying a broader sense of curriculum than most of the answers in the current survey. Many of those respondents indicated the importance of having "the respect of the students and control of the teaching/learning environment," being a master of the subject, understanding technology, and finding "a way to relate to the students initially and then adapt the curriculum with that in mind" (p. 28). They also mentioned group work, cooperative learning, and peer teaching as techniques that involved students in their own learning.

The third question asked teachers, "What factors have most contributed to your personal success as a music teacher in the urban setting?" Most responses fell into two categories: *personal traits* (flexibility, love of music teaching and/or children, patience, and stubbornness) and *professional traits and knowledge: teacher-ship* (ability to relate to students, having and communicating high standards, putting in extra effort, and being involved in the school community). A notable number of responses fell into the category of *professional traits and knowledge: musicianship* (knowledge of piano, knowing what students listen to). Other categories revealed in this question include *professional opportunities* (workshops, seminars, and earning a paycheck), *school environment* (mentioned by only four participants), and *prior experience* (having primarily to do with growing up in an urban environment). A few teachers (four out of 46) mentioned that administrator support and school size were important aspects of their success.

Fiese and DeCarbo's (1995) respondents indicated that support networks ("teachers, supervisors, mentors, and others") were very important to them. It is clear from their responses that going "beyond the classroom" to take classes, attend conferences, and contribute to the school community both inside and outside the building were factors that they considered key to their success (p. 29).

The next questions asked respondents for their opinions: "What general comments do you have related to improving music education in the urban schools?" A third of the respondents indicated that *facilities/supplies/funding* was their greatest need. Seventeen percent indicated a need for *professional development*, including understanding music in context of culture; eliminating bias against non-Eurocentric music; integrating music across the curriculum; having higher standards for students. *Support from administration and school community* was mentioned by 13% of respondents. Thirteen percent of respondents mentioned *scheduling* while 11% mentioned *class size* and another 11% suggested *coordination of the music teacher agenda* (networking and sharing ideas, centralizing supplies, maintaining high hiring standards, seeking a state mandate for music). Responses to this question were markedly similar to those of the focus groups discussed earlier.

While many of the responses from our participants indicated needs that were beyond themselves, the majority of suggestions from Fiese and DeCarbo's respondents were more personal. They noted the need for relevant training by qualified trainers in the area of management skills, repertoire choices, multicultural education, and "the psychology of urban students" (p. 29). Some suggested that they needed a greater understanding of how to reach low income students, and that such understanding needed to be integrated schoolwide. Finally, they noted the importance of relationships "among music teachers, administrators, and music supervisors." As Fiese and Decarbo note, "Having all of the constituencies involved in dialogue, rather than parallel monologues, for the advancement of the students' music education is perhaps one of the central features of successful urban school music programs, according to the respondents" (p. 30).

Two questions specific to this project asked participants' for their opinions about the needs assessment and about future professional development opportunities. When asked, "Which of today's activities was most valuable for you?" 50% responded that *networking* (*getting out of school—being with colleagues; talking to the person next to me, who does a job similar to mine, but on the other side of town*) was the most valuable part of the day. Other activities (*the jazz workshop, the mind-mapping exercises, the setting of priorities*, even *venting*) were also mentioned. It is notable that simply having an opportunity to interact with discipline-specific teaching peers was the activity these music teachers found to be the most useful. When asked, "What issues do you suggest we target for our next workshop?" the majority of respondents mentioned issues that implied action beyond the classroom. These included *policy issues* (bringing our needs to the larger educational community; state mandates; getting teachers to agree on a plan of action), *district-level issues* (educating administration as to the viability of music and its relation to education), and *building-level issues* (convincing and educating administrators and building-level peers, improving scheduling and facilities).

In New Jersey, schools that receive Title 1 funding or have acquired Abbott status are required to be involved in one of the whole school reform (WSR) models. Each of these models stresses the importance of teacher involvement in the reform process. A common feature of these models is site-based management, in which a small advisory team of teachers assists in the governance of the school. Each member of the advisory team creates a secondary team and all members of the school's faculty are required to serve on one of these teams. Collaborative planning is another feature of most school reform models. To investigate the kinds of opportunities these music teachers had for collegiality in and outside their buildings, four additional questions were posed:

1. How much planning time do you have in the school day?
2. How does this compare to the time given other teachers in your building?
3. How much time do you have time to plan/collaborate with music teaching colleagues? With grade-level colleagues?
4. How does this compare to the time given other teachers in your building?

Participants who responded to these questions indicated that while "prep time" is roughly equal for music teachers and grade-level teachers (one "prep" each day), it is not *equitable* in many of the buildings where they teach. Roughly half (15 out of 27 respondents) indicated that they had no time to collaborate with other teachers in their buildings (nine of the 27 indicated one collaborative planning period each week; an additional three indicated one period each month), and a large majority, 39 out of 47 respondents, indicated that they had no opportunities for collaboration with other music teachers during their work time. This is in stark contrast to grade-level teachers who have both daily "prep time" and weekly "grade-level" meetings for the purpose of collaboration.

An interesting example of the role special area teachers play in the WSR process was revealed in an earlier interview with a member of the advisory group. This is how one music teacher describes his involvement in his school's "special" teachers school reform team:

> see, what they do, in here, is that they put together the music teachers, the art teachers, and the gym teachers, and we all sit together and say "what are we doing here" and we write down some issues that nobody reads. You know . . . and that's not right.

Thiessen and Barrett (2002) suggest a very different reality; one in which reform-minded music teachers have opportunities to "work with colleagues and other stakeholders . . . in ways that

- Build their capacity for joint work;
- Focus on school-based, collaborative, and inquiry-oriented professional learning;
- Create a balance and connection between disciplinary and interdisciplinary curriculum practices; and
- Expand their involvement in and commitment to making shared decisions about classroom and school improvement." (p. 770)

DIRECTION FOR THE FUTURE

The results of the two stages of needs assessment used to provide direction for our partnership have implications well beyond this project. Our experience and the results of our needs assessment suggest that it is possible to create a partnership to meet the professional needs of music teachers from urban schools involved in whole school reform, but they also suggest that the definition of *need* and the role of music teachers in the reform process should be explored further by music teachers, teacher educators, and others who have a stake in urban education.

Sociologists use the term *capital* to describe the often intangible human resources that make people successful in their jobs and daily lives. Forms of capital include *human capital* (skills, knowledge, and expertise), *cultural capital* (ways of being), *social capital* (networks and relations of trust), and *economic* or *physical capital* (material resources). James Coleman (1988) is credited with the first application of this concept to education. He explains it this way:

> Social capital . . . comes about through changes in the relations among persons that facilitate action. If physical capital is wholly tangible, being embodied in observable material form, and human capital is less tangible, being embodied in the skills and knowledge acquired by an individual, social capital is less tangible yet, for it exists in the *relations* among persons. Just as physical capital and

> human capital facilitate productive activity, social capital does as well. For example, a group within which there is extensive trustworthiness and extensive trust is able to accomplish much more than a comparable group without that trustworthiness and trust. (pp. S100–S101, emphasis in original)

Spillane and colleagues (2003) studied the relationships between educators in eight Chicago public elementary schools to understand how capital and teacher leadership impact reform in urban schools. While school administrators in their study were considered leaders on the basis of who they were (their cultural capital), certain teachers were also considered by their peers to be leaders in the reform process. The researchers found that teachers were "more likely to be constructed as leaders on the basis of their human capital" (pp. 10–11), or the skills and knowledge they exhibited to their peers. As they describe it, "the social capital among teachers is a basis for the construction of leadership. The teachers in this group constructed each other as leaders on the basis of this social capital, facilitating the dissemination of human capital" (pp. 8–9). "Specialist" teachers were not seen by "ordinary" (i.e., grade-level) teachers as leaders because grade-level teachers defined leadership as the capacity to help them "learn about and change their teaching practices" (p. 11).

The majority of needs stated by the music teachers involved in this project (primarily facilities and supplies) are examples of *economic capital.* While these are very real needs, economic capital was not seen by the urban teachers in Spillane's study as indicative of leadership. Instead, teachers constructed those who shared educational insights and expertise as leaders. In sociological terms, the grade-level teachers from the Chicago schools constructed their peers "as leaders on the basis of their human capital" (p. 11), and the development of human capital was facilitated by social capital such as grade level meetings (p. 9). The music teacher responses to the *Sound Ways of Learning* questionnaire noted a desire for further opportunities to develop social capital—expressing that the most valuable part of the formal needs assessment for them was networking—but it is clear from their responses that they have little or no opportunity to develop the kinds of teacher-leadership skills that support the reform process.

Michelle Zederayko (2000), a researcher and art education professor from Toronto, Canada, had different but related results. She studied an urban high school in Canada where arts educators were credited with turning the school climate from one of failure to one of success. This school had not adopted a formal arts-based-reform model; it had simply made a decision to support the arts and arts participation for all students. The arts teachers responded by building strong programs that met the needs of as many students as possible.

Zederayko found that the music and visual art teachers in the school who were the catalysts for the successful reform effort *and were credited by their administrators as such*, did not see their efforts as teacher leadership. As Spillane and his colleagues note (2003): "The construction of leadership does not presume intent by leaders. . . . People are often unwitting leaders, and it is not surprising that when followers label someone a leader, the leader may respond by saying, "I am?" (p. 9). Zederayko warns that this difference in the definition of *leadership* as understood by administrators and arts teachers could undermine communication between these two groups. It was beyond the scope of our assessment to explore differences between administrators' and music teachers' perceptions of leadership, but the fact that more than half of the focus groups in our formal needs assessment mentioned administrative support as a concern, and that this concern was reiterated in individuals' responses to the questionnaire, suggests that communication between the music teachers and administrators in our partner districts may be a concern.

CONCLUSION

This discussion does not intend to play down the importance of materials, supplies, facilities, or program funds to urban music educators. All of those things are certainly critical for high-quality music programs. It does suggest, however, that "need" on the part of music educators involved in urban school reform encompasses several issues beyond the usual trappings of the music room. Coleman (1988) noted that *social capital* is a resource that people "can use to achieve their interests" (p. S101). But opportunities for building social capital, such as formal and informal interactions between music teachers with teachers and administrators at the building level, and with the larger educational enterprise, are almost entirely absent from the professional lives of these music teachers.

Thiessen and Barrett (2002) cite an idealized (and fictional) middle-school music teacher who has jumped into her school's reform efforts with both feet. Her professional life is strikingly different from the reality described by our participants. As she tells it:

> My life in school is very different now that my school has agreed to participate in a school reform network. The nature of my work includes more time with colleagues, more involvement in school-level decisions, more contact, and even partnerships with more people outside the school . . . all of which enrich and extend the professional role I play." (p. 767)

This kind of participation was not expected by, required of, or available to most of the music teacher participants in our assessment.

If music education is to become a critical piece of the urban school reform conversation, then the role of music educator in schools, urban and otherwise, must expand beyond the music classroom to include the corridors and community on both a micro and macro scale. Emphasizing *only* the classroom work of music teachers "fails to adequately acknowledge the work of teachers in other contexts and, consequently, underplays the inter-dependence of what teachers do inside and outside the classroom" (Thiessen & Barrett, 2002, p. 761). As Zederayko noted, the skills that many arts teachers use in their daily work have the capacity to make a positive difference in the climate of a school. But this will not happen if music educators do not have and do not take opportunities in their work lives to join the conversation.

The William Paterson Sound Ways of Learning partnership began with a generous grant from the New Jersey State Teacher Enhancement Consortium. The outreach part of the project continues to be supported by a grant from William Paterson University's Provost's Incentive Fund, while related research is supported by an Assigned Release Time Award. The author is grateful for this support.

REFERENCES

Altschuld, J. W., & Witkin, B. R. (2000). *From needs assessment to action: Transforming needs into solution strategies*. Thousand Oaks, CA: Sage.

Coleman, J. S. (1988). Social capital in the creation of human capital. *American Journal of Sociology,* 94 (supplement), S95–S120.

Conkling, S. W., & Henry, W. (1999). Professional development partnerships: A new model for music teacher preparation. *Arts Education Policy Review*, 100 (4), 19–23. Retrieved February 8, 2003, from www.hwwilsonweb.com.

Fiese, R. K., & DeCarbo, N. J. (1995). Urban music education: The teachers' perspective. *Music Educators Journal*, 81(6), 27–31.

Fowler, C. (1970). Teacher education: Stop sending innocents into battle unarmed. *Music Educators Journal, Special Issue*.

Frierson-Campbell, C. (2003). Professional need and the contexts of in-service music teacher identity. In H. Froelich, D. Coan, & R. R. Rideout (Eds.), *Social dimensions of music, music teaching, and learning*. Amherst, MA: University of Massachusetts.

Parsons, M. (1995). A PDS network of teachers: The case of art. In M. Johnston, P. Brosnan, D. Cramer, & T. Dove (Eds.), *Collaborative reform and other improbable dreams* (pp. 223–231). Albany: State University of New York Press.

Robinson, M. (2000). A theory of collaborative music education between higher education and urban public schools (unpublished doctoral dissertation, Eastman School of Music of the University of Rochester).

Spillane, J. P., Hallett, T., & Diamond, J. B. (2003). Forms of capital and the construction of leadership: Instructional leadership in urban elementary schools. *Sociology of Education*, (76), 1–17.

Thiessen, D., & Barrett, J. R. (2002). Reform-minded music teachers: A more comprehensive image of teaching for music teacher education. In R. Colwell and C. Richardson, *The new handbook of research on music teaching and learning*. New York: Oxford, 759–785.

Wynne, J. (2001). *Teachers as leaders in education reform. ERIC digest* (ERIC Document Reproduction Service No. ED462376).

Witkin, B. R. & Altschuld, J. W. (1995). *Planning and conducting needs assessments: A practical guide*. Thousand Oaks, CA: Sage.

Zederayko, M. W. (2000). The impact of administrator and teacher leadership on the development of an exemplary arts program and its role in school reform: A case study. *Dissertation Abstracts International*, 61, 04A (UMI number 9971274).

About the Contributors

Daniel Abrahams is currently a music specialist at Bryan High School in the Omaha Public Schools, where he has taught at the elementary, middle school, and high school levels. A native of Philadelphia, Mr. Abrahams holds degrees from Temple University and the University of Nebraska at Omaha. Currently, he is a doctoral candidate at Shenandoah Conservatory, where his research centers on the applications of differentiated instruction in urban music education programs.

Frank Abrahams is professor of Music Education and chair of the Music Education Department at Westminster Choir College in Princeton, New Jersey. An expert in the applications of learning styles to music teaching and learning, he has written and lectured extensively on Critical Pedagogy for Music Education. His latest book is *Case Studies in Music Education*, 2nd edition, published by GIA.

Carlos R. Abril is assistant professor of music education at Northwestern University. He has many years of experience teaching in urban schools and currently directs a music program for at-risk youths in the Chicago Public Schools. His research focuses on multicultural issues in music education and the general music curriculum.

Cathy Benedict is currently an assistant professor as well as the coordinator of Undergraduate Studies in Music Education at New York University. Her interests lay in the reciprocity of the teacher/student, student/teacher relationship and the difficulties in facilitating music education environments in which students engage in a transformative process so that they are encouraged to take on the perspective of a justice-oriented citizen.

Regina Carlow is assistant professor of Choral and General Music Education at the University of New Mexico. Her research interests include culturally responsive curriculum in music education, teaching bilingual and multilingual students in music classes, accommodating students with special needs in choral ensembles, and adapting a Kodaly-centered curriculum and teaching sequence to multicultural populations. She is a choral conductor, clinician, and adjudicator specializing in youth and children's choirs.

Jeanne Porcino Dolamore has degrees from the Crane School of Music and Long Island University, and studied violin pedagogy with Kato Havas in England. After teaching string music on Long Island and in Colchester, England, for several years, Ms. Dolamore began developing a unique string program in the Poughkeepsie City School District. She is founder and artistic director of the Flying Fiddlers String Chorale (FFSC), a not-for-profit community string ensemble for elementary and middle school students, which has been selected by both ASTA (2002) and MENC (2005) to perform and give demonstration seminars on Strings and Community.

Donna T. Emmanuel, currently an assistant professor at the University of North Texas, holds degrees from the University of Michigan and Michigan State University. She has taught in inner-city schools in Florida and Michigan, and worked extensively with the Detroit School District. She worked as a research associate with Dr. Hal Abeles in evaluating arts-centered education programs in Detroit, and was a research assistant for Dr. Richard Colwell with the second edition of *The New Handbook of Research on Music Teaching and Learning*.

Carol Frierson-Campbell, assistant professor of Music Education at William Paterson University, holds degrees from Tennessee Technological University, Ithaca College, and the Eastman School of Music. An active member of the William Paterson faculty, she teaches courses in music education and graduate research. Carol's professional activities focus on improving curricula and support for music education in urban settings.

Edward Green has taught at Manhattan School of Music since 1984, where he is a professor both of Music History and Composition. An award-winning composer, in 2004–2005 he was composer in residence for the Inter-School Orchestras of New York under a *Music Alive!* grant from the American Symphony Orchestra League. His scholarly publications range from the music of Franz Joseph Haydn and the contemporary Chinese composer Zhou Long to the aesthetic theories of Donald Francis Tovey.

Karen Iken has been an instrumental music teacher in the Green Bay Area Public School District since 1988. A variety of student populations compose the demographics of her many schools as she concentrates at the beginning level. Iken has Bachelor's and Master's of Science Degrees from the University of Wisconsin-Green Bay, serves as department chair in GBAPS, presents staff development opportunities, and organizes the Jazz Ensemble Summer Music Camp at UW-GB.

Elizabeth Ann McAnally is a graduate of Nazareth College of Rochester and Columbia University Teachers College. For the past 14 years, Elizabeth has served as a vocal/general music teacher in the School District of Philadelphia, where she feels privileged to work with incredibly creative and talented students.

Kevin Mixon began his teaching career in rural schools in Illinois and currently teaches instrumental music at Blodgett K-8 School, Syracuse City Schools, New York. His urban instrumental groups regularly receive the highest ratings at regional festivals and are widely recognized for achievement. Mr. Mixon publishes and presents regularly on topics related to music education, and a growing number of his published compositions for band and orchestra reflect and respect student diversity in urban schools.

Kathy M. Robinson is director of Umculo! Kimberley, a professional development program for inservice teachers featuring immersion in Kimberley and Galeshewe, South Africa. The project was developed while teaching at Temple University and the Eastman School of Music. Kathy's research focuses on world music in education, Music of Ghana and South Africa, culturally relevant pedagogy, and urban music education.

Patrick K. Schmidt is assistant professor of Music Education at Westminster Choir College in Princeton, New Jersey. A native of Brazil, Mr. Schmidt is a rising music education philosopher whose interests are in the relationship of social theory to music education. Mr. Schmidt is headmaster and lead teacher at Westminster Academy, the laboratory school of the Music Education Department at Westminster and a Ph.D. candidate in Urban Education at Temple University.

Alan Shapiro has taught junior and senior high school chorus and general music since 1987 in the New York City and Oyster Bay, New York, public schools. He has given staff development to music teachers in Manhattan and Brooklyn and, with composer Edward Green, has presented workshops at the summer and winter conferences of the New York State School Music Association. He has lectured on musical works by Wagner, Ellington, Rachmaninoff, Armstrong, Verdi, and others. He is a singer and an accomplished jazz pianist.

Janice Smith, after a 30-year career in the public schools of Maine, currently teaches general music methods, foundations courses, and graduate portfolio preparation at the Aaron Copland School of Music, Queens College, City University of New York. Her research interests include composition and children, teacher preparation, and stages of music teaching career development.